SMALL EARTHQUAKES

SHAFIK MEGHJI

Small Earthquakes

A Journey Through Lost British History in South America

HURST & COMPANY, LONDON

First published in the United Kingdom in 2025 by
C. Hurst & Co. (Publishers) Ltd.,
New Wing, Somerset House, Strand, London WC2R 1LA
Copyright © Shafik Meghji, 2025
All rights reserved.

The right Shafik Meghji to be identified as the author of this publication is asserted by him in accordance with the Copyright, Designs and Patents Act, 1988.

Distributed in the United States, Canada and Latin America by Oxford University Press, 198 Madison Avenue, New York, NY 10016, United States of America.

A Cataloguing-in-Publication data record for this book is available from the British Library.

This book is printed using paper from registered sustainable and managed sources.

ISBN: 9781805264033

www.hurstpublishers.com

Printed and bound in Great Britain by Bell & Bain Ltd, Glasgow

For Jean, Nizar and Nina Meghji, and Sioned Jones

CONTENTS

Map	ix
Author's Note	xi
Preface: 'Not Many Dead'	xiii
1. Forgotten Colony: Buenos Aires	1
2. Everything but the Moo: Uruguay	35
3. Y Wladfa: Argentine Patagonia	61
4. The Golden Fleece: Chilean Patagonia	85
5. 'Two Bald Men Fighting Over a Comb': Falkland Islands and South Georgia	113
6. End of the World: Tierra del Fuego	139
7. Stolen Friend: Rapa Nui	183
8. Jewel of the Pacific: Valparaíso	205
9. Ghost Towns: Atacama	225
Epilogue: Open Veins	253
List of Illustrations	259
Select Bibliography	261
Acknowledgements	283
Index	285

AUTHOR'S NOTE

Small Earthquakes is based on a series of research trips over the past fifteen years. Some names have been changed for reasons of privacy or security.

PREFACE

'NOT MANY DEAD'

In the late 1920s, sub-editors on the *Times* came up with a game to entertain themselves during tedious evening shifts. A prize was awarded to whoever wrote the dullest headline that made it into print in the following day's paper. In his autobiography, *In Time of Trouble*, the journalist and novelist Claud Cockburn claimed to have won the competition on one occasion with 'Small Earthquake in Chile. Not Many Dead'.

The anecdote may be apocryphal—no edition of the paper carrying the headline has been found—but has nevertheless entered Fleet Street folklore, popping up in countless articles and on journalism courses. It inspired the 'Not Many Dead' column in the *Oldie*, in which readers of the magazine send in 'items of non-news', and the title of a 1970s book by journalist, historian and one-time spy Alistair Horne.

The phrase characterises a certain British attitude to South America—a distant place of little relevance.

* * *

Some places feel like home even if you've never been there before. Buenos Aires was like that for me. I arrived at the end of my first

PREFACE

visit to South America, a life-shifting backpacking trip through Brazil, Bolivia, Peru, Chile and Argentina after giving up a job as a news and sports reporter for the *Evening Standard*. In some sense, part of me never left the city.

These travels cemented an interest in South America that developed in childhood from a disparate patchwork of sources. Growing up in South London, I was captivated by stories of the Amazon and the Inca Empire, by *The Mysterious Cities of Gold* cartoon, Willard Price's *Amazon Adventure* and fleeting clips of Diego Maradona, Gabriel Batistuta and Carlos Valderrama. Later I devoured Michael Palin's TV travelogues, David Attenborough's documentaries, Graham Greene's *Travels with My Aunt* and Paul Theroux's *The Old Patagonian Express*.

My time in South America also prompted a change of career. I moved into travel writing and ultimately relocated to Buenos Aires for a year. There, I frequently came across fragments of British history and culture: the English-language *Buenos Aires Herald* on the newsstands, a shuttered Harrods store on the main shopping strip, the nearby Richmond café. Close to my apartment in Villa Crespo were streets named 'Thames', 'Darwin' and 'FitzRoy'. Farther afield, there were intriguingly titled suburbs, towns and cities ('Hurlingham', 'William C. Morris', 'Temperley') and football clubs ('River Plate', 'Newell's Old Boys', 'Racing Club'). I came across British schools, polo clubs and rugby teams, as well as a Welsh-Argentine community in the south of the country. It soon became apparent that Britain and Argentina's links ran far deeper than simply conflicts in the South Atlantic and rivalries on the football pitch.

These experiences were echoed across the continent. Everywhere I went, I stumbled upon forgotten stories and unexpected connections between Britain and South America, a history I wasn't taught about in school and didn't see represented in the media or popular culture. As I travelled across Bolivia to research

PREFACE

my first book, *Crossed Off the Map*, I came across a graveyard of British-built trains on the edge of the world's biggest salt flat, a notorious Amazonian rubber trader with a home in Hampstead, a tall tale about a British diplomat stripped naked, tied to an ass and kicked out of La Paz. I read about Walter Raleigh's search for El Dorado in what would become the British colony of Guyana, a land laboured by enslaved Africans and indentured South Asians; British soldiers who fought alongside Simón Bolívar in the wars of independence; a town built by a British railway company in southern Brazil.

But the stories that most captured my imagination come from the Southern Cone: Argentina, Chile and Uruguay. Travelling from the Atacama to Tierra del Fuego, Easter Island to South Georgia, I slowly unearthed a shared history spanning five centuries and featuring nitrate kings and wool barons, footballers and pirates, polar explorers and radical MPs, cowboys and missionaries. From ghost towns in the desert to far-flung ranches in the sub-polar tundra. Rusting whaling stations in the South Atlantic to an isolated railway built by convicts. The southernmost city on the planet to a crumbling port known as the 'Jewel of the Pacific'.

On the way, I learned about Britain's enduring impact on Argentina, Chile and Uruguay—from sparking wars, forging national identities and redrawing borders to a tangled role in their colonisation and decolonisation—and how these countries have shaped Britain in profound and unexpected ways.

* * *

On a summer morning in 2015, as the idea for a book exploring Britain's ties to Argentina, Chile and Uruguay began to coalesce, I arranged to meet Andrew Graham-Yooll, former editor-in-chief of the *Buenos Aires Herald*. Launched in 1876 by William Cathcart, a Scottish resident of the city, it developed into the best-known and

PREFACE

most influential English-language newspaper on the continent, publishing uninterrupted until 2017. (The paper was subsequently relaunched as an online-only publication in 2023.)

I took a taxi to Graham-Yooll's house in Barracas, a neighbourhood in southeast Buenos Aires. He was in the process of moving to Entre Ríos, a province north of the city, but kindly made time to fit me in between a visit from the gasman and a trip to the doctor. 'We can go to this grotty little bar on the corner—half a block away—for a beer,' he told me over the phone. 'It's half Galicians, half truck drivers. I go there for a break.'

Given his storied career, I thought I should dress smartly for the occasion, but after a month on the road living out of a backpack while researching *The Rough Guide to Argentina*, the only vaguely appropriate item in my possession was a crumpled blue shirt. I needn't have worried. It was a stiflingly humid afternoon, and Graham-Yooll answered the door bare-chested. Low-voiced, slightly hunched and with shaved grey hair, he ushered me into an apartment filled with boxes and packing crates.

Putting on a shirt, he handed over copies of *The Forgotten Colony: A History of the English-Speaking Communities in Argentina* and *Uruguay: A Travel and Literary Companion*, two of the thirty-plus books he had written, in both English and Spanish. We then walked down the block to a café-bar, a simple place with a wooden countertop manned by a deaf waiter and a few scuffed tables and chairs. 'Grotty', it became clear, was an affectionate term. Graham-Yooll said hello to a couple of regulars who were drinking beer tempered with soda water from siphons and ordered us crustless ham-and-cheese *sándwiches de miga* and a large bottle of Quilmes to share. As the lunchtime traffic steamed past outside, we chatted about his background, life as a journalist and the British in Argentina.

Born in Buenos Aires to an English mother and a Scottish father in 1944, Graham-Yooll grew up in the southeastern sub-

PREFACE

urb of Ranelagh, which was originally developed by a British railway company. Speaking English with a slight Scottish accent, he explained that his father had emigrated from Edinburgh in 1928, working initially as a farmer in Patagonia before moving to the capital. As a fledging journalist, Graham-Yooll joined the *Buenos Aires Herald* and quickly moved up the ranks.

In 1976, a military coup overthrew the government of Isabel Perón, the wife and former vice-president of Juan Perón—who had died in office two years earlier—and the world's first female president. For the next seven years, Argentina was ruled by a brutal dictatorship that committed widespread and systematic human rights violations. Security forces and right-wing death squads killed or 'disappeared' around 30,000 people, many of whom are still unaccounted for. The period is often described as the 'Dirty War', though this mistakenly implies that two armies were fighting the conflict.

Despite—or, perhaps, because of—its relatively small circulation and status as an English-language publication in a Spanish-speaking country, the *Buenos Aires Herald* played an outsized role during those torrid years, courageously reporting on the junta's atrocities when many other media outlets fell silent. Graham-Yooll, by this stage the news editor, played a key role in this work, as he later documented in his 1986 book *A State of Fear*. He also secretly sent information about the situation in Argentina to human rights organisations such as Amnesty International. This work earned him beatings, threats, imprisonment, attempts on his life and, ultimately, after being forced to flee Argentina in 1976, eighteen years of exile in the UK. 'Of course we were afraid,' he later told the *Buenos Aires Times*, 'but it's one thing to be afraid and another thing to be a coward.'

We moved on to Britain and Argentina and the quasi-colonial relationship that existed between them for decades. 'This may sound overrated, but the British influence is everywhere in

PREFACE

Argentina,' he said. 'Their legacy is vanishing, but it still stands out ... If you look at sport, the schools, the clubs, the railway, everything ... you just can't avoid it.'

After an hour, we finished our beer and sandwiches. Graham-Yooll told me not to leave a tip as the old-school owners would take it as an insult, before wishing me luck with my research and hailing me a taxi. Four years later, as work on this book progressed, I saw on Twitter (now X) that he had passed away suddenly at the age of seventy-five and thought back to our chat in that 'grotty little bar' in Barracas. 'I feel myself very Anglo-Argentine,' he had said at the end of our conversation. 'I belong to two cultures.'

This book traces that shared history, uncovering the deep-rooted but overlooked British connections with Argentina, Chile and Uruguay.

1

FORGOTTEN COLONY

BUENOS AIRES

On a grey morning in the winter of 2024, as the rush hour gradually dissolved into a dull roar, a taxi dropped me off on the edge of Balvanera, a *barrio* just west of the centre of Buenos Aires. The driver was still grumbling after a much-delayed journey that featured several lengthy traffic jams and a stop by a truculent police motorcyclist, who queried the use of a temporary licence plate. Narrowly avoiding the heavily laden shopping trolley of a *cartonero*, one of thousands of *porteños*—as residents of Buenos Aires and port cities across South America are known—who search the streets for discarded plastic or cardboard to sell on to recycling centres, I found a quiet spot outside a Tudor-style school and glanced down. A set of pavement slabs had been removed and replaced with slate- and terracotta-coloured tiles with the names of teachers and students killed or 'disappeared' by the 1976–83 military dictatorship: Nélida Beatriz Ardito, Martha María Brea, Liliana Ester Almetta, Lila Epelbaum, Graciela Clarisa Monari, Susana Isabel Santillán.

SMALL EARTHQUAKES

I'd come to Balvanera to visit an incongruous site: the world's most beautiful water-pumping station, which sits on the opposite side of the road from the school. Buenos Aires is not short of striking architecture: the Casa Rosada, the salmon-pink presidential residence from the balcony of which Eva 'Evita' Perón addressed her adoring masses in the 1940s and '50s; La Bombonera, the cacophonous stadium of footballing titans Boca Juniors that takes its name from its resemblance to a chocolate box; the idiosyncratic Palacio Barolo, whose mishmash of influences includes Neo-Gothic designs, Indian-style domes and references to Dante's *Divine Comedy*; Edificio Kavanagh, a soaring modernist skyscraper; and Recoleta Cemetery, a vast city of the dead, including the tomb of Evita, now a place of pilgrimage.

But nothing quite compares with the Palacio de Aguas Corrientes. Spanning a block and dominating the surrounding area, the 'Palace of Running Waters' lives up to its exalted name, with a French Renaissance style interwoven with baroque flourishes. As well as an unexpectedly interesting tourist attraction, the pumping station provides an insight into a remarkable piece of British-Argentine history, which has been largely forgotten about outside of the dusty corners of academia.

Plans for the Palacio de Aguas Corrientes emerged during the 1870s, in response to the city's rapid population growth and serious outbreaks of cholera, yellow fever and typhoid. Designed by a Norwegian architect and British and Swedish engineers, it was completed in 1894, an architectural embodiment of the burgeoning confidence of Buenos Aires. The exterior is decorated with more than 300,000 terracotta tiles made by British ceramic companies Royal Doulton and Leeds-based Burmantofts, while the French-style mansard roof is covered with green slate. There are also stained-glass windows, wooden shutters and sturdy doors that look like they could withstand a battering ram. Inside is a stadium-sized iron structure with 180 columns supporting three floors of massive tanks, which could collectively hold more than 72 million litres of potable water. In his novel, *Santa Evita*, journalist and author Tomás Eloy Martínez describes the building as a 'ceramic absurdity'. It looks like the setting for a Wes Anderson film.

The pumping station operated until 1978 and, eleven years later, was designated a National Historic Monument. It now houses the offices of Agua y Saneamientos Argentinos (AySA), the state-owned water and sewage company. On the ground floor, queues of people holding sheaves of documents—evidence for querying bills or raising complaints—waited for their number to flash up on an electronic screen. AySA staff sat at desks in front of large stained-glass windows, which gave the building the hushed solemnity of a cathedral.

There was also a quirky museum. Displays on the history of water supply and sanitation in Buenos Aires sat alongside an eclectic array of exhibits, including hundreds of taps, faucets, valves and gauges; pieces of ceramic from the exterior coloured red, green and yellow and shaped like flowers, plants and palm fronds; and scores of pipe sections and U-bends that, in another context, would have been lauded as a contemporary art installation. One room was filled entirely with white porcelain toilets, bidets, bathtubs and sinks. The walls were lined with glossy photos of modern water treatment plants throughout Buenos Aires province, each with a list of their key stats, as if they were Top Trumps cards: while Hurlingham serves 450,000 people and can treat more than 5,000 cubic feet of water per second, La Matanza serves 1 million people and can treat double the amount of water per second as its counterpart. I wasn't expecting to see many other visitors, but there was a large group of Argentine pensioners roaring with laughter at a quipping tour guide, as well as a pair of photo-snapping Danes with expensive cameras.

* * *

SMALL EARTHQUAKES

Two weeks earlier, before I set off for Buenos Aires, I visited one of my regular writing spots, Manor House Library in Hither Green, southeast London, which has an improbable connection with the far more ostentatious Palace of Running Waters. The community-run library is based in a Grade II-listed mansion built for a wealthy merchant in 1771 and bought twenty-five years later in a coffeehouse auction by Sir Francis Baring, director of the East India Company and co-founder of Baring Brothers.

One of Britain's oldest merchant banks, Barings was a mainstay of the City of London and a major supplier of loans to foreign governments. According to an 1817 comment generally ascribed to French statesman the Duc de Richelieu, the bank was one of Europe's six great powers, alongside England, France, Russia, Austria and Prussia.

During the nineteenth century, Barings had a close relationship with Buenos Aires, with a series of 'both excellent and catastrophic investments', according to the bank's refreshingly candid archive. As the century progressed, Argentina developed into one of the key emerging markets of the day, and British capital poured into the country, led by Barings. By the 1880s, Argentina attracted 40–50 per cent of British foreign investment, most of which was ploughed into railways, ports and utilities. This was not universally welcomed: Barings was vehemently criticised for an exploitative £1 million loan to the government in Buenos Aires, as well as for political and economic meddling, scheming to topple governors and even promoting the 1864–70 War of the Triple Alliance, a devastating conflict between Argentina, Brazil and Uruguay on one side and Paraguay on the other.

A large chunk of Barings' investment went into the Buenos Ayres Water Supply & Drainage Co. On the surface, it looked like a sound move. The British firm had a concession to expand and operate the city's water and sewage system, which was originally designed by engineers from Ireland and Britain. Its high-profile board included figures from two valuable British enterprises in Argentina, the Bank of London and the River Plate and the Buenos Aires Great Southern Railway. An experienced Barings clerk, Nicholas Bouwer, had assessed the project and described it as indispensable to the city. Confidence was also high at Barings thanks to its recent over-subscribed floatation of shares in Guinness. But as historian H.S. Ferns noted in a piece for the *Journal of Latin American Studies*: 'Irish stout was one thing; Argentine water was another.'

Barings underwrote a £2 million Buenos Ayres Water Supply & Drainage Co. share issue, but the shares found few buyers among British investors. Meanwhile, an economic downturn in Argentina sparked widespread anti-government protests, mass strikes and the 'Revolution of the Park' uprising, which led to the resignation of President Miguel Juárez Celman in August 1890. To make matters worse, the Buenos Ayres Water Supply & Drainage Co. had underestimated the costs of developing the infrastructure—such as the Palace of Running Waters—and overestimated the willingness of *porteños* to pay for its services.

Combined with doubts over Barings' ability to meet its debt and rising interest rates, this was a 'classic recipe for bank failure', wrote Stephen Fay in *The Collapse of Barings*. The result was one of the biggest financial crises of the nineteenth century.

Known as the Baring Crisis, it feels like a strikingly modern episode. Barings was considered too big to fail—had it done so, it was feared other financial institutions would follow suit, threatening the global primacy of the City of London. In November 1890, a Bank of England consortium bailed it out, creating a template for future rescues of stricken financial institutions. Argentina was less fortunate. It fell into a sharp recession, the 'Panic of 1890', with GDP plunging 11 per cent. The crisis also rippled out across South America and beyond; according to financial services firm Morningside, it resulted in the seventeenth 'largest real decline in US stock market history'. The government that succeeded Celman responded by nationalising the Buenos Ayres Water Supply & Drainage Co., with the Palace of Running Waters transferred to the city's municipal authorities, steadying moves that helped to lay the foundations for decades of economic growth.

Barings also bounced back. It remained a major global player until 1995, when the estimated £830 million losses of another Nicholas—'rogue trader' Nick Leeson—sparked the bank's spectacular collapse. As for Manor House, it was sold to the London County Council in 1896. The building became a library, and the grounds were turned into a public park, with the requisite café, tennis courts and playground sitting alongside a 200-year-old ice house. Nearby is the Lord Northbrook pub, which shares its name with a title held by the Baring family. A further ten-minute walk takes you to Baring Road, which runs south to Grove Park, passing Northbrook Park en route.

* * *

My visit to the Palace of Running Waters in 2024 coincided with another period of political upheaval and economic chaos. In November 2023, Javier Milei, a far-right economist, ex-Chacarita Juniors goalkeeper (nicknamed 'El Loco' by his teammates), one-time tantric sex coach, former Rolling Stones cover band singer and self-described 'anarcho-capitalist', was elected president. Six months on, Argentina remained beset by hyper-inflation—the annual rate between March 2023 and March 2024 was almost 288 per cent, though it had slowed by the end of the year—and racked by mass protests and strikes.

Bearing east from the pumping station towards the city centre, along traffic-snarled roads and across Avenida de Julio—the world's widest avenue, with up to sixteen lanes of traffic—I passed two protests against Milei's pledge to take a 'chainsaw' to public spending, shrink the size of the state, restrict the right to strike, reduce salaries and pensions and slash funding to public universities. Outside a college building, a group of students congregated on the pavement, sipping *mate*, a caffeine-rich herbal tea, while handing out flyers and holding a banner with a red fist and the message: 'Milei has declared war on education.' A few blocks on, a group of retirees carried placards with the slogan: 'No to Milei's destruction of pensioners.'

Milei has also embarked on a mass privatisation spree, with the national airline and state radio and TV broadcaster among the targets. Also in line—in a coincidence that almost feels contrived—is AySA, some 135 years after its privatised predecessors sparked a transatlantic financial disaster.

* * *

The Palace of Running Waters symbolises a relationship between Britain and Buenos Aires dating back to the city's earliest days. When conquistador Pedro de Mendoza founded a settlement on the shore of the Río de la Plata, an area occupied by the Querandí people for millennia, in 1536, there were British sailors among his crew. The Spanish colonial city that later developed was initially little more than a waystation for enslaved Africans and Andean silver. It was governed by the Viceroyalty of the Río de la Plata alongside the sister port of Montevideo, now the capital of Uruguay, on the opposite shore of the Río de la Plata.

Over the following centuries, Britain's colonial and commercial interest in South America steadily grew. Under the 1713 Treaty of Utrecht, Spain granted Britain a licence to transport enslaved Africans to its Latin American colonies. The London-based South Sea Company bought the contract from the British government for £9.5 million, largely paying off the national debt in the process. Under the agreement, the firm could transport 4,800 enslaved Africans a year for the next three decades to ports such as Buenos Aires. Working with the Royal African Company and protected by the Royal Navy, the South Sea Company trafficked almost 42,000 Africans—7,000 of whom died en route—in horrific conditions across the Atlantic before its bubble dramatically burst in 1720.

Jumping ahead to the late eighteenth and early nineteenth centuries, the American Revolution and European blockades during the Napoleonic Wars intensified the British government's desperation for new markets, trading hubs and natural resources. Some influential figures touted creating a British colony on the Río de la Plata. These factors helped create the conditions for two invasions of the region, both of which ended in embarrassing defeats.

In the early 1800s, the population of Buenos Aires was an estimated 25,000 to 50,000, including a tiny contingent of Britons working as sailors, butchers, carpenters, cobblers and—much more lucratively—smugglers. In 1806, a 1,500-strong British expeditionary force captured the lightly defended city. The Spanish colonial authorities provided little resistance, characterised by Viceroy Rafael de Sobremonte's decision to flee, which was widely viewed as an act of cowardice. But the city's residents organised a militia and kicked out the invaders after just forty-six days.

The following year, British forces returned. After occupying Montevideo, they launched a second assault on Buenos Aires. Although larger and better equipped than the 1806 force, they too proved woefully unprepared for the ensuing urban warfare. A popular militia—including free and enslaved Africans and Indigenous peoples—rallied to the cause, and there were fierce bouts of street fighting. One British officer described gunfire 'from the tops of houses, whence we also received grenadoes and earthen pots [filled with boiling oil] ... which burnt several of our party'. Subterfuge was also deployed: in a famous incident, a resident named Martina Céspedes and her daughters captured twelve British soldiers after getting them drunk.

FORGOTTEN COLONY

Within days, some 2,500 British troops—half of the invading force—had been killed, wounded or captured. Around 1,600 of the city's militia suffered the same fate. Commanding officer Lieutenant-General John Whitelocke was forced to sign a humiliating armistice and withdraw from Buenos Aires and Montevideo before returning home to intense criticism and a court-martial.

The spirited defence of Buenos Aires was a seminal moment for the city and its residents. Achieved with little help from the Spanish authorities, it catalysed a nascent national identity and fuelled a desire for freedom from Spanish rule. This came to fruition in the 1810 May Revolution, which kick-started a war of independence. There was also a significant British involvement in this conflict. Many of Whitelocke's troops who were captured or had deserted decided to stay in Buenos Aires after the invasion. Some went on to serve under José de San Martín, an Argentine soldier, statesman and national hero who led the independence movement in southern South America.

The subsequent creation of the modern Argentine state was a belated silver lining for the vanquished British invaders. Spain lost its commercial stranglehold over South America, and Britain stepped in to fill the void.

* * *

The day after my visit to the Palacio de Aguas Corrientes, I travelled to the city's main square, the Plaza de Mayo, which takes its name from the May Revolution and is home to the Casa Rosada. Dodging tour groups and a gaggle of students on a school trip, I headed north through the financial district, whose tight streets were packed with austere banks, financial houses and the stock exchange. There was the odd space between the buildings where an old structure had been demolished, giving the area a gap-toothed look. The former post and telegraph office had been refashioned into the Centro Cultural Kirchner, a nine-floor arts, performance and event space named after a former president, and a Ministry of Human Rights office was draped with a banner with 'Freedom advances, salary recedes' daubed on it in green paint.

Around the corner, hemmed in by office blocks, was the Anglican Cathedral of St John the Baptist. A simple, well-maintained building, with six columns supporting the roof, protected by a black metal fence, it looked rather plain compared to the city's more flamboyantly decorated Catholic places of worship. Originally a church, it was completed in 1831, six years after the Treaty of Friendship, Commerce and Navigation granted British subjects in Argentina religious freedom and the right to build their own Protestant churches and cemeteries. This was the first time a non-Catholic faith was officially permitted to establish a presence in the country and reflected the growing size and status of the British community in Buenos Aires and the wider Río de la Plata region following the May Revolution.

Boosted by the arrival of merchants selling textiles and buying Andean silver, the community also benefitted from the support of Bernardino Rivadavia, a key independence leader, government minister and the first de facto president of the country. Rivadavia was regarded as an admirer of Britain: he had visited on a diplomatic mission, respected liberal philosophers such as Jeremy Bentham and James Mill and was keen to develop his country on British economic lines, which had involved arranging the £1 million Barings loan in 1824.

The church was upgraded to cathedral status in 1964 and remains in use today, holding weekly Sunday services, though the size of the congregation has dwindled over the years. Appropriately, given the British community's historic ties—for good and ill—to the city's banking and financial sector, it stands opposite a branch of the Banco del Chubut.

* * *

Life was more turbulent for the British community—and southern South America as a whole—under Juan Manuel de Rosas. For most of the 1829–32 and 1835–52 periods, the dictatorial ruler of Buenos Aires province (and, briefly, the Argentine Confederation) waged war against Indigenous peoples, perceived opponents, political rivals and the Peru–Bolivian Confederation, before finally being ousted. Despite facing an Anglo-French naval blockade during the 1839–51 Uruguayan civil war, Rosas was later given asylum in Britain and spent the last twenty-five years of his life in Swaythling, Southampton. After dying of pneumonia in 1877, he was buried in Southampton Old Cemetery, with his remains repatriated to Argentina in 1989.

The departure of Rosas coincided with the start of the 'Age of Mass Migration'. Between the mid-nineteenth and mid-twentieth centuries, a raft of political, economic and social crises and widespread ethnic and religious persecution in Europe, Russia and the Middle East prompted millions of people to travel to the Americas in search of a new life. Most headed to the United States: between 1892 and 1954, more than 12 million people passed through the immigration processing centre on New York's Ellis Island. The second biggest destination, for European emigrants at least, was Argentina. During the latter half of the nineteenth century, the country grew dramatically in economic, population and territorial terms, amid soaring exports of wheat and other agricultural goods. By the early twentieth century, Argentina had the seventh highest per capita income in the world; some academics argue it may even have been the fifth richest country on earth.

This growth was driven by immigration: an estimated 6.6 million people came to Argentina, mainly via Buenos Aires, in the 1850–1930 period. Successive governments actively encouraged European settlers, as well as European investment, providing new arrivals with subsidies, accommodation, help to find work and transportation to their final destination.

These policies had a distinct racial edge. In the second half of the nineteenth century, in a conscious echo of the westward expansion of the United States, the Argentine state brutally colonised the Pampas—the fertile grasslands spanning much of the centre of the country—and Patagonia to the south, carrying out a genocide against the Indigenous populations and seizing their lands. European immigrants were then sent out to colonise the regions, a deliberate policy 'for the whitening of Argentina, upon which a national identity of whiteness has been grafted,' as journalist and author Uki Goñi noted in the *New York Review of Books*.

There were also attempts to erase the country's African heritage. Between the sixteenth and nineteenth centuries, hundreds of thousands of enslaved Africans were brought to Río de la Plata region, including by the South Sea Company. In the early 1800s, a third of the population in Buenos Aires was Black. Yet the myth of a 'white' Argentina persists, despite a 2008 University of Brasília study pointing out that the average genetic makeup of Argentines today is 31 per cent Indigenous, 9 per cent African and 60 per cent European.

The British community in Argentina expanded significantly during the Age of Mass Migration, and by the turn of the twentieth century it was the biggest of its kind outside of the empire. Between 1857 and 1920, more than 60,000 people from Britain came to Argentina, according to the Department of Immigration; this figure only covers people who officially arrived in the country, so the true number is likely to be higher. Although far smaller than arrivals from Italy (2.3 million) and Spain (1.6 million), they had an outsized impact.

Many working- and middle-class British migrants arrived via the Hotel de los Inmigrantes, the Buenos Aires equivalent of Ellis Island. More than a million people from across the globe passed through this state-funded institution during its years of operation between 1911 and 1953. A half-hour walk from the

FORGOTTEN COLONY

Anglican Cathedral of St John the Baptist, it is located on the fringes of Puerto Madero, a glitzy, high-rise zone that rose up in the 1990s to replace a chain of obsolete nineteenth-century docks and warehouses. The hotel provided new arrivals with free lodging, meals, training and help to find work. In theory, the maximum stay was five days, but some people stayed for months, particularly those who had fallen ill on the voyage to Buenos Aires. It was not a benevolent government gesture: immigration was vital for economic growth, and by 1914 almost one in three Argentines were foreign born.

The hotel is now a museum, wedged between a naval base and a Department of Immigration complex. Negotiating my way past an irritable official, I crossed a grassy courtyard to a hulking, sand-coloured, four-storey building made from reinforced concrete. The museum was officially closed for the day, but Marcelo Huernos, a curator and researcher, had agreed to show me round. New arrivals, he explained, landed at the neighbouring pier and underwent health and immigration checks before being taken to the hotel, which could house 3,000 people at a time in a series of 250-bed dormitories. To cater for them, it had a huge kitchen and cavernous dining halls, plus a bakery, butchers, post office, bank, hospital and employment office.

Our footsteps echoed on the empty hallways, the tiled floors worn smooth by the feet of people hailing from virtually every corner of the globe. Some had carved their names and arrival dates into the dining tables; one had created a silhouette of a girl staring impassively into the distance, dreaming of home or looking to the future, depending on how optimistic you feel. The windows looked out on to the Río de la Plata, a vast brown soup that feels far removed from its 'River of Silver' title.

The word 'hotel' is similarly misleading, Marcelo emphasised: the facilities were basic, and 'guests' were obliged to follow a strict daily routine, which started at 6 am and involved chores such as laundry and childcare for the women and work placements for the men. Meals were served in shifts for a thousand people at a time, and there were courses and workshops on everything from domestic service to farm machinery, as well as lectures and film screenings on Argentine history, culture and geography (or, at least, the government's view of these contested issues).

Some of the dormitories have been kept in their original state; others now contain photos, displays, contemporary art and exhibits that tell the story of one of the most significant human population movements in modern history: a photo of a group of Sikh men on their way to the northwestern city of Tucumán; a battered leather suitcase; immigration cards for Albert Einstein ('Profession: Professor'; 'Health: Good'; 'Defects: None'), who travelled to Argentina on a lecture tour in 1925, and Spanish poet and playwright Federico García Lorca, who arrived in Buenos Aires for the Argentine premiere of his play *Blood Wedding* in 1933, three years before he was executed by a Fascist firing squad during the Spanish Civil War.

Marcelo showed me items left behind by, or donated by the families of, some of the thousands of British migrants who passed through the hotel. A crinkled British passport with a Foreign Office renewal stamp (12 August 1921), an unintelligible signature and a photo of a middle-aged man with a receding hairline, neatly knotted tie and dour expression. An advert for the Colegio Británico, 'a great boarding school' founded in 1868 and surrounded by 'beautiful parkland', and a photo of shy-looking pupils outside a Welsh school in northeast Patagonia. A poster for the White Star Line proudly noted its flagships *Olympic* and *Titanic* and boasted of the 'largest steamers in the world' and 'Services to all parts of the world.'

* * *

As the British community grew, so too did its political, economic and cultural clout. Investment spread from railways to 'tram and gas firms, water and sewage works [such as the Palacio de las Aguas Corrientes], along with meat packers, banks and insurance companies,' wrote historian David Rock in *The British in Argentina*: 'British shippers, warehousemen and importers occupied prominent positions on the waterfront, while British shopkeepers sold British goods along the city's congested streets.'

There are reminders of this legacy throughout central Buenos Aires, forming an essential, if often overlooked, part of the city's fabric. A fifteen-minute walk northwest of the Hotel de los Inmigrantes is the grand Estación Retiro. Designed by British architects in a distinctly Edwardian style vaguely reminiscent of St Pancras in London, its steel skeleton was made in Liverpool before being shipped across the Atlantic. Opening in 1915, Retiro was once the hub of the biggest railway network in South America, extending across more than 27,000 miles of track at its peak in the 1940s. From the late nineteenth century, trains had been central to the development of the modern Argentine state and its colonisation of Indigenous lands, transporting a steady stream of European migrants and an apparently never-ending supply of beef, lamb, wool, wheat and other produce to port for export. During this period, Argentina's agricultural output skyrocketed, and the country became known as the 'granary of the world'.

Railway historian Jorge Waddell, a professor of public policy and co-author of *A History of the Railways in Argentina*, described the railway network as 'a state instrument to develop and create a country which did not exist'. It was also emblematic of the connections, and tensions, between Britain and Argentina. From the mid-nineteenth century, British and Anglo-Argentine firms, investors, merchants, engineers and staff played a key role in the development of the network. By the 1910s, British railway firms dominated the sector and were among the most valuable companies in Argentina.

Understandably, this bred resentment, particularly when combined with British influence over other parts of the Argentine economy, a set of imbalanced trade and diplomatic agreements, the unscrupulous behaviour of large British landowners and the nefarious activities of British meatpackers, which were accused of manipulating prices and illegally moving their huge profits overseas. By 1929, some 12 per cent of British income from overseas investment came from Argentina. Trains were at the forefront. Many Argentines regarded railway companies as agents of imperialism and believed the country was being drawn into Britain's 'informal empire'. A popular satirical cartoon of the time depicted the railway firms as a 'Pulpo Inglés', an 'English Octopus' whose tentacles encircled Argentina, grabbing its resources and stifling its development.

This notion was developed by writer Ezequiel Martínez Estrada in his influential 1933 meditation on Argentine identity *X-Ray of the Pampa*, which described the railways as a 'spider's web'. Railway companies—predominantly British or Anglo-Argentine—were often granted a 'league' (around 3.4 miles) of land on either side of the tracks to exploit as they wished. These terms, argued Estrada, 'condemned us to perpetuate our original condition as a colony', benefitting the company, investors in the UK and the Argentine elite in Buenos Aires at the expense of the rest of the country: 'With their leagues of land the railroads ... established on their flanks a certain kind of natural frontier ... The area beyond the two leagues was fallowness, loneliness and ignorance.'

This was not merely an Argentine perspective, with the historian John King describing how in 1929, the British ambassador, Malcolm Robertson, remarked: 'Without saying so in so many words, which would be tactless, what I really mean is that Argentina must be regarded as an essential part of the British Empire.' A reaction was inevitable. In 1948, amid growing pressure in his party and beyond, President Juan Perón nationalised the rail network, taking British (and a smaller number of

French) companies into state hands as part of a populist programme focused on industrialisation, social justice and economic independence.

Today, the neighbouring, architecturally nondescript Retiro bus terminal is the area's key transport interchange, and rail services throughout Argentina are sadly diminished, covering only around 9,300 miles of track. There are commuter lines in Buenos Aires province, a handful of long-distance services and a few tourist-oriented heritage lines. The latter include the narrow-gauge *Tren de la Costa*, which travels from the suburb of Olivos to the island-town of Tigre, on the edge of the steamy Paraná Delta, South America's second biggest river system.

The Argentine network as a whole was privatised in the mid-1990s, before being nationalised again a decade later. During my visit in 2024, it appeared set to be pushed back into private hands as part of Milei's zealous privatisation drive. During the election campaign, he proclaimed: 'We had the best railroad system in the world back when it was British.' While the history may have been forgotten in Britain, it still has political power in Argentina.

* * *

Across from the station, beyond a steady thrum of traffic—black-and-yellow taxis, heaving city buses and long-distance coaches heading to Salta, Mendoza and Córdoba—is the Torre Monumental. Standing almost 200 feet, the clocktower was a gift from the British community to the city in 1916 to mark the centenary of Argentina's independence. Built from materials shipped over from Britain, it was originally called the Torre de los Ingleses, or English Tower. The base features the shields of Argentina and the UK, while its bells play the Westminster Quarters melody, the same chime as Big Ben.

Now dwarfed by shiny glass office blocks and hotels, the clocktower and the surrounding Plaza Británica were both renamed in the 1980s amid a bout of anti-British hostility in the wake of the Falklands War. In a pointed location opposite the tower, a large Argentine flag fluttered next to one of the country's many monuments to the 1982 conflict in the South Atlantic. Guarded by a pair of soldiers in ceremonial uniforms, immobile and clutching polished swords that glinted in the early winter sunshine, it paid tribute to the troops who lost their lives in the war while forcefully restating Argentina's claim to the archipelago.

Uphill, in leafy Plaza San Martín, office workers sat on benches eating takeaway lunches as homeless men slept on the neatly tended grass, a group of cycle couriers snatched a short break between deliveries and a carnival-style drum troupe embarked on a jam session, drowning out the incessant hum of traffic. In a corner of the square stood a statue of José de San Martín: the revolutionary leader was garlanded with flowers, but his proud bearing was somewhat undermined by the presence of a pigeon on his head, scanning the paths for dropped sandwiches and discarded empanadas. After helping several countries in South America to win their independence in the early 1800s, the Argentine-born San Martín grew frustrated with the internal conflicts across the continent and moved to Europe. In 1824, he visited his friend, James Duff, the fifth Earl of Fife, in Banff, Scotland, during which he was granted the freedom of the town. On 25 October 1950, an Argentine *Araucaria araucana*, or monkey puzzle tree, was planted in the grounds of Banff Castle by Argentine ambassador Carlos Hogan to mark the centenary of his death. There are also memorials to San Martín in London: a blue plaque marks a house—23 Park Road in Marylebone—where he stayed, while a statue of him stands in Belgrave Square, alongside fellow 'libertador' Simón Bolívar.

Southwest of Plaza San Martín, in the shadow of the soaring Edificio Kavanagh, a glorious Rationalist skyscraper built for an Irish millionaire in the 1930s, is the former five-star Hotel Plaza.

Completed in 1909, the hotel was the tallest building in the city before being surpassed by its 395-foot neighbour. Currently closed for renovation, its exterior was yellowed, rusted and partially hidden behind advertising boards for aftershave and perfume brands Kevin Red and Valeria.

On 20 March 1936, the hotel played host to the last moments of one of the most enigmatic characters in British-Argentine history: Robert Bontine Cunninghame Graham, whose implausible life story is largely forgotten today, at least in Britain. James Jauncey, his great-great-nephew and the author of *Don Roberto: The Adventure of Being Cunninghame Graham*, describes him as a 'fantastic combination of Don Quixote and Sir Gawain, Indiana Jones and the Lone Ranger'.

Cunninghame Graham was born in 1852 into a wealthy Scottish family; his great-great-grandfather, Robert Graham, owed his fortune to the transatlantic slave trade and sugar plantations in Jamaica worked by enslaved Africans. Claiming to be a direct descendant of King Robert II, Cunninghame Graham spoke Spanish as a first language thanks to his mother, Anne Elizabeth Elphinstone-Fleeming, the daughter of a Spanish noblewoman. Aged seventeen, he travelled to Argentina and fell in love with gaucho culture on the Pampas. Launching himself into cattle ranching, he became a cowboy himself, earning the nickname 'Don Roberto'. Friends with the likes of Robert Louis Stevenson and George Bernard Shaw, Cunninghame Graham was also a prolific writer, producing a multitude of books, essays, short stories, travelogues, works of history and biographies, many of which were inspired by his time in South America. His exploits strongly influenced Joseph Conrad's novel *Nostromo*, which is set in a fictionalised South American country.

Known as the 'Gaucho Laird', Cunninghame Graham later moved back to Britain and into politics. He is commonly regarded as Britain's first socialist MP, having been elected to parliament in 1886, though he was officially a member of the Liberal Party at the time. The following year, he became the first MP to be suspended from parliament for swearing during a speech; the offending word was 'damn'. Two months later, he was arrested and given a six-week prison sentence for taking part in the banned Bloody Sunday demonstration, a protest in London's Trafalgar Square against unemployment, repression in Ireland and the jailing of Irish MPs, as well as in defence of freedom of speech. In 1888, he co-founded the Scottish Labour Party, alongside Keir Hardie. Forty years later, as a strong advocate for Scottish independence, he co-founded the National Party of Scotland, a forerunner of the modern Scottish National Party. As well as calling for land reform, the abolition of the House of Lords and the creation of national parks, he was, wrote Jauncey, a 'champion of the oppressed, a crusader for social justice ... and a vehement anti-imperialist'.

After dying of pneumonia aged eighty-three following a visit to the birthplace of his late friend W.H. Hudson, the Anglo-Argentine author and naturalist, his body lay in state at the Casa del Teatro, where mourners included the Argentine president, Agustín Pedro Justo. He was later buried at the ancient monastery of Inchmahome Priory on an island in the Lake of Menteith, near Stirling. The cattle brand from his Argentine ranch is imprinted on the gravestone.

* * *

Immediately south of the Hotel Plaza, I walked down Calle Florida, one of the city's key shopping streets, a pedestrianised zone dotted with crumbling relics of the Anglo-Argentine relationship. Comparable to London's Oxford Street, it remained a busy commercial artery, despite Argentina's present economic malaise, lined predominantly with pricey chain stores and packed with tourists. Every few metres, I encountered a moneychanger calling out '*cambio*' (change) or 'dollars' at passers-by. They offered 'blue market' deals for foreign currency that were as much as 20 per cent higher than the official exchange rates accessible through licensed bureaux de change or cash machines. Illegal but commonplace and broadly tolerated, the moneychangers led punters to side streets or unmarked, minimalist shops known as 'caves' to conduct transactions. Unless you've been scammed, you leave with a large wad of cash that feels like it should have been handed over in an unmarked envelope in the car park of a motorway service station. A few days earlier, I had exchanged a $100 note for 1,100 Argentine pesos, which were bound together by an elastic band and created a suspicious, and slightly unsettling, bulge in my jacket pocket.

Alongside the moneychangers, shops, cafés and fast-food outlets, sandwich boards advertised tango shows and open-topped bus tours, while stalls—and sometimes simply blankets unfurled on the pavement—offered incense sticks, counterfeit football shirts and fluffy yellow chick toys entitled 'Patitos Tik Tok'.

Beyond these familiar scenes is an anomaly. Midway along Calle Florida, I found a large, abandoned department shop with a faded green exterior and a recognisable copper-coloured sign: Harrods. The once impressive Belle Époque exterior retained only a hint of its former lustre, with a tangle of barbed wire over the main entrance, graffitied metal shutters encircling the ground floor, and upper floors with several lost or broken windowpanes, providing easy access to a roost of resident pigeons. Opposite this unlikely outpost of Britain's most famous luxury store were shops stocked with Japanese manga and offering to buy and sell gold. The empty, shuttered shell was quiet and rather sad—a long way from the boom years of the early twentieth century when it hosted a live Indian elephant and red London double-decker bus as publicity stunts, later providing the backdrop for films and TV programmes.

SMALL EARTHQUAKES

The first overseas branch of Harrods opened in Buenos Aires in 1914 and once virtually spanned an entire block. It was subsequently sold to a local retailer but retained the iconic name; Mohamed Al Fayed, who bought Harrods in London in 1983, tried to recover sole rights to the name but lost a legal battle in the 1990s. It was a short-lived victory for the Buenos Aires branch, which closed in 1998, blighted by debts. Despite various attempts to re-open it over the years since, and the occasional temporary exhibition, it remains closed and near derelict.

Harrods was one of scores of British shops and businesses in downtown Buenos Aires in the early twentieth century. The *South American Handbook* for 1924 listed Anglo-Argentine pharmacies, jewellers, stationers, wine merchants, booksellers, newsagents and clothes shops, British banks with branches in London and across South America, and railway operators, freight companies and shipping lines. There were adverts for an array of British products that may have come in useful for the discerning South American traveller. These included 'Dinner Toast' biscuits to aid digestion; magnesium supplements to soothe 'heartburn, headache, gout, biliousness, acidity of the stomach'; Webb's Indian Tonic; Lipton's tea; Ross' Belfast ginger ale ('Favourably known all over the World'); Allen & Wright Ltd briar pipes; portable Remington typewriters; Snugfit hosiery; British Admiralty charts; Fry's 'exquisite fancy boxes' of chocolate; and Nobel Industry explosives, detonators, safety fuses and cables.

A short walk west from Harrods, I found the former site of Café Richmond, a much-loved literary hangout dating back to 1917 and once frequented by the likes of Jorge Luis Borges, Lawrence Durrell and Graham Greene, who featured it in his novel *The Honorary Consul*. The ex-*Buenos Aires Herald* editor Robert Cox claimed it was the only place in the city you 'could get a decent cup of tea'. The café-bar was controversially closed and replaced by a Nike store in 2011. The site is now occupied by a womenswear shop named BIBA selling pink puffer jackets, cable-knit jumpers and distressed jeans.

* * *

Thankfully, some café-bars with British connections have survived. Recrossing the Plaza de Mayo, I headed south into Montserrat, the oldest section of the city and site of furious fighting during the British invasions. Calle Defensa, a narrow, cobblestone street whose name commemorates the successful resistance, was lined with townhouses, churches, mid-level office blocks and grey-faced banks. Many once elegant nineteenth-century buildings were now ramshackle. One mansion block was on the verge of collapse, its balcony rusted, window frames rotted, an ancient a/c unit ready to topple into the street, held in place only by a thick layer of dust. Despite the crumbling architecture and its proximity to the city centre, Montserrat felt calm and quiet, though politics was never far away. Milei-related graffiti covered the walls: 'Money for the public, not for the private sector'; 'Boys, we're organising again now.'

Continuing south, I reached neighbouring San Telmo, one of the most beautiful and touristy *barrios* in Buenos Aires. Many of its historic buildings have been renovated, leaving behind just enough traces of urban decay to provide an edge. The neighbourhood is known for flea markets, antique stores and designer clothes, and there are plenty of boutique hotels, restaurants and bars, often covered with distinctive *fileteado porteño*, colourful stylised lettering and flowery designs that traditionally appear on shopfronts and buses. Tourists thronged the pavements, streaming in and out of souvenir shops selling overpriced jars of dulce de leche—a thick, super-sweet caramel-like confection—*mate* paraphernalia and football shirts.

Beyond the bric-a-brac, orange juice sellers and buskers of Plaza Dorrego, I crossed an underpass towards working-class La

SMALL EARTHQUAKES

Boca, irrepressible mosquitoes nipping at my neck. On the edge of Parque Lezama, the spot where conquistador Pedro de Mendoza, the founder of Buenos Aires, first landed in the sixteenth century, is one of the city's *'bares notables'*, a collection of classic café-bars dating from the late nineteenth or early twentieth centuries.

Opened in 1928, Bar Británico took its name from a group of British First World War veterans who lived in a nearby lodging house and were once regular patrons (the name was briefly changed to 'El Tánico' during the Falklands War). It has been threatened with closure on various occasions, most recently during the COVID-19 pandemic, but has always found a way to survive, thanks to the affection of the local community. A constellation of literary and cinematic connections—author Ernesto Sabato wrote much of his novel *On Heroes and Tombs* in the bar, which also featured in the 2004 Che Guevara biopic *The Motorcycle Diaries*—probably helped too.

In the late afternoon sunshine, Bar Británico had a sepia-tinged look: *fileteado porteño* designs on the windows, a checkerboard tiled floor, wood panelling, scuffed mirrors, vintage Cinzano signs and tango posters, black-and-white photos of San Telmo street scenes and assorted footballing memorabilia—a chunky pair of boots from the 1970s, a signed Club Atlético San Telmo shirt (a pointed presence given that we were barely a corner kick away from the Boca Juniors stadium, La Bombonera). There was a mix of locals and tourists, drinking tea with lemon or the first Quilmes of the day and finishing a late lunch special of Spanish-style lentils or grilled hake. The service was brisk, the coffee passable. It felt like the kind of place Cunninghame Graham would have liked.

On the outside wall was a plaque with lyrics from the song 'Vals municipal' (Municipal waltz) by María Elena Walsh, an immensely popular writer, poet, composer, singer and musician with English, Irish and Spanish heritage. Famous, above all, for her much-loved children's books, stories and songs, she was also a critic of the 1976–83 military dictatorship and was eventually forced to flee the country. Many of her works, for adults and children, were regarded as subversive by the junta and censored or banned. Inevitably, this succeeded only in turning them into symbols of democracy and resistance, notably her cover of the US Civil Rights anthem 'We Shall Overcome'.

* * *

By the time Bar Británico opened, the British community was already in decline. Political instability, authoritarian governments, the Wall Street Crash and the Great Depression, as well as mounting discontent within Argentine society at British dominance over large swaths of the economy and infrastructure, all played a part, alongside the presidency of Juan Perón. In his first spell at the Casa Rosada between 1946 and 1955, he 'disrupted the liberal society the British helped to construct. By the time of Perón's fall in 1955, their once salient economic presence had shrunk to a negligible level from which it never recovered,' argued Rock.

But the community did not disappear completely. For an insight into the situation today, I reached out to John Hunter, president of the British Cemetery of Buenos Aires and former chair of the Argentine-British Community Council (ABCC). We met across the city in the *barrio* of Palermo, which gave me an excuse to visit Estación Constitución, another grand railway terminus with the scale and sensibility of a cathedral. Built by Buenos Ayres Great Southern, one of the major British-owned railway companies in the nineteenth and early twentieth centuries, the station opened in 1865 before being rebuilt and expanded in the 1920s. The foundation stone for the current incarnation was laid in the presence of Edward VIII, then the

Prince of Wales, during an official visit to Argentina. Joining a pack of commuters heading home, I took the Subte, the oldest underground railway in Latin America, north towards Palermo. Launched in 1913, the network's first line was built by the Anglo-Argentine Tramways Company, which had a near monopoly on the city's tramways at the time, with almost 400 miles of track. In 1922 alone, 46 million passengers travelled on the firm's trams, resulting in an annual turnover of £4.5 million.

I met Hunter at a coffee shop on a residential street, a pleasant but less characterful venue than Bar Británico. To a soundtrack of '80s British pop and rock—the Cure, Buck's Fizz, Queen—we spent the next hour and a half in a freewheeling conversation about the British connections to Argentina. Engaged and informed, Hunter provided a string of interesting and often unexpected facts, from the number of bag-piper bands in Argentina (eight) to the story of how a lowly football team in Buenos Aires province came to be named Club Atlético Douglas Haig (it was founded days after the end of the First World War by a group of railway workers, whose British boss insisted they honour the commander-in-chief of British forces in France for much of the conflict).

Hunter's personal story echoed that of many Anglo-Argentine families. His maternal grandfather arrived after the First World War and initially worked as a farmer in Río Negro, a province in northern Patagonia. 'My grandmother, when she was pregnant, sailed back to Scotland, heavily pregnant, to have her kids. My mother—Andrew Graham-Yooll's cousin—was born in Edinburgh and six months later came back to Argentina and was raised here.'

His paternal grandfather emigrated to work on the railways, and his father was raised in a southern suburb of Buenos Aires called Temperley, which was founded by Newcastle-born merchant George Temperley in the 1890s and is still home to an area called the Barrio Inglés. (Several neighbourhoods in Buenos

Aires are named Barrio Inglés; some were actually once home to British residents or had a strong British link. In other cases, such as in the *barrio* of Caballito, it was simply a marketing ploy to make the area seem more desirable.)

There are still three British-founded churches in Temperley, an Anglican, a Presbyterian and a Methodist, while neighbouring Lomas de Zamora is home to Barker College, founded in 1897 and one of several British schools operating in and around Buenos Aires. 'There are massive links between Britain and Buenos Aires: clubs, sports, schools, railways, as well as the Anglican cathedral and the British Hospital,' said Hunter. He also highlighted the Hurlingham Club, founded in 1888 to host polo, cricket, tennis, golf and social events. 'The British and Irish contributed a lot to Argentine independence, too. An Irishman, William "Guillermo" Brown [born in County Mayo and later press-ganged into the Royal Navy], was the first admiral of the Argentine Navy, and the majority of his officers were British.'

There are no precise, up-to-date statistics on the number of Argentines with British heritage (let alone data on those who actively identify as such); figures of around 100,000 people with Scottish ancestry and 70,000 with Welsh ancestry have been touted in the past. Whatever the true numbers, fundraising events organised by the ABCC, a non-profit that coordinates social, cultural and welfare activities, get a good turnout, said Hunter. Across Buenos Aires and its suburbs, 'there are car boot sales, bagpiping and Scottish dancing sessions, a Christmas fair, golf events at the Hurlingham Club, and food events—curry lunches, sausage and mash. They're open to all, not just those of British origin.' As well as marking events such as Remembrance Day, the ABCC has a newsletter, online magazine and YouTube channel. When he chaired the organisation, Hunter says one of his main aims was to 'show that British immigration was positive on Argentina and to try to present, remember and celebrate the British legacy'.

SMALL EARTHQUAKES

As we finished our coffees and the café's soundtrack shifted into the 1990s with Oasis's *Definitely Maybe,* Hunter mentioned there were varying attitudes in Argentina to England, Scotland and Wales:

> If you say you're from Scotland, people say, 'Ah, whiskey, bagpipes, golf, beautiful country.' If you say you're Welsh, they say, 'Ah, Gales [Wales in Spanish], Patagonia, Lady Di, Welsh cakes, how beautiful.' But if you say you're of English origin, they say, 'You're a pirate, you are against Argentina, you took away the Falklands.'

He broke off in laughter before adding:

> I'm generalising, of course. But it would be very unusual, at some community event in Argentina that we as the British community could parade with the Union Jack—that would be contentious. Scottish, Welsh and Irish flags fly anywhere, no problem. But not the British, not yet at least. Maybe in twenty years' time. In the meantime, as I see it, as the British community, we must celebrate our contribution and not let the Falklands War shade it all out.

* * *

One of the ways Hunter commemorates this connection with Argentina is through the British Cemetery of Buenos Aires, which was founded in 1820 near the Plaza de Mayo before moving to its present site in Chacarita, northwest of the city centre, in 1892. It sits beside the similarly sized German Cemetery in the shadow of the far larger Chacarita Cemetery, which spans 95 hectares and houses the tomb of tango legend Carlos Gardel.

On the afternoon I visited, there was no one else there, save for a handful of staff. Trains rumbled in the distance, fittingly, given the deep British involvement in Argentina's railway network. The cemetery was suitably peaceful and immaculately kept, with a small church and a memorial paying tribute to the nearly 900 members of the British community in Argentina who died in the First and Second World Wars. 'There were almost 10,000 volunteers in total,' Hunter told me. 'The RAF in the Second World War even had a squadron named the Argentine-British Squadron, the No 164. It's a shame there's no recognition of them in Britain.'

I spent an hour in the cemetery, losing myself in the stories of its most noted residents, potted biographies of whom were available via QR codes beside their headstones. My first stop was Alexander Watson Hutton, arguably the Briton who made the biggest contribution to Argentine society. Born in Glasgow and orphaned at a young age, he emigrated to Buenos Aires in 1882 to teach at St Andrew's Scots School in Olivos, Buenos Aires province. Two years later, he founded Buenos Aires English High School in Belgrano, with physical education central to its curriculum. Watson Hutton subsequently brought over the first footballs to Argentina, created the country's first football pitch and encouraged his pupils to play the game.

In 1893, he founded the Argentine Football Association (AFA), one of the oldest in the world outside of the UK, and the Alumni Athletic Club. Better known simply as Alumni, his team was predominately made up of former Buenos Aires English High School students and dominated the league before being disbanded in 1913 due to financial and recruitment issues. As a result, Watson Hutton became known as the 'father of Argentine football'. In 2023, the AFA celebrated his contribution on the official football for its cup competition, the Copa de la Liga Profesional.

The introduction of football is the most visible legacy of the British in South America, and there are equivalents of Watson Hutton throughout the continent, as I was to find across the Río de la Plata in Uruguay and over the Andes in Chile. Many of the early players were British, numerous clubs that exist today had British or Anglo-Argentine founders—such as Newell's Old Boys in the city of Rosario—and British-owned railway lines carried the sport to the farthest points of the country. Britain also played an important role in the development of Argentine culture and national identity, as football writer Jonathan Wilson pointed out in *Angels with Dirty Faces*. He highlighted the attitude of influential football magazine *El Gráfico* in the 1920s, which 'created an identity for Argentinian football—and to an extent Argentina itself—in opposition to the British', an echo of the wider concerns of overbearing Anglo influence across society at the time. A century on, 'Whoever doesn't bounce is an Englishman' remains a popular chant among Argentine football fans and is a cue for the whole stadium—sometimes including the players—to jump up and down.

Buried nearby, and a near contemporary of Watson Hutton, Cecilia Grierson had a similar impact. Born in Buenos Aires to Irish-Scottish parents in 1859, she was the first female doctor in Argentina, though this title rather undersells her myriad achievements. Originally a teacher, Grierson went on to graduate from the hitherto male-only Buenos Aires School of Medicine. A pioneering feminist who rallied against the misogynistic prejudices and strictures of the time, she founded the School of Nurses and Massage Therapists, as well as working as a 'sculptor, activist for educational spaces ... philanthropist and a great participant in the debate on public policies', according to Beatriz Morrone, author of *Cecilia Grierson: Soy una obrera del pensamiento* ('Cecilia Grierson: I am a worker of thought'). 'She did not recognise limits in her profession and broke new ground with great courage,' wrote Morrone. 'She was fundamental in creating specialities that did not exist in Argentina, such as gynaecology, obstetrics and neonatology. She was also key in other areas, such as the education of the blind and mental health issues.'

There were also other, less feted but still fascinating figures buried in the cemetery. They included Frank Brown, who was born in Brighton in 1858 to a family of clowns, mastering skills such as conjuring, horse riding and the trapeze before touring

FORGOTTEN COLONY

Europe, the United States and Central America with a circus. After settling in Buenos Aires, he became known as the 'English Clown'—with fans including two Argentine presidents, Carlos Pellegrini (whose grandfather was an English engineer) and Domingo Faustino Sarmiento—and carved out a successful career as a circus impresario.

Elsewhere, I stumbled upon the grave of Fanny Haslam de Borges, the grandmother of the most famous Argentine author of the twentieth century, Jorge Luis Borges. Born in Staffordshire, she was a 'great reader' who emigrated to Argentina to join her elder sister, whose husband 'brought the first horse-drawn tramcars to Argentina', Borges wrote in *The New Yorker*. Fanny later married a colonel, Francisco Borges, in the early 1870s. Meanwhile, Borges' great-grandfather, Edward Young, was the editor of one of Argentina's first English-language newspapers, the *Southern Cross*. 'Perhaps, without knowing it, I was always a bit of a Britisher; in fact, I always think of Waterloo as a victory,' he added.

* * *

I headed back to Palermo via my old neighbourhood of Villa Crespo. The working-to-middle-class residential and largely tourist-free *barrio* felt comfortingly familiar, though there were signs of creeping gentrification, notably a Starbucks. When I moved here, I mistakenly thought that an English-language travel writer would be a rare commodity in the city, only to quickly discover a large pool of British and American journalists, including a Lonely Planet author who happened to live in the apartment directly above mine.

Most of us would have been considered digital nomads, had the concept existed at the time, or perhaps 'expats', a euphemistic term for economic migrants that is only ever applied to certain groups of people. With the privilege of a British passport that ensured a hassle-free route though immigration, I had the luxury of just thinking of myself as a traveller. I didn't apply for a working visa or residency permit; the first time I visited a Department of Immigration office was en route to my tour of the Hotel de los Inmigrantes. Instead, I picked up a free three-month tourist visa on arrival at Ezeiza airport, which I then renewed periodically by catching a ferry across the Río de la Plata for the short hop to Uruguay, spending the night before heading back to Buenos Aires. Some of my British and US friends returned the same day, often spending less than ten minutes on Uruguayan soil before catching a ferry in the opposite direction. A few didn't even bother to do that, so confident were they that overstaying their tourist visa would earn them nothing more than a smack on the wrist.

After a nostalgic glance at my old apartment, I followed Calle Serrano northeast towards my guesthouse in Palermo, past a store selling the blue-and-yellow shirts of local football team Atalanta, the kiosk where I used to buy the *Buenos Aires Herald* and a once much-frequented café-bar serving afternoon teas known as *meriendas*. Crossing into the Palermo Soho district, a hub of pricey hotels, restaurants and bars, the road changed its name to Jorge Luis Borges, who was born and brought up in the then working-class neighbourhood at the turn of the twentieth century.

Argentina is a country of late eaters, so at 8.30 pm there was only one other diner, a Dutch tourist, in the *parrilla* just off Plaza Serrano. The walls of the steakhouse were a mini shrine to Maradona—a framed Argentina shirt, cuttings from Italian newspapers marking his signing for Napoli, a photo of him leaning on a goalpost in his Barcelona kit, wearing a pair of unfeasibly short shorts—and a match between Estudiantes and Deportivo Riestra played out on a muted TV. I ordered a *bife de chorizo*, roughly equivalent to a sirloin, and a carafe of malbec, which came in a white penguin-shaped jug, the traditional Argentine vessel for serving house wine. The steak came with a tangy chimichurri sauce, classically a combination of chopped parsley, oregano, garlic, vinegar, oil and sometimes chilli. (The origin of the word 'chimichurri' is contested. It probably derives from Quechua or Basque, but some claim it takes its name from an Irish immigrant named Jimmy Curry, while others argue it originated from the failed British invasions of 1806–7, when captured soldiers asked for some 'curry' to liven up their meals.)

Alongside football and tango, beef is a central part of Argentine culture, highlighted in travel articles and tourist literature to the point of cliché. But steaks, ranches, gauchos and the Pampas are equally central to neighbouring Uruguay, which has traditionally had one of the highest per-capita rates of beef consumption in the world (alongside Argentina, the United States and Australia). Just like its larger, more boisterous counterpart on the opposite shore of the Río de la Plata, Uruguay was transformed by the cattle industry in the nineteenth and early twentieth centuries. During this period, it gave birth to an iconic British food brand and changed the way we—and the rest of the world—eats.

2

EVERYTHING BUT THE MOO

URUGUAY

'Welcome to the "killing room",' said Diana Cerilla, guiding me into a cavernous warehouse with a grisly array of hooks, pulleys, wheels, chains, conveyors and scales. At one stage, as many as 1,600 cows a day—plus thousands of sheep, pigs, chickens and other animals—met their end in this slaughterhouse, she explained matter-of-factly. I scanned the rusting machinery, immobile but ominous, and started to shiver. Shards of sunlight pierced the broken windows, illuminating concrete troughs and white-tiled basins. Worn signs warned workers to maintain the equipment and wear protective trousers and boots, adding sternly: 'Continuing work for all depends upon the performance of each individual.'

With a sandy blonde bob, oval glasses and pristine white polo shirt, Cerilla spoke in a mix of English and Spanish, typically finishing her sentences with a quizzical, 'You understand?' The carcasses, she explained, left the 'killing room' to be processed, packaged and exported around the world. As well as helping to turn Uruguay into an agricultural powerhouse, the plant supercharged the globalisation of food production, transforming the diets of people across Europe and beyond. It also produced some of the most famous British products—from corned beef to stock cubes—of the twentieth century, while foreshadowing our current era of unaccountable, tax-avoiding multinationals. In the process, the otherwise nondescript town of Fray Bentos became a household name.

Crucially, added Cerilla, nothing was wasted: 'The company claimed it used every part of the cow except for the moo.'

* * *

Wedged between two far larger neighbours in Argentina and Brazil, Uruguay is the second smallest country in South America after Suriname. A little bigger than England and Wales combined and with a population of fewer than 3.5 million people, it is often overlooked by travellers.

On our first visit, my girlfriend and I spent a night in Colonia del Sacramento, a charming city across the water from the Argentine capital, before catching a bus east across the undulating hills of Nueva Helvecia, which was colonised by Swiss settlers in the mid-nineteenth century and is now known for its dairy production. We stayed at a Hostelling International outpost, a rustic lodge on a small farm, passing the time by cycling to neighbouring cheesemakers, lounging in hammocks in a flower-filled garden patrolled by tiny hummingbirds and playing with a boisterous Alsatian named Tupac. Evenings were spent eating fondue and drinking unlabelled bottles of tannat made by a local winemaker who had relocated from France; while half the bottles were corked, the rest were sensational. Fist-sized tarantulas occasionally scurried into our room, but the owner calmly stomped on them in her heavy work boots.

One evening, I fell into conversation with one of her friends. As we watched a pair of piebald horses graze in a neighbouring field, he mentioned in passing the nineteenth-century British invasions of the Río de la Plata, the second of which involved an occupation of Montevideo. It was the first time I'd heard about the conflict, and I began to wonder what other aspects of British history in South America had been similarly obscured or overlooked.

* * *

Britain's earliest connections with what is now Uruguay parallel those with Argentina. The first encounter of note occurred during the second invasion of the Río de la Plata in 1807, when the region was a Spanish colony. On 3 February, a British expeditionary force besieged Montevideo, which sits on the north shore of the river and had a population of around 10,000 at the time, roughly a third of whom were enslaved Africans. The city fell within hours, and the British also captured the smaller port of Colonia del Sacramento, 100 miles to the west.

The commanding officer, Lieutenant-General John Whitelocke, used Montevideo as a base to launch a second invasion of Buenos Aires in July. After another bruising defeat on the southern shore of the Río de la Plata, his troops were forced to abandon Montevideo and Colonia del Sacramento, as well as Buenos Aires. Although often overlooked by British historians, Andrew Graham-Yooll argued in *Uruguay: A Travel and Literary Companion* that this event was widely regarded on the Río de la Plata as 'the turning point in colonial rule that put Spanish America on the path to independence'.

Yet the relief was short-lived in Montevideo. Over the next twenty years, the city was occupied by forces from Spain, Argentina, Portugal and Brazil. Uruguay finally claimed its independence in 1828, with Britain playing a significant role. Eager to create a buffer state between Brazil and Argentina and boost free trade—which, of course, would benefit Britain above all—a British envoy, Anglo-Irish diplomat Lord Ponsonby, brokered a peace deal, an incident cited as evidence of Britain's 'informal empire' in the region. 'Britain could not envisage war between two good potential customers with the memory so fresh of a Europe closed by Napoleon,' wrote Graham-Yooll. 'Independence [for Uruguay] came only after the British intervention.'

But the next two decades were similarly turbulent, as a byzantine web of local independence leaders and Argentine and Brazilian factions vied for control, while Britain and France repeatedly intervened to advance their own commercial and strategic interests. The crisis built up to the start of a civil war in 1839. Also known as the Guerra Grande ('Great War'), the polarising conflict involved rival independence leaders and their international allies. There was a nine-year siege of Montevideo by an Argentine–Uruguayan army and a retaliatory Anglo-French blockade of Buenos Aires before the war eventually came to an end in 1851. But the lack of a clear winner, and the extent of the destruction, saw conflict flare up again over the following decades.

Nevertheless, as the nineteenth century progressed, the British presence in Montevideo grew steadily and, while small in numbers, exerted a profound influence.

* * *

The Ciudad Vieja, the oldest part of Montevideo, covers a peninsula jutting into the Río de la Plata, so wide at this point it resembles the sea. Cobbled streets were lined with sprouting palm trees and nineteenth-century townhouses, their walls covered with murals and calligraphic graffiti tags. The scent of barbecued beef drifted over on the afternoon breeze, and a pulsing, emotive rhythm sounded in the distance—the kind of music you feel before you really hear it.

In 2018, seven years on from my first visit to Uruguay, I arrived in Montevideo to delve into its British connections. At first glance, the capital, particularly the elegantly crumbling architecture of the Ciudad Vieja, had much in common with Buenos Aires. Football, tango and world-class steaks were all present and correct, too, and you were more likely to see Montevideanos strolling around with a *mate* than a takeaway coffee. But beyond the surface similarities, the Uruguayan capital was far smaller and calmer, with its own distinct character and pace of life. Despite its riverside location, Buenos Aires largely turns its back on the water. While it retains a busy port, Montevideo feels more like a seaside resort, with a series of beaches along its southern flank and the serpentine Rambla, which extends for more than 13.7 miles, drawing runners, cyclists, fishers, dog-walkers and families. It is regarded as the longest continuous sidewalk in the world.

Montevideo is regularly named as the most 'liveable' city in South America, thanks largely to Uruguay's political and economic stability and broadly progressive outlook—same-sex marriage and recreational cannabis use were both legalised here in 2013. A UNESCO City of Literature—a status symbolised by an array of gorgeous independent bookshops—it also has a rich musical heritage. Montevideo is widely known as one of the two birthplaces of tango (alongside Buenos Aires), but few people outside of Uruguay are aware that the city is also intrinsically linked to another form of music and dance: candombe. Originating among communities of enslaved and formerly enslaved Africans and now recognised by UNESCO as part of Montevideo's intangible cultural heritage, it is based on a trio of drums, the *piano*, *repique* and *chico*. Featuring elaborately costumed dancers and a strong, and often satirical, storytelling element, candombe—not to be confused with the African-Brazilian religion Candomblé—is central to Montevideo's famous carnival, which, at forty days, is the longest in the world.

A short walk from my simple Ciudad Vieja hotel was the Mercado del Puerto, a covered market with a striking cast-iron structure reminiscent of a Victorian railway station, the metal-

SMALL EARTHQUAKES

work originating in a foundry in Liverpool in the 1860s. A hive of activity, particularly on weekends and when cruise ships have docked, it was packed with smoking steakhouses whose waiters reeled in customers with complimentary tasters of *medio y medio*, a blend of dry white and sweet sparkling wines.

Passing through a mix of gentrification (boutique hotels, fancy coffee shops, renovated *palacios*) and urban decay (blacked buildings, broken windows, disintegrating walls), I stumbled upon the former offices of two British businesses from the late nineteenth and early twentieth centuries, the Banco de Londres and the Montevideo Waterworks Co. Nearby, a flea market spread across the Ciudad Vieja's main square, selling an eclectic range of items—glassware, licence plates, old jewellery, *mate* gourds.

On the southern edge of the Ciudad Vieja, the Rambla takes the name Gran Bretaña and stretches south towards the old British-run gasworks, the last remnant of which is an empty gas holder. Before you reach it, you find the rather austere Anglican church. The Cathedral of the Most Holy Trinity—locally referred to as the 'Templo Inglés'—was originally built in 1844 before moving to its current site in 1935 to make way for the Rambla. Once the focal point of the religious life of Montevideo's British community, it was locked behind a rusted, padlocked fence, overlooking a patch of freshly mown grass dotted with palm trees, scattered with rubbish and dwarfed by a glass-and-concrete hotel. Its sides were graffitied with tags and doodles, and one corner had recently been singed by a fire, whose grey ashes still spiralled in the wind. Nearby, a homeless man had constructed a rudimentary shack from bits of scrap wood and a length of purple tarpaulin. The cathedral looked abandoned, but a sign at the back said it was open for Sunday services.

Back in the centre of the Ciudad Vieja was Montevideo's oldest surviving café-bar. Opened in 1877, Café Brasilero sat on a side street off a square, a low-lit, wood-panelled, quietly sophisticated joint covered with paintings, prints, black-and-white photos and crinkled newspaper clippings. It was a favourite haunt of Uruguay's best-known author and journalist, Eduardo Galeano. Early in his career, he used the pseudonym 'Gius', an approximation of the Spanish pronunciation of his middle name, 'Hughes', which came from his Welsh great-grandfather.

A playful, poetic writer, Galeano's work spanned capitalism and colonialism, culture and football. His most famous book, the anti-imperialistic polemic *Open Veins of Latin America*, was published in 1971. Banned by the military dictatorships in Uruguay, Argentina and Brazil, it sold more than a million copies and became one of the most influential South American books of all time. The author was jailed and then forced into exile during this period but refused to be silenced.

'No history is mute,' wrote Galeano, who died of lung cancer in 2015. 'No matter how much they own it, break it, and lie about it, human history refuses to shut its mouth. Despite deafness and ignorance, the time that was continues to tick inside the time that is.'

* * *

On a grey, drizzly, distinctly British-feeling Saturday morning, historian Álvaro Cuenca arrived at my hotel and upbraided me on my accommodation choice. 'I think you've made a lousy selection,' he said with a chuckle, escorting me to his car. 'You will see tomorrow. On Sunday everything in the Ciudad Vieja is closed. All you will hear are your own footsteps.'

The Anglo-Uruguayan Society had put me in touch with Cuenca, and he proved to be an excellent guide to Montevideo's lost British connections—knowledgeable, enthusiastic and equipped with an ironic sense of humour. Setting off in his Fiat hatchback—which he affectionately described as a 'Ferrari'—he explained that his interest in the subject was organic:

SMALL EARTHQUAKES

I have no British heritage: my family came from Spain, France and the Basque country. My father was an engineer, the director of public works for Montevideo. If I had been a typical son, I would have gone to a state or Catholic school. But my father died when I was young, and I wanted to go to an English school. I loved reading and history, and my interest [in the British in Uruguay] started from there. I was particularly interested by the world wars and the empire.

As we drove, Cuenca bemoaned the lack of good, modern travelogues about Uruguay and dismissed the books of late nineteenth- and early twentieth-century British-South American writers such as Robert Bontine Cunninghame Graham and W.H. Hudson as 'terrible, unreadable'. The latter, born on an Argentine ranch to American parents before moving to Britain where he found success as an author and naturalist, wrote about Uruguay in his 1885 novel *The Purple Land that England Lost*, reissued nine years later under the verbose title *The Purple Land, Being One Richard Lamb's Adventures in the Banda Orientál, in South America, as Told by Himself.* In it, Lamb, a young Englishman who flees to Uruguay, states:

> I cannot believe that if this country had been conquered and recolonised by England, and all that is crooked in it made straight according to our notions, my intercourse with the people would have had the wild, delightful flavour I have found in it. And if that distinctive flavour cannot be had along with the material prosperity resulting from Anglo-Saxon energy, I must breathe the wish that this land may never know such prosperity.

At its height, Cuenca explained, the British community in Uruguay was around 2,000 strong and concentrated in Montevideo and on ranches in the surrounding region. Members were predominantly 'businessmen and adventurers, and usually some combination of both'. Cuenca was keen to emphasise that it was a 'colony' rather than a community: 'A colony is not the same as a community: in the former you have leadership, common values—common Victorian values in this case. We had a British colony here from around 1880 to 1918, after which it declined.' One of the leaders, he added, was Walter Baring, a scion of the banking dynasty who served as British consul-general to Uruguay.

Although small in size—less than a fifth of the number of Lithuanians, for example—the Britons in Uruguay wielded significant political and economic clout. As in Buenos Aires, British investors dominated much of the local economy during the late nineteenth and early twentieth centuries—particularly in the areas of finance, utilities and communications—and owned large tracts of land in the wider region. British products flooded into the country, and by the time the Baring Panic struck in 1890, 'Uruguay's public debt was held in London,' said Cuenca. Members of the colony also reached high office. Born in Buenos Aires to a Scottish father and a Uruguayan mother, Duncan Stewart had a brief spell as interim president of Uruguay during a political crisis in 1894.

Alongside vast slaughterhouses, there was heavy investment in the railway network, which flourished in the early twentieth century before being nationalised and gradually withering away over the following decades, Cuenca explained as we arrived at the Estación Central General Artigas. Once Montevideo's main station, the elegant structure was built in 1897 by the London-registered Central Uruguay Railway Company, which also constructed around 1,000 miles of tracks across the country. Despite being designated a national monument, the station was closed in 2003. Now fenced off, its cavernous hall was occupied by homeless people, while the sculptures of British railway pioneers George Stephenson and James Watt that decorate the façade were soot-smudged from a recent fire and covered with pigeons.

As well as schools, clubs and a hospital, the British residents of Montevideo founded English-language newspapers—the

SMALL EARTHQUAKES

Montevideo Independent, *River Plate Times* and *Montevideo Times*, the latter of which ran until 1934—and a host of musical and theatrical societies. The latter often performed at the Victoria Hall, a community venue built to mark Queen Victoria's Diamond Jubilee in 1897. Yet the building quickly became a burden: it was only completed in 1902, a year after the monarch passed away, and the loan and interest repayments proved onerous. Later known as Teatro Victoria, it served as a masonic lodge for a period and was then largely vacant for decades before being turned into a theatre in the mid-1990s.

Cuenca drove west along the coast road, a fierce wind whipping across the Río de la Plata, lashing the shore with waves and sending up great clouds of chocolatey water that doused passing cars. 'The River Plate is always brown, but it's less brown on the Montevideo side—more of a brown-blue colour. But today it's very brown because we're getting all of the Buenos Aires water,' he insisted, as we arrived at the smart seaside *barrio* of Pocitos. A series of glass-fronted hotels and apartment blocks with balconies faced the river; the latter had aspirational names: Mirador, Regatta, El Dorado. Scraps of election posters were taped to lampposts, rippling in the wind.

Despite the inclement weather, a volleyball game was underway on the beach, kite-surfers zipped across the water and a dog-walker trudged along the Rambla. Cuenca continued:

> In the late nineteenth century, the British came up with the idea of creating 'Brighton in the south' in Pocitos. At this time, the Uruguayan aristocracy used to go to the countryside for their holidays, not the beach. The British built a huge hotel, the Gran Hotel de los Pocitos, an exact copy of Brighton pier and a tramway to get there. People started to go for the day or the weekend and a new neighbourhood formed around it.

Sadly, the pier was destroyed by a mighty storm in 1925, but some of the building names hint at the neighbourhood's British heritage: Balmoral, Exeter, The Prize. A later remnant of British-Uruguayan history also remains in Pocitos. Beyond Plaza Winston Churchill, a small square with a bust of the former prime minister, created in 1955 to mark his eightieth birthday, and a generic 'MONTEVIDEO' sign of the type that has sprung up in seemingly every city, town and resort worldwide in recent years, stood the Museo Naval. Facing the Río de la Plata, its grounds were strewn with assorted anchors, cannons, bows, torpedoes and gun emplacements, as well as a tattered Uruguayan flag on a pole, a black-and-white *Tintin*-style mural celebrating the 'Uruguayan pioneers of Antarctica' and, somewhat incongruously, a children's playground. Near the entrance of the museum was a long, grey gun that once sat on the *Admiral Graf Spee*, a casualty of the Battle of the River Plate, the first naval conflict of the Second World War.

Between September and December 1939, during the so-called 'Phony War', the period following the Nazi invasion of Poland in which there was little land-based fighting, the *Graf Spee*, a German pocket battleship, sunk or captured a series of British merchant vessels in the South Atlantic. In response, the Royal Navy dispatched seven 'hunting groups' featuring twenty-three warships in hot pursuit. Commanded by Captain Hans Langsdorff, the *Graf Spee* destroyed a further three merchant vessels, before clashing with HMS *Exeter*, HMS *Ajax* and HMS *Achilles*, forcing the former to flee to the safety of the Falkland Islands. Langsdorff then headed to the port of Montevideo in neutral Uruguay, pursued by light cruisers *Ajax* and *Achilles* under the command of Commodore Henry Harwood.

International law permitted the *Graf Spee* to remain in a neutral port for twenty-four hours. Despite British diplomatic efforts, Langsdorff managed to extend the stay to seventy-two hours to repair damage to the ship but eventually departed on 17 December. In the meantime, the Royal Navy spread misinformation about a large fleet gathering nearby. The ruse appears to have worked. Rather than risk the lives of his crew for little military gain, Langsdorff decided to scuttle the *Graf Spee* in the estuary of the Río de la Plata, providing the British with a significant propaganda and military victory. The crew of the *Graf Spee* were taken to Buenos Aires, where Langsdorff shot himself in his hotel room.

By contrast, Harwood's efforts earned him a knighthood and a promotion to rear admiral. His dress uniform is on display in the museum's large display on the Battle of the River Plate, alongside assorted items salvaged from the *Graf Spee*—a sextant, a pair of binoculars, a telephone, a twisted shard of metal from the hull—and a stentorian documentary playing on loop.

Around 130 *Graf Spee* crewman decided to stay on in Argentina, settling in the Córdoba province town of Villa Calamuchita, whose population already had a sizeable German, Austrian and Swiss contingent. Later renamed Villa General Belgrano, it now has an ersatz Germanic vibe, with mock castles, Alpine-style buildings, beer halls, shops selling cuckoo clocks and troll dolls, and restaurants serving sausages, sauerkraut and black forest gateau, as well as a raucous Oktoberfest.

* * *

Our final stop was the British Cemetery, which dates back to 1828. The outside walls were topped with barbed wire and covered with graffiti, but the interior was tranquil and well tended. A monument to Queen Victoria and a tribute to Queen Elizabeth stood at the entrance, and there were more gardeners than mourners, mowing the lawns, watering the flowers, trimming the hedges.

The names on the gravestones told stories of both immigration and integration: Cooper, Lumb, Humphreys, Cutler, Clark, Coates and Attree, as well as Ruiz-Balbi, Keller, Arechavaleta and Clark-Vidal. Showing me round, Cuenca told me about some of the more notable residents. They included John Christie, the 'jute-wallah of Uruguay', and Elizabeth Birdsall, 'the first woman from the Americas to conduct a symphony orchestra'.

We stopped at the grave of footballer Henry Stanley Bowles, who symbolises British sporting links with Uruguay. In 1842, when Montevideanos were largely occupied with Spanish-origin sports such as bullfighting, a group of British residents set-up the Victoria Cricket Club. Among them was Liverpool-born Samuel Lafone, a prominent cattle merchant with extensive investments in Uruguay, Argentina and the Falkland Islands. He was a driving force behind the development of the neighbourhood of La Teja and the Anglican church in Montevideo, while laying the groundwork for a new settlement 80 miles west on the peninsula of Punta del Este, now one of the glitziest beach resorts in South America.

The Victoria Cricket Club only lasted a few years, but many of its founders were involved in the creation of the Montevideo Cricket Club (MVCC) in 1861. Bats, balls, stumps and other sporting equipment was imported from Britain, and the membership was soon bolstered by staff from a recently opened branch of the Bank of London and by employees of the Montevideo Waterworks, a British company that secured a tender from the Uruguayan government to provide the city with drinking water. A match against the newly formed Buenos Aires Cricket Club (BACC) was originally scheduled for 1864, but political unrest led to its suspension until 1868. Held at the MVCC's La Blanqueada ground, the first international cricket match in South America was won by the BACC, as was the rematch in Buenos Aires the following year; all of the players had British heritage. (These results largely continued until the Second World War, with the MVCC winning only six of twenty-nine matches against its Argentine rival.)

Despite its name, the MVCC was a multi-sports organisation. Alongside cricket, members took part in athletics, cycling and rowing and played tennis, golf, hockey and rugby—the MVCC is the oldest rugby union club still in operation in the Americas and the eighth oldest in the world. Unlike cricket, a niche interest in present-day Uruguay, the sport is still popular, though the most famous Uruguayan rugby story occurred off the pitch in 1972, when an air force plane carrying members of Montevideo's Old Christians Club rugby team crashed in an Andean valley en route to Santiago, Chile. Against the odds, sixteen young men endured seventy-two days in extreme conditions, forced to eat the flesh of their dead teammates to survive, before being rescued in what became known as the 'Miracle of the Andes'. But as in Argentina, football was the sport that transcended its origins to become a central part of Uruguayan culture.

Sports, games and activities involving rubber balls have long been played in Latin America—famously in highly ritualised forms in Mesoamerica among societies such as the Maya and Mexica (commonly known as the Aztec), as well as among communities across the Amazon—but the modern incarnation of football had British roots. It took hold in Uruguay (and Argentina) as the nineteenth century wore on. During this period, the British population in Montevideo grew through the opening of British schools (in which sport was central to the curriculum, at least for boys) and the development of the railway network, which was dominated by British and Anglo-Uruguayan firms. The MVCC initially held intra-club matches before playing against an outside opponent, a team drawn from the crew of a visiting British ship, in 1878. In *From Beauty to Duty: A Footballing History of Uruguay 1878–1917*, author Martin da Cruz quotes one of the players from that day, Pedro Campbell Towers: 'It was a very rough game in those days. Football had not yet been properly defined ... it was played almost like rugby.' The first match was a draw, the second a win for the home team. Three years later, in 1881, the MVCC played the Montevideo

Rowing Club in the first football match involving different Uruguayan teams.

Originally limited to players with British heritage, football gradually spread throughout the wider Uruguayan population. Its popularity was driven forward by William Leslie Poole, an Anglo-Scottish teacher born in Kent. After emigrating to Uruguay at the age of eighteen, he founded Montevideo's English High School and became Uruguay's equivalent of Argentina's Alexander Watson Hutton. Known as the 'father of Uruguayan football', Poole championed the sport to such an extent that one of his former pupils, Henry Lichtenberger, who had British, Brazilian and Alsatian heritage, founded the country's first football club, Foot Ball Club (later renamed Albion Football Club) in 1891. An accomplished player in his own right before becoming a referee and then president of the forerunner of the Uruguayan FA, Poole had a more open-minded approach to participation than some of his peers, according to the Scottish Football Museum: 'Poole insisted on the participation of both [British] nationals and foreigners with no distinction of race, language, religion, political opinion or economic position.'

British railway companies and their employees also played an important role. Founded in 1891, the Central Uruguay Railway Cricket Club's football team later took the name of the working-class Montevideo neighbourhood in which it was based: Peñarol. 'The club's players sported a black and yellow striped kit, based on the colours of George Stephenson's [ground-breaking locomotive] *Rocket*,' wrote Andreas Campomar in *¡Golazo! A History of Latin American Football*. Peñarol steamed ahead, becoming one of the most successful teams in South America, with five Copa Libertadores victories to date.

Other clubs had indirect British inspiration. Based in the Montevideo *barrio* of Nuevo París, Liverpool FC were originally a team of Catholic school students before formalising as a club in 1915. The name comes from the city's strong maritime tradition rather than the Merseyside club: ships carrying coal regularly sailed from Liverpool to Montevideo in the early twentieth century. According to legend, one of the club's founders, Jose Freire, 'had pinpointed Liverpool on a map and noted its link to his hometown, which he confirmed by consulting a local priest,' reported the *Liverpool Echo*. The club, which plays in blue-and-black kits, unlike their red namesakes, won their first Primera División title in 2023. 'Back in the day, I remember a red flag with an LFC crest being taken to every game. Nowadays, you can see a banner that reads "Nunca Caminarás Solo" (You'll Never Walk Alone). There is also a Liver Bird a mythic symbol of both the city and Liverpool FC on it, painted in black on a blue background,' its communications and marketing officer, Nicolás Aranco, told the website This Is Anfield.

In theory, there could be a South American-flavoured Merseyside derby, as Everton de Viña del Mar play in Chile's Primera División. Based some 900 miles west of Montevideo in the upscale seaside resort town of Viña del Mar, the club dates to 1909, reputedly taking its name from one of its Anglo-Chilean founders, David Foxley, whose grandparents were from Liverpool. Nicknamed the Ruleteros (roulette players), thanks to early financial backing from the Viña del Mar casino, they played their English namesakes in a pre-season friendly for the Brotherhood Cup at Goodison Park in 2010: the home side won 2–0. The two clubs have since had a partnership to 'share knowledge in a variety of areas including youth coaching, marketing and retail and fan base development, as well as talent identification,' the *Liverpool Echo* reported.

On the international stage, Uruguay has always punched above its weight, winning the World Cup in 1930—a tournament it hosted—and 1950, while reaching the semi-finals on four other occasions. Its first international goal was scored by Bowles, who was born in Brighton in 1871. As a youngster, he turned out for

EVERYTHING BUT THE MOO

Preston North End before taking advantage of family contacts to move to Montevideo, where he worked for the Eastern Telegraph Company and earned a place in the MVCC team. In 1889, the skilful forward scored for a select XI picked from Montevideo's clubs against their counterparts in Buenos Aires. Held to mark the opening of the MVCC's new football pitch, the contest was 'the first of its kind in the Río de la Plata ... The celebration took place on the 70th birthday of Queen Victoria, whose portrait was placed on one of the VIP seats', according to the MVCC's official history.

Tragically, Bowles didn't have long to enjoy his success. 'In 1899, he goes to play golf at the course in Punta Carretas, and in comes a tornado, which killed him,' explained Cuenca. There are varying accounts of what exactly happened: some say Bowles was carried away by the tornado after deciding to walk to the clubhouse rather than shelter in a bunker with his friends; others say the tornado struck a hut in which he was sheltering or hit the changing room in which he was getting ready to play.

Bowles' untimely death, shortly after his wife gave birth to their son, could be seen as an omen signalling the beginning of the end of the British domination of football in Uruguay and throughout South America, as the sport steadily spread beyond the confines of the Anglo clubs, schools and companies. 'In the twentieth century,' wrote Campomar, 'football would become both a passion and a religion that would get into the blood of the whole of the continent.'

Before heading off, Cuenca showed me the chapel, which contained a reminder of the most significant British connection with Uruguay. As the squawks of monk parakeets drifted in from the heights of the towering palms outside, I found a small plaque on the wall entitled: 'Fray Bentos Roll of Honour 1939–45' with the names of six men who died in the Second World War.

* * *

SMALL EARTHQUAKES

The story starts in 1816, when Europe experienced the 'year without a summer', triggered by the most powerful volcanic eruption in recorded history. The previous year, Mount Tambora on Sumbawa in present-day Indonesia blasted apart, killing more than 10,000 people in the surrounding area and spewing 36 cubic miles of rock, ash, aerosols and other debris into the atmosphere. A giant volcanic cloud drifted across the northern hemisphere and blocked out the sun, causing summer temperatures in Europe to plunge and sparking crop failures, food shortages and famine.

The event had a profound impact on Justus von Liebig, who was thirteen at the time and living with his family in Darmstadt, now in the German state of Hesse. Liebig grew up to become a ground-breaking scientist: his myriad achievements include founding the first university-based research laboratory, modernising chemistry education; conducting some of the earliest research into fertilisers; and making breakthroughs in organic compound analysis. Memories of the dark days of 1816 also inspired an interest in food chemistry and nutrition. As well as inventing infant formula, Liebig developed a process for producing a concentrated meat extract as a cheap and tasty source of nutrition for people who were malnourished, sick or convalescing, as was much of Europe's working class during the Industrial Revolution. Chunks of beef were salted, boiled and broken into slithers before being set in their own fat. Liebig's Extractum Carnis went on sale in 1847, at a time when meat was prohibitively expensive for most people in Europe. But the product required around 30 kilos of beef to make one kilo of extract, so producing it using European meat proved commercially unviable.

The solution was provided almost two decades later by a young German (or Belgian; there are conflicting accounts) railway engineer who had worked in South America, George Christian Giebert. He had read about Liebig's work and approached the chemist with a proposal to set up a factory in Uruguay. The booming leather industry on the Pampas produced as a by-product an abundance of meat, much of which was left to rot in this era before the development of refrigerated shipping. In 1863, Giebert bought a tract of land on the banks of the Río Uruguay, 180 miles northwest of Montevideo, and founded a ranch and factory. Two years later, he and Liebig registered the Liebig Extract of Meat Company (LEMCO) and secured a £150,000 loan in London. Later that year, 1,760lbs of Liebig's Extract of Meat were exported to Europe.

The venture was a huge success, with the company making exalted boasts about the product's health benefits. Liebig even declared it could cure typhus. The medical and nutritional claims were called into question, but this did not dent sales: London's St Thomas Hospital reportedly used 12,000 pots of Liebig's Extract of Meat a year. LEMCO responded to the criticism by shifting focus, with adverts describing the product as 'invigorating for the weak and ailing' and an 'invaluable tonic', as well as an easy way for cooks to add flavour to their meat stews. It also released collectable trading cards and cookbooks—such as *Lemco Dishes for All Seasons* by Eva Tuite, which features recipes for everything from macaroni cheese to veal cutlets—to boost public interest.

In the process, a town grew up alongside the Río Uruguay factory, as workers flocked from across Uruguay and around sixty other countries. Originally called Villa Independencia, the settlement was later renamed after a religious hermit called Fray Bentos ('Friar Benedict' in English), who reputedly lived in a nearby cave. Over time, LEMCO refined the manufacturing process, solidifying the liquid extract and creating Oxo, crumbly cubes of stock that could be sold in smaller quantities at a cheaper price, thus expanding the market. It also started churning out other products, including tinned corned beef and tongue, while taking advantage of the development of refrigerated cargo ships ('reefers') in the late nineteenth century to export frozen meat to Europe.

These products became staples for working-class people across Europe for whom meat had previously been a luxury item. Oxo was an official sponsor of the 1908 London Olympics; marathon runners were even offered Oxo-flavoured drinks to give them an energy boost during the race. The products also provided inexpensive, long-lasting and easy-to-carry rations for polar explorers such as Robert Falcon Scott and Ernest Shackleton, as well as British soldiers during the Boer War and British and German troops in the First World War. In 1917, the crew of a tank known as 'Fray Bentos'—named by its captain, a Nottingham grocer who sold the products in his shop before the war—spent more than sixty hours in no-man's land under heavy fire during the Battle of Passchendaele. The men inside became the most decorated tank crew of the war.

In 1924, LEMCO's Fray Bentos plant and associated ranches and assets—including its cold store on London's South Bank, of which the iconic Oxo Tower was once part—were bought by the British Vestey Group and renamed Frigorífico Anglo del Uruguay (though the Fray Bentos trademark was retained by LEMCO). The company dated back to the 1890s, when William and Edmund Vestey founded the Union Cold Storage Company in their home city of Liverpool, built cold stores across Europe, Russia and China and developed a fleet of refrigerated ships, the Blue Star Line, through which they supplied meat, fish and eggs to customers in the UK and globally. The brothers later moved into cattle ranching, meat production and processing in Argentina, Brazil, Venezuela, Australia and New Zealand, as well as Uruguay. Alongside canning plants and commercial property, they also built up a large chain of butcher shops in the UK. The brothers sought to control the whole supply chain and wield huge market power while driving competitors out of business and creating monopolies.

EVERYTHING BUT THE MOO

The company became the world's largest private conglomerate, and the brothers grew fabulously wealthy, mingling with the royal family and acquiring a peerage for William. As journalist Phillip Knightley reported in his book *The Rise and Fall of the House of Vestey*: 'They did not live on the income; they did not live on the interest from their investments; they lived on the interest on the interest.' By the 1940s, the Vesteys were estimated to be the second richest family in the UK, after the royals.

During this period, their Uruguayan plant—commonly known as El Anglo—was exporting more than 200 different products, from leather to soap, sausages to jams. In 1943 alone, 16 million tins of corned beef were shipped from Fray Bentos, the vast majority used to power the Allied war effort. The products even earned a royal following: 'I remember eating corned beef until it came out of my ears,' King Charles, then the Prince of Wales, told reporters when he visited Uruguay in 1999.

* * *

Today, the plant is open to the public as an improbable tourist attraction. The Paisaje Industrial Fray Bentos (Fray Bentos Industrial Landscape) site is an impressive display of once cutting-edge, now slowly rusting Edwardian- and Victorian-era technology. It even has an eerie beauty, at least for anyone with a passion for industrial archaeology.

The office buildings have been renovated and now house a museum with exhibits from the plant's heyday, including vintage typewriters, classic posters, rudimentary firefighting equipment and rickety delivery trucks. Another section has been taken over by a local university, keeping alive the plant's technological traditions. But most of the rambling complex has been left as it was, and wandering through these vast, silent, low-lit buildings was a haunting experience. The engine room looked like a scene from a steampunk comic, with rusted diesel-powered generators, huge turbines and steam compressors festooned with levers, valves and wheels connected by a multitude of winding pipes and chimneys. On the walls next door were marble-panelled units covered with the dials and switches that controlled the plant's electricity production: in 1883, this became the first place in Uruguay to generate electricity. 'The factory reminds me of the Charlie Chaplin film *Modern Times*,' said Cerilla, the museum manager, as she and guide Nicolás Cremella showed me round.

Outside, a soaring water tower loomed over a crowd of interlinked brick, concrete, glass and corrugated-iron buildings. Many are off-limits for safety reasons, including the monolithic cold store, which once held up to 18,000 tonnes of frozen meat. But it is possible to poke round the Casa Grande, the manager's house, an opulent mansion with stained-glass windows, two pianos, hardwood floors and a gong to signal the start of a meal. 'This was the industrial revolution in Uruguay,' said Cremella. 'Fray Bentos was really important to Uruguay—it was the country's real capital, not Montevideo. It was the only industrial meat company and provided jobs throughout the country.' But while the company may have provided work locally, employing around 5,000 people at its height, the profits headed overseas.

Fray Bentos products remained popular in post-war Europe but slowly fell out of favour as food technology developed and eating habits changed. The Anglo plant was passed on to the Uruguayan government in the late 1960s and eventually closed in 1979. 'It was a company town, and it was terrible for people when it finally shut down,' said Cerilla, whose father and grandfather worked at the plant. 'Lots of people left, and many emigrated.'

Despite the initial gloom, Fray Bentos recovered. Today, it has a large paper pulp industry—which has provoked controversy because of concerns over water pollution—and in 2015 UNESCO granted World Heritage Site status to the Anglo plant and nearby Barrio Anglo, a suburb of around 300 homes built for senior staff. In the late afternoon, I walked back into town via the neighbourhood. The smell of mowed grass, tree blossoms and barbecue smoke hung in the air as I wandered past clusters of simple bungalows with corrugated-iron roofs and luxuriant gardens. Nearby were the golf, tennis, football and rowing clubs that once formed the focal point of life for the community.

An insight into this period is provided by S.W. Johnson, a British manager at the plant in the 1930s. In an account featured in *Uruguay: A Travel and Literary Companion* by Graham-Yooll (who worked as a trainee auditor at the Anglo meatpacking company in Buenos Aires before moving into journalism), Johnson emphasises that he and his compatriots led 'a very active life':

> We had the 'Anglo Social and Athletic Club', with its hall for dances, a snooker/billiards room, bridge room, library which only carried English books and magazines ... and a bar (the Uruguayan attendant also accepted bets on the then illegal *quiniela* or numbers game) ... As we were not then blessed or cursed with television, and the radio [was] mainly used for listening to the BBC, which brought news from 'home'.

During Johnson's spell in Fray Bentos, British staff—who, together with their families, numbered around sixty to seventy— 'retained all the key posts' and tended to avoid mixing with local Uruguayans, who were firmly excluded from the array of leisure activities. The result, Johnson continued, was a 'suffocating British colony atmosphere' that left him eager to break out.

By the time I reached the town centre, it was early evening and life was returning as locals rose from their afternoon siestas. Guests at my hotel posed for photos beside a 6-foot cardboard reproduction of a 1930s advert for corned beef, and a middle-aged man in karate whites and flip-flops carried a holdall of nunchucks and wooden swords. Nearby, a group of children played hide-and-seek in the main square, Plaza Constitución, ducking down in the cast-iron bandstand, donated by the company to the town in 1902 and a replica of one that once stood at the Crystal Palace in London. Parents gathered on benches to sip *mate*, while monk parakeets cawed from their perches in the palm, willow and palo borracho trees.

For my final dinner in Fray Bentos, it seemed fitting to sample the product that, above all others, put the town on the map. Uruguayans eat more beef than virtually anyone else in the world, and the livestock industry remains a cornerstone of the economy: there are currently around 12 million cows in the country, outnumbering the human population by almost four to one. But while Fray Bentos remains synonymous with corned beef in the UK, few locals eat it today. 'We don't like eating meat from tins, we like fresh meat,' said Cremella. 'People in Fray Bentos may have tins of corned beef at home, perhaps on the shelf as a souvenir [or trinket], but not to eat.'

Sure enough, none of the restaurants I visited had corned beef on the menu, nor did the first three supermarkets I stopped in. Eventually, as I was on the verge of giving up, I found a small general store with a couple of tins for sale—'Marca Uruguay—Industria Brazil', the label read: 'Uruguay Brand—Made in Brazil'.

* * *

In the UK, Fray Bentos products remain a cultural touchstone and have even undergone a crisis-driven renaissance in recent years. Although demand for corned beef has waned, Baxters—the Scottish-based food company that now owns the Fray Bentos brand—reported a 'surge' in demand for its tinned pies in 2019 as customers stocked up amid fears of food shortages in the wake of a no-deal Brexit. The following year, another wave of stockpiling took place during the early stages of the COVID-19 pandemic, as anxiety-driven nostalgia for comfort foods and tightening household finances combined to push sales of canned meat products up by almost a quarter.

Fray Bentos products have also been co-opted into confected right-wing 'culture wars': the *Sun* claimed the launch of Fray Bentos' full English breakfast pie 'put two sausage-shaped fingers up to the smashed avocado brigade', while the *Daily Mail* lamented the redesign of the 'iconic metal tins after a half a century because millennials don't know how to open them'. They also regularly appear in the satirical photo collages of artist Cold War Steve:

> I started to introduce tinned pies into my work, following the announcement of then Brexit Secretary Dominic Raab that there will be 'adequate food' after our departure from the EU. Fray Bentos pies, Vesta Curry, Ye Olde Oak tinned ham, are all perfect foodstuffs for stockpiling—they are also brands which hark back to a glorious pre-ethnically diverse Britain, of insipid food and insipid high streets.

Nevertheless, the Fray Bentos range has attempted to move the brand with the times. You can now buy a chicken curry pie or a tub of 'meatball arrabbiata'. And the brand that once boasted it used 'every part of the cow except for the moo' even sells a vegan steak and kidney bean pie that was named the 'best of the year' at animal rights organisation PETA's 2019 Vegan Food Awards.

* * *

As for the Vesteys, their family's international business empire was once worth an estimated £2 billion. But in 1980, a *Times* investigation revealed 'a complex tax-avoidance scheme (using overseas trusts) that meant some of their British-based businesses had paid almost no tax for almost 60 years. The loophole was eventually closed in 1991.' A revenue official is said to have compared dealing with the tax affairs of the Vesteys to 'trying to squeeze a rice pudding'.

In *Treasure Islands: Tax Havens and the Men Who Stole the World*, Nicholas Shaxson argued that William and Edmund

Vestey were ahead of their time, describing them as pioneers of 'today's global tax avoidance system'. 'When the Queen finally started paying income tax in 1993 after a public outcry,' he added, 'the latest Lord Vestey smiled and said: "Well, that makes me the last one.".'

Meanwhile, the town of Fray Bentos now lies within a free trade zone, which largely exempts companies operating within it from taxation, a development you suspect would have found favour with the Vestey brothers. The Uruguayan government claims free trade zones will help diversify the national economy, which still relies heavily on livestock, a dependence spurred by LEMCO back in the late nineteenth century.

* * *

In 1865, as the fledgling Fray Bentos plant began shipping Liebig's Extract of Meat across the Atlantic to Europe, a small band of Welsh men and women sailed in the opposite direction, seeking freedom in Patagonia.

3

Y WLADFA

ARGENTINE PATAGONIA

A pair of bus-sized shadows slid beneath the boat, crushing together, breaking apart, almost close enough to touch. Moments later, an ink-black torso broke the surface of the water, its white-smudged head encrusted with barnacles and pockmarked with callouses. Finally, a giant fluke erupted upwards, a few feet away, creating a cascade of waves that rocked the boat and drenched everyone on board. For a couple of minutes, the behemoths disappeared from view before reappearing beneath us, spiralling silently through the water. Given that they each weighed 60–70 tonnes, the mating ritual of these southern right whales was a predictably momentous, but also unexpectedly elegant, affair.

The waters surrounding Península Valdés, a hammerhead-shaped landmass extending into the Atlantic at the northeastern tip of Patagonia, are a globally important breeding ground for this species of whale. Between June and December, more than 1,000 of the endangered cetaceans—so-named because whalers considered them the 'right' ones to hunt, thanks to their plentiful oil and baleen, the bristle-filled plates used to filter krill and other planktonic crustaceans from the water—gather offshore in the bay to the south of the peninsula, the Golfo Nuevo.

Designated a UNESCO World Heritage Site, this part of coastal Patagonia is populated by multitudes of seabirds, while the beaches are blanketed with large colonies of sea lions and elephant seals, their inquisitive pups occasionally preyed upon by stealthy orcas. When the naturalist and writer Gerald Durrell visited in the 1950s in search of animals for his zoo on Jersey, he was astonished by the abundant birds, animals and marine creatures. 'It was almost as if the peninsula and its narrow isthmus was a *cul-de-sac* into which all the wild-life of [the region] had drained and from which it could not escape,' he wrote in *The Whispering Land*.

A century earlier, a converted tea clipper named the *Mimosa* arrived in the Golfo Nuevo from Liverpool at the start of the breeding season for the southern right whales. On board were around 153 people from Wales who would transform the fate of Patagonia.

* * *

A region long mythologised by outsiders, Patagonia always feels just out of reach. Divided between Argentina and Chile, it spans more than 400,000 square miles—twice the size of Spain—and encompasses most of southern South America. Patagonia's precise boundaries are fuzzy and contested, sometimes fiercely. Broadly speaking, the large area east of the Andes is part of Argentina, while the narrower portion to the west of the mountain chain is part of Chile. In the north, it stretches from the Río Negro in Argentina—and anywhere from the city of Temuco to the town of Hornopirén in Chile—south to the Strait of Magellan; the archipelago of Tierra del Fuego, which lies south of the channel at the southern tip of the continent, is often also included as part of Patagonia. A dizzying array of landscapes lie

Y WLADFA

within the region: ragged granite massifs, volcanoes, temperate rainforests, icefields, arid steppe, fertile valleys, tablelands, canyons and beaches.

Studies suggest the first human inhabitants arrived 14,500 to 17,000 years ago. A window into the culture of early Patagonians is provided by the Cueva de los Manos, which is located in an isolated spot 500 miles southwest of Península Valdés. The 'Cave of the Hands' contains some of the world's oldest surviving forms of artistic expression, dating back 9,500 to 13,000 years. Alongside depictions of hunting scenes, stylised humans and animals such as guanacos—wild relatives of the llama, still found across Patagonia—there is a mesmerising collection of stencilled red, white, yellow and black handprints, created more recently but still some 5,000 years old.

The cave painters were probably ancestors of the Tehuelche, who once ranged across much of Patagonia and are known in the southwest of the region as the Aónikenk. While sharing a common language and way of life, there was a wide range of dialects and cultural practices among Tehuelche nomadic societies. In his fantastical account of the 1519–22 Magellan–Elcano expedition, which featured British sailors and travelled along the Atlantic coast of Patagonia on what would ultimately become the first circumnavigation of the globe, Venetian chronicler Antonio Pigafetta refers to the Tehuelche as 'giants'. Some of them, he claimed in his account of the voyage, were so 'tall that the tallest of us only came up to his waist', creating a myth that proved stubbornly persistent in Europe. As well as kidnapping a Tehuelche man (who subsequently died on board) from an area now occupied by the town of Puerto San Julián, the expedition's leader, Ferdinand Magellan, gave the region its modern name by calling its inhabitants 'Patagones'. The etymology is disputed: the name probably came from a contemporary Spanish novel, *Primaleon*, which featured the fearsome giant Patagón, though some argue it refers to 'Land of the Big Feet', deriving from the Spanish word for foot, *pata*, as the Tehuelche's hefty guanaco-skin shoes left behind large prints.

Magellan and Pigafetta's mythmaking was dismissed by Francis Drake when he sailed along the Patagonian coast on his own circumnavigation in 1577. In *The World Encompassed by Sir Francis Drake*—which was compiled by Drake's nephew (who, confusingly, was also named Francis Drake) and based on the notes of the fleet's pastor, Francis Fletcher, as well as Drake's journal and snippets from his crewmen—the Tehuelche are described as relatively tall but 'nothing so monstrous and giant-like as they were represented'. Yet Drake was far from a benign visitor: he killed a Tehuelche man after two of his crew were fatally shot with a bow and arrow, shortly before executing his former friend Thomas Doughty for mutiny and treason, an act that also took place in the future site of Puerto San Julián.

Over the following centuries, the Spanish Empire and, subsequently, the independent Argentine and Chilean states consolidated their hold over southern South America. But by the mid-nineteenth century, Patagonia largely remained beyond their control, despite sporadic, unsuccessful, efforts to found colonies, trading settlements and fortresses. The idea of staking a British claim to Patagonia was also promoted on various occasions, inspired in part by the travels of Thomas Falkner, a surgeon on a slave ship that arrived in Buenos Aires in the 1730s. Ill health forced him to convalesce in the city, and he ended up spending the next four decades in South America, during which he became a Jesuit and travelled widely in northern Patagonia as a missionary. In *A Description of Patagonia, and the Adjoining Parts of South America*, he wrote enthusiastically about the possibilities for British trade, advocated a strategic alliance with the Spanish Empire and discussed the benefits of establishing a settlement in Patagonia that 'would be much more convenient for ships going to the South Seas than that of Buenos Ayres'.

Y WLADFA

Despite a history dating back millennia, the Tehuelche and other Indigenous peoples in Patagonia and neighbouring regions to the north and south were disregarded and dismissed, their ancestral lands deemed empty and ripe for exploitation. Over the preceding centuries, Tehuelche culture had been transformed by horses, the descendants of animals brought over to South America by Europeans in the sixteenth century, which escaped or were abandoned and steadily multiplied and spread across Patagonia. The Tehuelche became expert horsemen and women, which allowed their nomadic societies to expand in size and range, increasing interaction between different Indigenous groups and cultures, including the influential Mapuche.

* * *

The first half of the nineteenth century was also a turbulent time in Wales. During the mid-1830s, Chartism—a mass working-class movement demanding democratic reforms, including universal male suffrage (voting at the time was limited to male property owners) and the abolition of the property qualification for prospective MPs—took hold in the rapidly industrialising valleys of South Wales. There were large public meetings, marches and clashes with the authorities. In the Newport Rising of 1839, more than twenty protesters were killed when soldiers opened fire on a crowd, while local Chartist leaders were convicted of treason and exiled to Australia.

There was similar strife in rural areas. Between 1839 and 1843, the Rebecca Riots took place in Pembrokeshire, Cardiganshire and Carmarthenshire, a chain of protests by tenant farmers, farm workers, labourers and others, ostensibly against burdensome road tolls imposed by groups of businessmen called Turnpike Trusts. Known as Merched Beca (Rebecca's Daughters)—probably a reference to Genesis 24:60, in which Rebecca is told 'may your descendants possess the gate of those who hate them'—male protesters disguised themselves in women's clothing and attacked tollgates.

Although road tolls were the catalyst, the uprising was an expression of wider discontent over deteriorating socio-economic conditions in the Welsh countryside. Most farmers did not own their land and faced debilitatingly high rents from wealthy landlords. Alongside falling livestock prices, failing harvests and the loss of communal grazing grounds, they had to pay tithes valued at 10 per cent of their annual produce to the church, even though most of them went to Nonconformist chapels instead. This was combined with the 1834 Poor Law, which instituted the much-despised workhouses, and a growing rural population, despite large-scale emigration to industrialising cities in South Wales and England.

There was a predictable response from the British—or, rather, the English—establishment. The unrest was blamed on a lack of education and a government inquiry was launched, led by three male, middle-class Anglican commissioners, none of whom spoke Welsh. The subsequent report caused outrage and became known as the 'Brad y Llyfrau Gleision', the 'Treachery of the Blue Books'. As well as criticising the state of teaching and school buildings in Wales, it lambasted the morals of the Welsh people, their Nonconformity—a mass Protestant movement that broke away from the established Anglican doctrines and was practised by over three-quarters of worshippers in the country, with its chapels becoming a key part of Welsh identity and culture—and, above all, the Welsh language, which was spoken by most people in Wales at the time. Urging the adoption of English, the commissioners asserted in a tone that would become common across the British Empire: 'The Welsh language is a vast drawback to Wales, and a manifold barrier to the moral progress and commercial prosperity of the people. It is not easy to over-estimate its evil effects ... As a proof of this, there is no Welsh literature worthy of the name.'

Part of a longstanding tradition of discrimination against the Welsh language that included a sixteenth-century law mandating that English was to be the language of the courts in Wales, the 'Treachery of the Blue Books' had a lasting impact. It was compounded by practices such as the 'Welsh Not', in which pupils in many schools in the nineteenth and twentieth centuries were punished for speaking Welsh by having a wooden board hung around their necks; they were often caned, too. Increasing English migration into Wales to feed the ever-increasing demand for workers during the industrial revolution also fed into wider concerns about the suppression of Welsh language, culture and identity.

It was in this context that plans for a Welsh colony overseas began to take shape. During the nineteenth century, there was significant Welsh emigration to Anglophone parts of the British Empire such as Australia and Canada, as well as the United States and, to a lesser extent, South America. But there was a sense that the Welsh language and cultural identity was being lost in the process, and a desire grew to create a 'little Wales beyond Wales'. In 1850, a London-born Welshman, Thomas Benbow Phillips, attempted to found a small Welsh settlement named Nova Cambria ('New Wales') in southern Brazil, but it survived less than five years.

A later South American effort proved more successful. Reverend Michael D. Jones, a Welsh Congregationalist minister from the village of Llanuwchllyn near Bala, was the driving force behind it. He spent a period in Ohio, where he set up societies to help Welsh migrants maintain their culture. Despite these efforts, he noted both the hardships they faced and the speed and ease with which they assimilated into American life, a process that eroded their language and thus their identity.

Back in Wales, Jones began calling for the establishment of a self-sufficient Welsh-speaking colony away from the domineering influence of the English language. He set up an emigration society, gave speeches, wrote articles and a book, gathered funds and sought out settlers while vigorously rebutting criticism that the project was an unpatriotic venture. Several locations were touted, including in Australia, New Zealand, Vancouver Island and Palestine, before Patagonia was decided upon because of its sparse Indigenous population and isolation from other colonial settlements. After lengthy negotiations, a deal was struck with the Argentine government granting each Welsh settler family a *cuadra* (roughly 100 acres) of land in the Chubut River Valley (whose name derives from its Tehuelche name, *chupat*, meaning 'transparent'), close to the Atlantic coast in northeast Patagonia. The Argentine government also reportedly paid some compensation—perhaps totalling 300,000 pesos—to Tehuelche leaders in the region to ensure cordial relations with the Welsh colonists.

At this stage, eastern Patagonia had not been colonised, but both the Argentine and Chilean governments were keen to stake their claims. In a bid to expand 'civilisation' against the supposed 'primitiveness' of the native population and cement its territorial claim against the Chileans, the Argentine government actively encouraged European migration to what it regarded as the vast, empty expanses 'for the purpose of tilling the soil, improving industries, and introducing arts and sciences', as the constitution stated. The government's approach followed the famous dictum of influential nineteenth-century political theorist Juan Bautista Alberdi: 'To govern is to populate.' Dismissing Indigenous people (and, more widely, non-Europeans in general) as 'barbarians', Alberdi called for Anglo-Saxon immigration, a designation that included the Welsh in his eyes, as these 'people are identified with the steam engine, commerce and freedom'.

In 1862, Jones dispatched Sir Love Jones-Parry, a wealthy member of the emigration society and later Liberal MP for Caernarvonshire, and Lewis Jones, a printer, editor and staunch advocate of the colony project, to Argentina. After signing a deal with the interior minister, Guillermo Rawson, in Buenos Aires, they sailed south to scout out Chubut. There, a storm drove them into the Golfo Nuevo, on whose shore a later settlement would be named Porth Madryn, after Jones-Parry's estate. Back in Wales, their misleadingly positive reports on the area—which built on similarly overly optimistic talk from Jones and his colleagues—were used to promote the colony and attract settlers.

In Argentina, there were conflicting views over the terms of the agreement, with the government ultimately forced to row back on the degree of political autonomy granted to the colony, as members of congress thought it would be 'dangerous to allow Protestant and "English" immigrants to settle so close to the already British-occupied Falkland Islands,' wrote Geraldine Lublin in *Memoir and Identity in Welsh Patagonia*.

On 28 May 1865, the *Mimosa* departed from Liverpool on a two-month voyage to the Golfo Nuevo. Each of the roughly 153 Welsh passengers on board had paid a fare of £12 per adult, £5 per child (though, in practice, anyone who was willing to go was taken, even if they could not afford the fare). Four children died en route, and two babies were born. Most of the settlers came from the mining areas of South Wales and English cities and had already migrated for work at least once in the past. Around 25 per cent came from a single town, Mountain Ash in the Rhondda. There were miners, carpenters, cobblers, brickmakers and tailors but only a handful of farmers.

The *Mimosa* arrived in a bitterly cold winter, and the Welsh settlers found themselves woefully underprepared for the rugged, semi-arid environment of northeast Patagonia. The first Welsh birth (Mary Humphries, on 10 August) and death (Catherine Davies, on 21 August) in Patagonia took place on the shore of the Golfo Nuevo. (Humphries became a major figure in the community: as well as delivering around 3,000 babies as a midwife, she founded a hospital and helped to put down a diphtheria epidemic using remedies taught to her by the Tehuelche.)

The settlers soon headed inland to the Chubut River Valley, the only fertile area in the region. They trekked for 45 miles through dust storms across a 'sterile, waterless track of land,' wrote William Casnodyn Rhys in *A Welsh Song in Patagonia*. One man attempted to transport his possessions in a wheelbarrow before abandoning it after a few miles due to the inhospitable terrain.

The first years were tough, but the settlers' early letters to their loved ones back in Wales tended to skirt over the hardships and put on a brave face. Writing to his family in November 1865, three months after arriving in Patagonia, Lewis Davies described the land as 'first rate', before adding: 'I believe that we will do okay here as the place develops and new people join us and, in time, we don't have any doubt that we'll make our fortune.' The same month, R. Berwyn Jones told his brother: 'I am quite comfortable here and have plenty to eat. Ducks, ostriches, armadillos and rabbits. The rabbits are the size of hares.' Another settler emphasised the quality of the environment: 'It's a healthy place. The healthiest [air] that man has ever breathed.'

Along the banks of the narrow Chubut River, Davies, Jones and the other settlers founded a series of villages and towns—Porth Madryn, Rawson, Gaiman, Trelew, Dolavon—with farms on the plots allotted to each family by the Argentine government fanning out across the surrounding valley. More than 7,000 miles from their homeland, and some 200 miles from the nearest Argentine outpost, it became known as Y Wladfa (The Colony).

* * *

Today, approaching Chubut by air gives you a sense of the harshness of northeast Patagonia. The small city of Trelew, 800 miles south of Buenos Aires and home to the region's main airport, is surrounded by a band of cultivated fields, copses of trees and the odd lake. But the greenery is dwarfed on all sides by seemingly unending brown, stony steppe—largely flat, treeless, no water sources, no life and no roads beyond the main highway.

Y WLADFA

I caught a bus to Puerto Madryn, an hour away along a highway lined with barbed-wire fences snagged with scraps of paper and squashed plastic. The route was dotted with roadside shrines for car crash victims: they resembled bird houses and were topped with crosses and surrounded by wilted flowers, wine and beer bottles and an image of the Virgin Mary. A line of wind turbines rotated languidly in the grey sky. Beyond them was a building that looked like a prison, with high fences and guard towers. A tangle of power lines was held up by pylons resembling weary men with broken arms. A new highway was being built, but there was no sign of the workers.

On the horseshoe-shaped shore of the Golfo Nuevo, the low-rise city of Puerto Madryn—the Hispanicised version of Porth Madryn—is now a tourist hub, popular with scuba divers and a jump-off point for wildlife-watching trips to Península Valdés and Punta Tombo, a raucous penguin colony to the south. Overlooking the beach, the waterfront streets were lined with apartments, hotels, restaurants, bars and beach clubs, which get lively during the peak summer season.

I found plenty of reminders of the city's Welsh origins. On the waterfront, near Avenida Gales (Wales Avenue), stood a bronze statue of a Welsh woman gazing inland, her dress fluttering in the wind, the centrepiece of a monument erected in 1965 to mark the 100th anniversary of the *Mimosa*'s arrival. On the base of the statue were stylised representations of the settlers and their—romanticised—relationships with local Tehuelche communities. Weather-beaten models of a penguin and a whale were set up beside the monument to advertise sightseeing cruises, and in the adjacent skate park teenage boys filmed themselves attempting BMX tricks.

A forty-five-minute walk south along the coast—past souvenir shops selling fleeces and penguin wine jugs ('15 per cent cash discount'), boat clubs, a stream of runners, rollerbladers and dog-walkers, and a woman juggling for tips at a set of traffic lights—brought me to a headland, Punta Cuevas. A Welsh Patagonian flag—a red dragon in the centre of the sky blue and white stripes of the Argentine flag—fluttered on a pole. It overlooked a curl of grey sand covered with seaweed, on the edge of which was a set of hollows in the rock. The Welsh settlers spent their first days in Patagonia sheltering in these humble crevices before constructing rudimentary huts on higher ground to provide a slightly greater degree of comfort, the foundations of which have survived to the present day. The late afternoon glow and clusters of brilliant pink wildflowers gave the site—now part of a modest 'historic park'—a far brighter look than it would have appeared back in the austral winter of 1865.

Above the caves, in the pocket-sized Museo del Desembarco, I chatted to curator Eduardo, a friendly guy with plug earrings the size of 5p pieces. Although he had no Welsh heritage, he told me he was fascinated by the language and had been studying it for several years. It was a difficult but rewarding process that had helped him converse with a couple from the town of Blaenau Ffestiniog in North Wales the previous day, he added.

Spread across a handful of rooms, the museum told the story of the Welsh arrival in Patagonia and its legacy. It was an important tale, Eduardo emphasised, well known today throughout Patagonia, though less so in Argentina more generally. The exhibits were evocative and sometimes moving—a passenger list from the *Mimosa*, crinkled newspaper extracts and adverts and diaries of early settlers alongside sewing machines, mangles, ceramic bottles and an old leather boot. There was the Sillón Bardico, a beautifully decorated wooden chair awarded to one of the winners of a 1920 *eisteddfod*, a festival of Welsh culture with poetry, literature and musical competitions. Jars of 'Mimosa marmalade' were on sale at the reception desk.

Just up the hill from the museum, a stone monument commemorated the 150th anniversary of the arrival of the Welsh with a list of the original settlers, as well as a memorial from the descendants of the local Tehuelche communities. At the summit was a stylised bronze statue of a Tehuelche man, standing on top of a plinth of rocks, holding a longbow and scanning the horizon. Nearby, a congregation of Argentines gathered on deckchairs to watch the sunset, drinking beers from coolers, passing around *mate* cups and flasks and gazing back across the bay to the vanishing city beyond.

* * *

In *Hanes y Wladfa Gymreig yn Patagonia* (History of the Welsh colony in Patagonia), preacher Abraham Matthews, who arrived on the *Mimosa*, described the region as an 'empty country ... where the Welsh could settle and rule themselves', repeating the sentiments of the Argentine government. But despite initial mutual suspicion, the Tehuelche played a crucial role in the survival of the early Welsh settlers, not least by showing them how to hunt the native guanacos and ñandus, a flightless bird related to the ostrich.

Nevertheless, in the early years, the Welsh settlers struggled with both the desert-like environment and periodic devastating flash floods. There were also failed harvests, internal disagreements over land usage and distribution and only irregular subsidies and supplies from the Argentine government in distant Buenos Aires. Some called for the colony to move; others abandoned it altogether. By 1869, the population had fallen to ninety, endangering the whole project. Yet over the following decades, the situation stabilised, thanks in large part to the local Tehuelche communities.

This relationship, however, is often heavily romanticised. As Lublin noted in *Planet* magazine, Hugh Hughes' 1862 *Handbook of the Welsh Colony* expressed some sympathy for Patagonia's Indigenous inhabitants, drawing parallels between their portrayal by outsiders as 'half beasts' with negative English depictions of the Welsh as 'savages'. It stated: 'We cannot disregard the rights of the Indians of the land but ... we should attempt to make friends of them, giving them whatever is honest, whatever is just.' Yet the book also asserted that the settlers aimed to 'defeat the Indian through kindness'.

The Welsh were both colonised and colonisers. They 'felt their nation to be stripped of sovereignty, socially disparaged, culturally quashed, and in many ways colonised' and chose in response 'as their key strategy the creation of a new homeland through an act of colonisation,' according to Lucy Taylor, a Latin American studies lecturer at Aberystwyth University. As with the millions of other Europeans who emigrated to South America during this period and, indeed, throughout history, a desire to escape economic hardships and seek greater freedom and opportunities were motivating factors, too. They were not free of prejudice and, in Argentina, also 'benefitted from geopolitical hierarchies of race and civilization' of the period, Taylor wrote in the *Journal of Global History*.

There was relatively little reported violence between the Indigenous communities and the Welsh, aside from a famous clash in 1883 in which three Welshmen were killed by an unidentified group of assailants during a prospecting trip in western Chubut. This may be because the Argentine government paid Tehuelche leaders some compensation for their land; the Tehuelche valued the trading relationship with the Welsh or viewed them as a lesser evil than the Argentine state; and/or the relatively benign attitudes of the Welsh community. Or it may be that incidents of hostility and violence have been dismissed, overlooked or airbrushed from the historical record.

* * *

The frustrating lack of first-hand Indigenous sources from this era makes it difficult to discern the truth about the views of the

Tehuelche and other native Patagonians, who are too often mischaracterised as passive actors. But a few contemporaneous documents provide a window, albeit through frosted glass. Taylor quoted a letter to Lewis Jones in December 1865 in which a Tehuelche *cacique*, or chief, named Antonio asserted his community's ownership over the Chubut region: 'I know very well that you have negotiated with the [Argentine] Government to colonize Chupat, but you also negotiate with us, who are the owners of the lands.' Antonio may have been unable to resist the ever-encroaching forces of the Argentine state, but his letter expressed a desire to make the best of a bad situation. He hoped the Welsh would prove better trading partners than the treacherous residents of the nearest Argentine outpost of Carmen de Patagones, almost 250 miles to the northeast, who 'steal our horses', while tavern owners 'rob and cheat us'.

Antonio outlined the goods on offer from his Tehuelche group: ñandu feathers and guanaco skins and wool. They could also turn the latter into loose, cape-like cloaks known as *quillangos*, which, he added, were sold by traders 'to rich people who put them as carpets'. The goods sought in return included tobacco, sugar, flour, ponchos, blankets, yerba mate and alcohol, as well as 'paper or silver money'. 'If you treat us well ... and if your traders do not cheat us, we shall always negotiate with you,' he added.

In time, a comprehensive trading relationship developed between the Welsh and the Tehuelche, as well as some friendships and marriages. The Welsh ploughed the profits into their farms. A vital step forward was the construction of a large-scale irrigation system spanning hundreds of miles of canals, which ensured a constant supply of water for crops and livestock. In 1872, Y Wladfa produced its first crop of wheat, which became a mainstay of the local economy; by 1885, production topped 6,000 tonnes. Four years later, Welsh Patagonian wheat won a gold medal at the Paris Exposition.

SMALL EARTHQUAKES

The colony grew steadily: more than 500 people arrived from Wales in 1875–6 alone. Chapels and schools were built, villages and towns were expanded, and a railway network, gold mining venture and cooperative societies were founded. There were also annual *eisteddfodau*, helping to ensure Welsh culture continued to flourish. Despite an official Argentine government visit and flag-raising ceremony in September 1865, shortly after the arrival of the *Mimosa*, the colony was largely autonomous for the first decade and a half. In the first year, all men and women over the age of eighteen were granted the right to vote in its council elections. It was a progressive move for the time, coming more than six decades before women in the UK would finally earn the right to vote on the same terms as men.

But the colony's freedom to run its own affairs began to erode in the 1880s, as the Argentine government launched its genocidal 'Conquest of the Desert' to secure control over eastern Patagonia, while Chile pursued a similar policy in the west. This brutal military campaign seized vast tracts of fertile land, displacing the Tehuelche, Mapuche, Rankülche, Puelche, Pehuenche and other Indigenous peoples from their ancestral lands in Patagonia and the Pampas to the north. 'Official, if dubious, figures for the conquest claimed that the Argentine army and navy captured or killed over 2,500 [Indigenous] warriors,' wrote Carolyne R. Larson in *The Conquest of the Desert: Argentina's Indigenous Peoples and the Battle for History*. 'State figures also indicated that more than 10,000 women and children were "placed under state supervision".' Under this euphemistic term, families were broken up, with women and children sent to prison camps or forced to work as domestic servants. Captured men were conscripted and forced to serve in the very army that displaced them. Many others were forced into virtual slavery on farms and ranches. There was also a concerted effort to prevent Indigenous people from having children.

Y WLADFA

Chubut was not spared. In 1883, the military attacked the Tehuelche communities with whom the Welsh had formed trading relationships, massacring scores of people and capturing many more. In response, the Welsh community wrote a joint letter to the local Argentine military commander, emphasising that they had received 'much kindness' from the Indigenous communities since their arrival in Patagonia and urging him to 'leave our old native neighbours in their homes while they remain as peaceful and harmless as has been their custom'. The letter fell on deaf ears. Instead, rumours circulated that the Welsh had actually aided the Indigenous communities, including by supplying them with rifles, claims that were strongly denied.

By the following year, the 'Conquest of the Desert' had come to an end. The name is a misnomer on various levels, not least because much of the captured land was fertile. Large parcels were sold on to ranchers and farmers, and the 'conquered' territory helped to transform Argentina into an agricultural powerhouse and one of the early twentieth-century's richest countries on the planet. 'Those were terrible days for the [Welsh] Colony, for our sympathies were with the Indians,' wrote Casnodyn Rhys. 'Some of the bravest fought to the last, preferring death to captivity.'

* * *

After the 'Conquest of the Desert', Argentina extended its authority across Patagonia, and the distinctly Welsh character of the Chubut Valley began to dissolve. An Argentine governor was appointed in 1884, the government subsequently introduced a law mandating that primary school education across the country must be in Spanish, and migrants from elsewhere in Argentina, as well as Europe and the Middle East, began to settle in the region. At the same time, the rate of emigration from Wales slowed and eventually dried up completely (the last Welsh migrants arrived in 1911), while some community members emigrated to Australia and Canada. There was another blow in 1899, when the Chubut River burst its banks and flooded the valley, destroying houses, farms and crops, and forcing residents to temporarily flee to higher ground.

Despite these setbacks, Welsh remained widely spoken in Chubut, and key religious and cultural events, most notably *eisteddfodau*, continued to take place. Geographically, the Welsh footprint in Patagonia also expanded. In 1885, a band of settlers rode west to the lush foothills of the Andes, where they found a bucolic area reminiscent of their homeland, which they named Cwm Hyfryd, or Beautiful Valley. This became the site of a second Welsh colony. The first settler families arrived in 1889 and went on to found the towns of Trevelin and Esquel. In a further boost, gold was subsequently discovered in the region.

The Welsh colony also played a key role in determining Patagonia's national borders. Its agricultural success in Cwm Hyfryd drew the attention of the Chilean government. 'Rainfall on the western slopes of the Andes feeds the rivers that flow through the valley,' wrote Chris Moss in *Patagonia: A Cultural History*. 'If strict watershed rules were followed, the Chileans argued, Cwm Hyfryd would be part of Chile.' As tensions mounted, Britain was engaged as a mediator in the border dispute. In 1902, an arbitration commission sought the opinions of the Welsh settlers, an overwhelming majority of whom said they preferred to remain part of Argentina. This helped to influence the commission's ruling, which awarded most of the disputed territory to Chile but allowed Argentina to keep the most fertile areas, including Cwm Hyfryd.

As the first generation of Welsh migrants passed away, connections with the homeland began to weaken. In 1950, the Welsh-language intermediate school in Chubut was forced to close for more than a decade because of a lack of pupils. But celebrations in 1965 to mark the centenary of the *Mimosa*'s arrival and the founding of the colony provided a boost for Welsh identity in the region and Argentine (and British) awareness of the settlement. Tourism began to grow, boosted by the publication of Bruce Chatwin's influential travelogue *In Patagonia* in 1977, in which the Welsh community of Chubut and its history—or, rather, Chatwin's heavily editorialised version of them—featured prominently. Almost half a century on, well-worn copies of the book remain mainstays of hostel book exchanges across Patagonia.

The 1995 visit of Diana, Princess of Wales also provided a major publicity boost, and the first quarter of the twenty-first century has seen a 'quasi-miraculous revival of Welsh culture in Patagonia', according to Lublin. Devolution and the revitalisation of the Welsh-language movement in Wales played a key role in the process, alongside renewed attention on the colony thanks to the 150th anniversary celebrations in 2015. Although the number of first-language Welsh-speakers has fallen in Patagonia, the language was given a major boost by the 1997 launch of the Welsh Language Project. Operated by the British Council in conjunction with the Welsh government and organisations including the Wales–Argentina Society, its activities include sending Welsh-language teachers to Chubut to work with children and adults and supporting a network of Welsh-language tutors throughout the region.

Today, around 50,000 to 70,000 people in Chubut have Welsh heritage, and estimates suggest as many as 6,000 speak the language. Lublin argued that many in Wales view them as 'a sort of capsule of Welshness isolated in South America, construed in the Welsh imagination as a purportedly uncontaminated cultural reservoir' on the other side of the Atlantic. Despite being tiny in numerical terms—an estimated 2,000 people are believed to have migrated from Wales to Chubut in total—the colony is viewed in Argentina as 'a paradigmatic example of mass European immigration' that established the first permanent non-Indigenous settlement in eastern Patagonia in a period when there were 'serious concerns that the region could be claimed by Chile or even Britain'.

* * *

From Puerto Madryn, I headed inland into the lower Chubut Valley, changing buses in Trelew. Named after Lewis Jones, who founded it in 1886, 'Lewis Town' became an important transport hub following the completion of a rail line to Puerto Madryn, which was a huge boost for Welsh Patagonian agricultural exports. A statue of Jones stands in the centre of the main square, which hosts the province's biggest *eisteddfod*, during which the prestigious Sillón Bardico (Bard's Chair) award is handed out for the best poetry in Welsh, while the Corona del Poeta (Poet's Crown) is given for the best in Spanish. Nearby, a phalanx of flags celebrates the nationalities of the town's residents, including the red dragon of Wales.

While waiting for my connection, I grabbed a coffee and a *medialuna* in Hotel Touring Club, a faded, faintly Art Deco café-bar-guesthouse with an illustrious history. Former guests include the French writer and aviator Antoine de Saint-Exupéry, author of the novellas *The Little Prince* and *Night Flight*. The latter was inspired by his experiences flying airmail routes in Argentina, from Patagonia to the high-altitude deserts of the far north, between 1929 and 1931. Butch Cassidy and the Sundance Kid, who hid out on a ranch in the western reaches of Chubut before robbing a bank in the city of Río Gallegos in southwest Patagonia on Valentine's Day 1905, also reputedly called in (similar claims are made by establishments across Patagonia, with varying degrees of veracity).

A 28 de Julio bus—named after the date of arrival of the *Mimosa* and filled with teenagers in shiny pink dresses and baggy suits heading back from a graduation party—dropped me off in

Gaiman, a smaller, quieter and more attractive settlement than Trelew. On the surface, it looked little different from small towns across Patagonia, but there was a distinctly Welsh flavour. Set along the poplar-lined banks of the Chubut River, Gaiman's street names emphasised a mixed heritage: Michael D. Jones, A. Matthews, J.C. Evans, D. Roberts, Evan Thomas and Bryn Gwyn, alongside San Martín, Belgrano, Jorge Luis Borges and Carlos Gardel. There was a panoply of red dragons and a sturdy, well-maintained chapel built in 1913. The park had a circle of Gorsedd stones for use during the annual *eisteddfod*, and the cemetery was lined with tombstones fashioned from slate brought over from Blaenau Ffestiniog expressly for the purpose.

Within Argentina, Gaiman is famous for its Welsh tearooms. The first *casa de té* opened some eighty years ago, and there are currently four in operation. My favourite was Ty Nain ('Grand-mother's House'), a handsome house built in 1890, clad with ivy and surrounded by flowerbeds, which has since sadly closed. The interior felt like a museum, crammed with old household items: oil lamps, irons, sewing machines and a gramophone, plus a Winchester 45 rifle, a mini cannon, a deer head, a puma pelt and a set of *bolas*, a Tehuelche weapon consisting of linked cords with heavy balls at the ends, used for hunting guanacos. There were needlework depictions of classic Welsh scenes, chapels in the Chubut Valley and the *Mimosa*, as well as a picture of Edith Mary Evans, the first woman of Welsh descent to be born in Gaiman.

Ty Nain was owned by Evans' descendants, their surnames Jones and Doyle, the waitress explained, as she served a classic *té galés*, an immense feast that could have fed a small army. A platter was piled high with ten different cakes: bara brith, Welsh cakes, a fruit cake called *torta galesa*, apple tart, chocolate cake, walnut cake, Swiss roll, bread-and-butter pudding, custard tart and—in a nod to Argentine tastes or a symbol of assimilation—a dulce-de-leche-based confection, plus sweet and savoury scones, slices of buttered brown and white bread, homemade strawberry and cherry jam, and a pot of tea with a pink-and-white cosy.

As I ate, I read yellowed copies of US newspaper articles about the café and the visit to Gaiman of Diana, Princess of Wales in 1995, during which she tucked into a *té galés*. Welsh-language folk songs, including a version of 'Hallelujah', played in the background. On the next table, an Argentine couple from Rosario told me the café was exactly the same as when they visited twenty-five years earlier. After an hour of what felt like steady eating, I'd barely made a dent in the *té galés*, but the waitress, who also had Welsh heritage, kindly bagged up the remainder for me to take away. I waddled around Gaiman, stopping off at its oldest house, built in 1874 for David D. Roberts and now open to the public. A simple, low-ceilinged dwelling that required me to almost bend double to enter.

A short walk to the east, the old railway station, built in 1889, was the site of the Museo Histórico Regional. Its exhibits traced the history of Welsh Patagonia, from a ticket from the *Mimosa* and copies of the original plans for the colony to schema for the mass irrigation projects, copies of court records and council meetings, a few editions of the *Y Drafod* newspaper and a letter from the daughter of Prime Minister David Lloyd George to the community during the First World War. These items were mixed with butter churns and cheesemaking equipment, personal possessions such as a black lace shawl, a piano once owned by Lewis Jones and wooden chairs and crowns given to *eisteddfod* winners.

* * *

There have been increasing calls for a reassessment of Y Wladfa in recent years, amid wider demands for an honest reckoning with Britain's imperial history and legacy. Many in Wales are looking beyond the simplified, sugar-coated portrayals of the colony (which is often coded as a settlement). 'The actions of the

Welsh in colonising Patagonia don't need to be romanticised,' argued writer and academic Ian Johnson in an opinion piece for *Nation Cymru*. 'They can and should be held to the same standards as every other examination that we make of Western action in recent centuries. We shouldn't be scared to do that.'

In Argentina, Indigenous voices are also challenging long-held assumptions. The 'Conquest of the Desert' is often regarded as a full stop. As president of Argentina in 2018, Mauricio Macri declared 'in South America we are all European descendants', whitewashing the continent's Indigenous (and African) heritage. His words reflect a sentiment shared by many in Argentina who see the country as a part of Europe that has somehow broken free and drifted across the Atlantic.

The data tells a different story. According to the 2022 census, 1,306,730 Argentines—2.9 per cent of the population—identified as Indigenous or as having Indigenous heritage (interestingly, more than double the number of the 2004 census). They included 145,783 Mapuche (the largest Indigenous group), 23,416 Mapuche Tehuelche and 17,420 Tehuelche. In Chubut, almost 8 per cent of the population are Indigenous. Moreover, Indigenous peoples in Patagonia continue to demand their rights, assert their identities and attempt to recover their lands and political autonomy in the face of racism, ignorance, violence and demonisation. In Chubut, there is increasing conflict over issues such as mining and deforestation.

The struggle is led by people like Moira Millán, a prominent Mapuche author, activist, land defender and *weychafe* (protective warrior) from Chubut who founded the Movement of Indigenous Women and Diversities for Good Living. The Mapuche nation, she told a reporter, 'does not feel either Argentine or Chilean. It is Mapuche.' Describing the aims of her movement, which carried out a peaceful occupation of the Ministry of the Interior in 2019, she continued: 'We are very clear that our anti-patriarchal struggle is an anti-colonial struggle; it is a libertarian struggle, for the self-determination of our bodies, of our territories, and for the self-determination of our peoples.'

* * *

On my final day in the region, I visited El Pedral, a private wildlife reserve at the southern tip of the Golfo Nuevo. It is home to a rowdy colony of Magellanic penguins, which provide another link with Wales. During Drake's voyage through the Strait of Magellan at the southern tip of Patagonia, he came across immeasurable colonies of 'strange birds, which could not flie at all, nor yet runne so fast as that they could escape'. On the islands, 'infinite were the number of fowle, which the Welsh men named Penguin ... It is not possible to find a bird of their bignes to have greater strength than they.'

According to the *Oxford English Dictionary*, this was the first written citation of the word 'penguin'. The etymology is contested, but many believe it derives from the Welsh name for the great auk, a flightless, black-headed bird with white eye patches that ranged across the north Atlantic before becoming extinct in the 1840s. In Welsh, pen means 'head' and gwyn means 'white'. The fly in the ointment with this story is that Magellanic penguins—the species predominantly found in this area—have largely black heads, albeit with distinctive white borders.

After visiting the shingle beach—where groups of penguins pottered about, dithered for a bit and then dived into the water, where they were creatures transformed, swift, graceful onyx torpedoes—I sat down for a slice of *torta galesa* with Gastón, one of the reserve's guides. He didn't have any Welsh heritage but brought up Y Wladfa unprompted. 'Those Welsh pioneers came from so far away and had to work so hard when they got here—it was difficult to find fresh water, to find food. But they stayed, worked and helped to lead to all this.' By sparking the colonisation of Patagonia and helping to shape its borders, he continued, the Welsh 'changed this part of the world'.

4

THE GOLDEN FLEECE
CHILEAN PATAGONIA

A burnt-orange glow illuminated the steppe as our jeep bounced along a stony track flanked by patches of white-flowering *mata negra* bushes. The dawn horizon was dominated by the Condoreras, a jagged golden ridge that stretches across Estancia Cerro Guido, one of the largest ranches in southern Patagonia. Chile's trekking hotspot of Parque Nacional Torres del Paine, which attracts hundreds of thousands of tourists each year, was only a few miles away, but it felt as if we had the area all to ourselves.

At the base of the Condoreras, I joined puma tracker Ricardo Muza, who was patiently scanning the striated rock face with binoculars for a tell-tale flash of movement. 'Pumas are perfectly evolved for this landscape,' he said, nursing a flask of coffee to stave off the early morning chill. 'They blend right into the landscape. You can be right next to them and not see them—but they can see you.'

Muza is one of three puma trackers employed by Estancia Cerro Guido as part of a pioneering conservation project that aims to transform attitudes in a region where the big cats have long been viewed as a menace. Their fortunes, and Patagonia as a whole, were transformed in the late nineteenth century by the arrival of a quintessentially Welsh animal in an area originally known as Sandy Point.

* * *

Nearing the western end of the Strait of Magellan in early 1587, crossing from the Atlantic to the Pacific with the aim of plundering Spanish treasure, Thomas Cavendish spotted a haunting sight on the north shore: an abandoned settlement. The Suffolk-born privateer—essentially a pirate with a letter from a monarch or government designating their robbing and pillaging as legal when targeted at foes—had arrived at the ruins of the hubristically titled Ciudad del Rey Don Felipe ('City of King Philip'). It was founded three years earlier by the Spanish sailor, soldier and historian Pedro Sarmiento de Gamboa, shortly after he had established the settlement of Nombre de Jesús at the eastern entrance of the Strait of Magellan. The aim was to fortify the channel and protect Spanish ships from privateer-pirates such as Cavendish and his counterpart Francis Drake. But the settlement quickly collapsed as a result of water shortages, crop failures and harsh winters. Most of the 337 inhabitants starved or froze to death.

Cavendish—who was involved in the establishment of the similarly ill-fated Roanoke Colony, the first permanent English settlement in North America, in 1585—dubbed the site Port Famine ('Puerto del Hambre' in Spanish). Having picked up one of the handful of survivors, he collected half a dozen of the settlement's cannons and swiftly moved on to raid ships and ports along the Pacific coast of the continent. He ultimately completed the third circumnavigation of the earth, capturing a 600-tonne, treasure-laden Spanish galleon en route.

Nombre de Jesús fared little better than Ciudad del Rey Don Felipe, and while the area had been successfully inhabited by

THE GOLDEN FLEECE

Indigenous peoples such as the Tehuelche for millennia, it was more than 250 years before another colonial outpost was founded in this harsh terrain. Concerned about both rising Argentine ambitions and Royal Navy activities in the region, the Chilean government dispatched the *Ancud* in 1843. The ship was captained by John Williams Wilson, one of the many Britons who fought in South America's wars of independence. Williams was born into a seafaring family in Bristol (or perhaps South Wales; there are conflicting reports) in 1798. Later known as Juan Guillermos, he joined the Chilean navy in his twenties, moved up the ranks and took part in the 1826 liberation of the mist-shrouded archipelago of Chiloé, the last outpost of the Spanish crown in Chile.

Subsequently named maritime governor of Chiloé's main island and promoted to lieutenant commander, Williams played an important role in Chile's colonisation of western Patagonia. He landed the *Ancud* at the blustery promontory of Punta Santa Ana, just south of Port Famine, and oversaw the construction of a fort, Fuerte Bulnes, which gave Chile a stronghold in the region. Williams was rewarded for his efforts with the role of maritime governor of the port of Talcahuano in the Biobío region. He also had the southern Patagonian island of Juan Guillermos named after him, as well as the city of Puerto Williams in Tierra del Fuego. In 1944, a 30-*centavo* stamp was even issued in his honour. His son, Juan Williams Rebolledo, also became a noted naval officer, serving in the 1879–84 War of the Pacific against Peru and Bolivia and eventually rising to rear admiral.

Replacing Chiloé, which lies more than 900 miles north, as the southernmost Chilean enclave at the time, Fuerte Bulnes lasted slightly longer than its more illustriously named predecessors. Despite hopes of developing it into a town, the arduous conditions acted as an understandable deterrent for potential

SMALL EARTHQUAKES

Chilean settlers. In 1848, the fort and its inhabitants were relocated to a more favourable location 35 miles north with easier access to fresh drinking water and known by British mariners as Sandy Point, the Hispanicised version of which became the city's modern name: Punta Arenas. With Chileans and European migrants still unwilling to settle in the far reaches of Patagonia in any great numbers, the government decided to remove the element of choice by establishing a penal colony alongside the fledgling town and port.

The timing proved fortuitous. As global maritime trade grew dramatically through the following decades, the Strait of Magellan route between the Atlantic and Pacific became increasingly important, with steam ships calling in to Punta Arenas to pick up supplies such as coal, which was mined locally. As in Y Wladfa during this period, there was also a profitable trade in Indigenous products such as guanaco skins and *ñandu* feathers, as well as sea lion hunting. Boosted by state subsidies, the population grew to around 1,100 and included a handful of Britons. But attempts to encourage greater European settlement through land grants largely floundered, while farmers who had moved south from Chiloé struggled with the unproductive land.

Given the fate of previous colonial settlements in the area, it was little surprise when disaster struck. Three years after Punta Arenas's foundation, a prison riot led by a disgruntled lieutenant was only contained by chance, thanks to the crew of a passing Royal Navy sloop, *Virago*. But in 1877, a larger revolt, driven by artillerymen unhappy with their salary and working conditions, virtually destroyed the town. A visiting *Times* reporter described the immediate aftermath:

> A mutiny had broken out among the artillery men ... they rose and set free the convicts, some 80 or 90 in number, and then together had pillaged and burnt the town ... All the respectable inhabitants

have lost heavily, and nearly all the Europeans are left houseless and destitute of food or clothing.

After the revolt, the authorities changed tack. As Argentina waged the 'Conquest of the Desert', the Chilean government 'legally redefined' Indigenous land in western Patagonia as 'state property and ... vacant territory,' wrote historian Alberto Harambour-Ross in his paper 'Sheep Sovereignties'. 'From that point forward, authorities began granting it to foreign cattlemen, fundamentally Europeans.' This process was echoed by the Argentine government in eastern Patagonia.

Inspired by the success of British sheep ranchers on the Falkland Islands, Punta Arenas governor Don Diego Dublé Almeyda returned from a visit to the archipelago in 1877 with a 300-head flock purchased by a Yorkshire-born merchant. Henry Reynard had recently relocated from a ranch in northeast Argentina and was granted a concession on an island just north of Punta Arenas named Isabel. His wool-producing business quickly proved a success and inspired countless imitators across Patagonia. The growth rate was startling: the few hundred sheep in Magallanes (the region around Punta Arenas) in 1877 grew to some 40,000 within a decade. By the early twentieth century, the number topped 2 million, dwarfing the number in the Falkland Islands. There was similar expansion in the Argentine section of Patagonia, and by 1910 there were 12 million sheep across the region as a whole. In the early 1950s, the number peaked at around 22 million.

The industry had a distinctly British character. As the nineteenth century drew to a close, British- or part British-owned ranches were responsible for almost half of the land use in Magallanes and the Chilean section of Tierra del Fuego to the south, and nearly three-quarters of the sheep. By 1906, more than 60 per cent of the region's shepherds were British, most of them Scots. By the 1920s, an estimated 90 per cent of the largest sheep farms in the region were managed by British subjects, according to the *South American Handbook* of 1924.

The industry proved so profitable that wool was dubbed, predictably enough, the 'golden fleece'.

* * *

In mid-August 1834, during his voyage around South America in the *Beagle*, Charles Darwin set off on an adventure in central Chile. Cheered by 'quite delicious' balmy weather, a meeting with an old school friend and a horse-riding trip through banks of fertile hills and bands of palm forests, he hiked up Cerro La Campana, a 6,299-foot mountain north of Santiago. 'We spent the day on the summit, and I never enjoyed one more thoroughly,' he wrote. 'Chile, bounded by the Andes and the Pacific, was seen as in a map.'

I got a similar sense of the country's scale and topographical diversity on the three-hour flight south from Santiago to Punta Arenas. The country unfurled like a sail, the capital's urban sprawl giving way to lush green valleys, which were slowly replaced in turn by the glacial lagoons and frosted volcanic peaks of the Lake District. As we crossed into northern Patagonia, the landscape grew more rugged. Mountain ridges, enveloped in snow and ribbed like washboards, rolled in waves towards the Southern Ocean. Their grooves and niches were filled with water—navy blue, turquoise, pale green.

After two hours in the air, cloud briefly obscured the views, and by the time it cleared we were over southern Patagonia. The land crumbled into islands, headlands, peninsulas and channels. There were sweeps of untrammelled snow and finger-shaped glaciers, the colour of blue toothpaste, poking into lakes, as if testing the temperature. They are part of the Hielo Continental Sur, the largest ice field in the southern hemisphere outside of Antarctica. There were also expanses of brown-and-tan steppe, the colour of old boots, scattered with ranches and veined with the occasional spindly road, like unravelled balls of string. Flashes of greenery appeared as we came in to land, and, in the distance, the Strait of Magellan.

The baggage claim at Punta Arenas's airport was filled with glossy adverts for new apartment complexes. Two small dogs in carriers circled on the carousel, yelping plaintively before being collected by their owner, who placed them on a trolley and balanced a box of Dunkin' Donuts—unavailable this far south in Chile—on top.

I took a taxi into the city, whose springtime temperature of 8°C was a barely a third of that in the capital. The road initially skirted the shoreline of the Strait of Magellan, the scrubland littered with yellow-flowering bushes, the brightest things in the vicinity. Trees were few and far between, growing at erratic angles, shaped by the Escoba de Dios—God's Broom—Patagonia's famously fierce wind. Signs declared we were in 'Magallanes—Land of Pioneers' and 'Magallanes—Door to the End of the World'. Beyond a naval base, we passed the University of Magallanes campus and the Zona Franca, a duty-free zone of warehouses and compendious superstores enclosed by high fences topped with barbed wire, and then a collection of hospitals and clinics.

Born and bred in Punta Arenas, the taxi driver insisted the whole world was getting worse, vigorously shaking her head for emphasis. Santiago was a den of crime, inflation was too high, house prices were through the roof. Handing me a chocolate wrapped in silvery paper from the glove box, she peppered me with questions. Who is the British prime minister? Why are you dumping so much sewage into your rivers? Why aren't you staying at a nicer hotel?

A fifteen-minute walk took me from my hilltop guesthouse to the centre of Punta Arenas, whose colourful mismatched houses hinted at the city's frontier past. Some had clapboarded walls and corrugated-iron roofs; others were modern and angular with large sunrooms; a few had faux castle-like turrets. Monkey puzzle trees were commonplace in the gardens, and all of the dwellings appeared to have a pet dog, an ongoing DIY project and a 4X4. It was too hot in the sunshine, too cold in the shade, trapping me in a constant cycle of putting on and taking off my jacket.

A small park was dedicated to the poet Gabriela Mistral, who in 1945 became the first Latin American to win the Nobel Prize for Literature. She was born in the bucolic Elqui Valley on the southern fringes of the Atacama Desert but spent two years as the principal of a girls' high school in Punta Arenas. During this period, she produced her debut anthology, *Desolación*, in which she describes southern Patagonia as a land that 'knows no spring' and whose 'long night' wraps her in a maternal embrace.

The surrounding streets had outdoor gear stores, chocolate shops and a disproportionate number of pharmacies. Pavement vendors sold boxes of fresh cherries, toffee apples and a cage of golden retriever puppies that had supposedly been abandoned outside a church. A 1980s-style boombox pumped out 'Rhythm Is a Dancer' and graffitied slogans called out: 'Without the fight there is no dignity' and 'Free abortion'. Some fancy cafés, a zero-waste shop and a clutch of Chinese-language signs outside tourist restaurants had popped up in the five years since my last visit. But the busiest spot was Kiosko Roca, a miniature Chilean take on a US diner, filled with football memorabilia—pennants, badges, shirts—and waitresses doling out the house speciality: bite-sized chorizo sandwiches and glasses of banana milk.

The architecture grew steadily more impressive as I neared Plaza Muñoz Gamero, the main square. Trees in full bloom shaded an evangelical group playing acoustic guitars. An old man listened to a football phone-in on a portable radio. A pair of toddlers unsuccessfully pursued a flock of pigeons. The centrepiece was a statue of Ferdinand Magellan, inaugurated in

1920. His foot rested on a cannon, eyes raised to the horizon. Beneath the Portuguese navigator, on the base of the statue, were stylised depictions of a pair of Indigenous men, one representing the Tehuelche of Patagonia, the other the Selk'nam of Tierra del Fuego.

According to local legend, if you want to return to Punta Arenas you should touch (or, some say, kiss) the toe of the Selk'nam statue. A line of Antarctic cruise passengers, mainly North American and European retirees wearing headsets so they could hear the guide and dressed in a patchwork of fleece, puffer jackets and Gore-Tex, took it in turns to grasp the appendage. The statue is symbolic of the few public references in Punta Arenas to Patagonia's original inhabitants: anonymised, swirled in mysticism, confined to the past. Beyond a handful of murals and mosaics, and brief displays in the local museums, the only real mention of the region's Indigenous heritage were the names of a few tourist businesses (one travel agency was called 'Turismo Selknam') and on the shelves of souvenir shops, which sold figurines, toys and postcards; one had a poke-your-head-through-the hole board, allowing passers-by to cosplay as a Selk'nam couple.

As well as the cathedral, the square was overlooked by opulent mansions built in the early twentieth century by Patagonia's dizzyingly wealthy and intractably intertwined sheep-ranching oligarchy. Designed in the Neoclassical style, generally by French architects, they included Palacio José Menéndez, the former residence of the Spanish-born 'King of Patagonia' and now a club for military officers. Nearby, Palacio Sara Braun's eponymous former owner arrived in Patagonia as a child after her family fled antisemitic persecution in the Russian Empire. It is now home to the Hotel José Nogueira—named after Braun's first husband, a Portuguese livestock and shipping tycoon whose estate she inherited after his death in 1893—and a basement bar with the look of a private members' club. Just off the square, the equally lavish Palacio Braun Menéndez was built for Braun's brother, Mauricio, and his wife, Josefina Menéndez, daughter of the 'King of Patagonia'.

Initially business rivals, Sara and Mauricio Braun and José Menéndez eventually joined forces through the Sociedad Explotadora de Tierra del Fuego, which became the dominant landholder and livestock producer in southern Chile and Argentina. Its territory extended across 3 million hectares of Patagonia and Tierra del Fuego—an area the size of Belgium. As a result, the Sociedad exercised considerable political and economic power. The company had a strong British dimension: its first president was Peter H. McClelland of the influential Chile-based trading company Duncan Fox, and much of the capital came from the UK, too. Many of its senior employees—notably ranch and factory managers and administrators—were also British (or from countries within the British Empire), as were most of its shepherds, engineers and technicians. All of whom stamped their mark on Punta Arenas.

The Palacio Braun Menéndez now houses the Museo Regional de Magallanes, which has preserved some of the extravagant living areas—airy rooms filled with stiff family portraits and items imported from Europe and Asia, including billiard tables, Chinese vases, crystal chandeliers and mahogany furniture—as well as the modest, cramped, light-deprived quarters for the mansion's small army of servants. There are also exhibits on southern Patagonia's history and the seismic impact of Menéndez, Braun and their sheep-ranching counterparts on the region, though they underplayed their impact on the Indigenous population.

* * *

A couple of blocks from the main square, the British School of Punta Arenas was momentarily calm as its 750 pupils started their first lesson of the day. Union and Chilean flags fluttered on poles outside the entrance of the main building, a modern concrete structure beside the wood-panelled original, which was whitewashed with blue trim around the windows and doors. The reception walls were covered with posters of musicals: *Mamma Mia!*, *The Lion King*, *Grease* and, somewhat surprisingly given Chile's longstanding rivalry with its Argentine neighbour, *Evita*. There was also a portrait of Queen Elizabeth II and a table-top Christmas tree. As we walked to the archive, the receptionist, Paula, told me about her British-Croatian heritage; one of her ancestors, a man named Beauchamp, hailed from 'somewhere near London'.

The school opened in 1896 as an offshoot of the neighbouring Anglican church, St James, which was inaugurated the year before. Initially known as St James College and sponsored by the South American Missionary Society, it catered predominantly to the local British community—whose population peaked at almost 1,200 in 1907—and provided a British-style education in English for its first few decades.

Most of the teaching is now in Spanish, and the students, most of whom have no British heritage, study the International Baccalaureate. But it retains a keen awareness of its roots, explained headteacher Alejandra Barrios Harmer, whose maternal ancestors were English: 'The British story is very important to us, and the archive is the heart of our school. We still think we are part of your country. At the start the school was just for British families but now it is for everyone. We're a school of families.'

Harmer was from Santiago but travelled south to Punta Arenas 'for love'. Her husband, son and daughter had all attended the school. Students often carry the Union flag during local parades to mark national holidays, she explained, and when Queen Elizabeth II died in 2022, a special assembly was held so students 'had the chance to say goodbye to her'.

The one-room archive was a treasure trove. There were photos and portraits of the royal family, alongside figures such as

Churchill and Darwin. Cabinets were topped with sporting trophies for volleyball, athletics and skiing, as well as tea-stained songbooks, musical scores, head boy badges, pennants, a 1945 rule book, a collection of typewriters, a rocking chair and a school register from 1939. There were several items linked to the school's founder, Reverend John Williams of St James Church (no relation, as far as I've been able to discern, of Captain John Williams Wilson, who founded the settlement that became Punta Arenas), including a selection of his books: Bibles, hymn collections, *Studies of Arianism* and *History of the Christian Church*.

There were oddities donated by former students: a set of dolphin teeth, a bag of fossils, the statute books of the Corporación Britanica de Punta Arenas and a 1935–81 guest register from the British Association of Magallanes. The latter was founded in 1899 and originally based upstairs from a branch of the Bank of Tarapacá and London. Its first president was Henry Reynard, Patagonia's original wool producer. Membership was initially restricted to 'British males, generally of the upper class', though English-speaking Chileans were later admitted too, according to an account on the Patagonia Bookshelf website. The 'premises were furnished in the plush style of a gentleman's club, complete with bar, library and billiard tables'.

I was drawn to copies of the English-language *Magellan Times*, whose tagline was 'The farthest south British newspaper'. The front-page adverts of one issue provided a window into everyday life in and around Punta Arenas in the 1930s: Young's Sheep Dip ('the cheapest and most economical on the market'), the British Hotel ('Guests will receive excellent meals and every comfort') and the Trocadero Tea Room ('Lunches, Teas and Dinners served at any reasonable hour').

On an earlier visit to Punta Arenas, I'd met up with John Rees, the British honorary consul, whose wife and children had attended the British School. Residents in the city were 'very much aware' of the British role in southern Patagonia's history, he said. 'The British were fundamental here. Sheep ranching, business, shipping, doctors, everything. Most of the farm hands who came out were Scottish. We have a lot of "Mac-somethings" here in Punta Arenas.'

* * *

The municipal cemetery in Punta Arenas provided a grand but melancholy illustration of this history. A Patagonian equivalent of Buenos Aires' famed Recoleta cemetery, where Evita's ornate grave continues to attract a steady stream of devotees, it spans 4 hectares and is often described as a 'city of the dead'. The necropolis is named after Sara Braun, who funded the perimeter walls and the striking portico at the entrance, reputedly on the understanding that once her coffin passed through the gateway, as it did in 1955, no others would follow. That particular entrance has duly remained closed ever since.

The cemetery is now something of a local attraction. On the Sunday morning of my visit, there were tourists taking photos, several dog-walkers and a group of children kicking around a football. Braun, Menéndez and fellow members of the Patagonian sheepocracy occupied ostentatious chapels, tombs and mausoleums topped with golden domes, plastered with sorrowful angels and set along paths lined with immaculately trimmed and sculpted pine trees. But the modest burial plots—simple gravestones, dating back a century or more, and the more recent rows of small, mailbox-style graves lining the far wall and decorated with plastic flowers, Bible quotations and photos of the deceased—offered a more interesting insight into Punta Arenas's multinational history. There was a strong Croatian, German, Spanish and Italian presence, alongside a sizeable section of British graves. Ranchers, shepherds, traders, factory managers, teachers, missionaries, sailors: McCall, MacLeod, MacDonald,

SMALL EARTHQUAKES

MacKay, Davidson, Fell, Haddow, Robb, Fenton, Armstrong, Spencer, Bishop, English, Kearney.

There were also monuments to British residents of Punta Arenas who died in the First and Second World Wars and the 143 crew members of HMS *Doterel*, who perished after the Royal Naval sloop sank off the coast of the city in 1881 following an explosion of coal gas in the bunkers that was originally erroneously blamed on Irish republicans.

I fell into conversation with a friendly woman named Doreen who was tidying the graves of some of her relatives. Brushing away dirt and pulling out weeds, she explained that her great-grandfathers were both Scottish. One came to Patagonia via the Falkland Islands, but the other arrived by chance. Born in the Isle of Lewis, he was planning to emigrate to Australia but after stopping in Punta Arenas en route, his onward ship never arrived. 'He found work on a sheep ranch and, after returning home to Lewis briefly to marry, he and his wife returned to Patagonia permanently.'

Keen to explore her genealogy, Doreen had connected to some of her cousins in Stornoway after writing a letter to the local paper. Another potential relative got in touch via Facebook and asked her to take a DNA test, but the post office had subsequently lost it. Her son now lived in Glasgow, she added, switching from Spanish to English, but was due to return for a visit soon. 'Enjoy Patagonia. Hopefully the weather will stay calm like today. Otherwise you'll need to put stones in your pockets to stop yourself blowing away.'

Afterwards, I stopped off at the most popular part of the cemetery for Chilean visitors. The 'Unknown Indian' statue represents a Kawésqar man from Isla Diego de Almagro, northwest of Punta Arenas, who was buried without a tombstone in 1929. It now has a similar status to the Selk'nam sculpture in the main square. Over the years, local residents came to believe that the

THE GOLDEN FLEECE

'Unknown Indian' could bring them good fortune and started to leave offerings, especially on All Saints' Day. A bronze statue was later placed on the site, and it is now surrounded by ceramic tiles from devotees expressing their thanks or desires. A bunch of yellow flowers was placed under his right arm, and his left hand was worn smooth and golden, the result of countless touches from visitors for luck.

* * *

The Ruta 9 heads out of Punta Arenas, briefly tracing the shoreline of the Strait of Magellan, before striking northwest through a vast stretch of grassy steppe, almost all of which is fenced in. Flat and virtually treeless, the terrain was speckled with clumps of scrub and occasional sprays of purple, cone-shaped flowers. There were a few flocks of sheep and smaller groups of white-and-cinnamon-shaded guanacos.

Two hours after leaving Punta Arenas, my bus approached the first wrinkles in the landscape, a belt of low hills. They were followed by clusters of homesteads, sheltered from the wind by thickets of trees, sometimes with a small cattle herd or tethered horse. Periodically, we passed a lonely bus stop: surprisingly ornate octagonal buildings with cream walls and pale blue or terracotta roofs. At one stop, we picked up a young man wearing a gaucho beret and with a knapsack thrown over his shoulder.

Nearing our destination, the hills and trees increased in height and number. Snowy mountains loomed on the horizon, and between them stretched an icy ribbon of water, Seno Última Esperanza, or 'Last Hope Sound'. The mountain-fringed fjord's inauspicious name derives from a sixteenth-century Spanish sea-captain, Juan Ladrillero, for whom it represented his 'last hope' of finding a passage to the Strait of Magellan. While he managed to replenish his depleted stock of provisions, Ladrillero was dismayed to discover that the route in fact ended at a giant glacier rather than the strait. It is glorious setting for such a wistful title.

SMALL EARTHQUAKES

The shoreline of Seno Última Esperanza was the site of the next key stage of the Patagonia sheep-ranching boom, driven—inevitably—by the Sociedad Explotadora de Tierra del Fuego. As the twentieth century progressed and refrigerated shipping technology developed, the focus of the industry shifted from wool to meat. As in Fray Bentos, state-of-the-art meat-processing plants known as *frigoríficos* sprung up in southern Patagonia. Improbably, a reminder of this history can be found at a five-star hotel.

In 1905, the Sociedad Explotadora de Tierra del Fuego purchased a small slaughterhouse, set up a few years earlier by a German settler at a waterfront site known as Puerto Bories, some 150 miles north of Punta Arenas. Over the next ten years, the company built one of the most advanced industrial complexes of the era. In 1915, it opened the plant, which would operate at close to full capacity for nearly seven decades, powering the surrounding region's economy in the process. Employing 100 people throughout the year (and 400 during the busy January–April period), it processed a staggering 150,000 to 250,000 sheep annually, with the meat (and wool) exported to Europe.

In 1996, the Chilean authorities named the cold storage plant a National Historic Monument. It was later painstakingly restored over a decade and transformed into a high-end lodging, the Singular Patagonia, by a team including the descendants of José Menéndez and John MacLean Fraser, a Scottish sheep rancher whose son, Rodrigo MacLean Cameron, worked at the plant for forty years. Alongside luxurious rooms overlooking the fjord and an upmarket restaurant and bar, the hotel has a fascinating museum dedicated to the site's industrial history.

The reception led into the old *frigorífico*, a series of echoing brick buildings housing a treasure-trove of Edwardian design and technology. It vaguely resembled the site at Fray Bentos, but here the machinery was so polished and well maintained it appeared ready to spring back into action at a moment's notice. I wandered through a tannery, blacksmith and fat-rendering facilities, and engine and boiler rooms filled with interconnecting pipes, turbines, wheels, pistons, dials, gauges, condensers and motors. Much of the machinery was made in Britain and shipped over to Patagonia: a royal green compressor from the Haslam foundry in Derby; a cream-and-red refrigeration unit from the UD Engineering Co. in Park Royal, West London.

There was also plenty of equipment from the railway that once ferried workers to the complex from Puerto Natales, which lies 3 miles north along the shore and was developed, essentially, as a company town for workers at the plant. The pride and joy of the line was a Bristol-built steam engine named *McClelland*, in honour of the company's first chairman. Black-and-white photos provided a glimpse of the complex in its heyday: a ship bound for the UK being loaded with frozen lamb at the dock while manufactured goods from the UK travelled in the opposite direction.

For the owners, Frigorífico Bories opened at a opportune time. The outbreak of the First World War meant food imports were a matter of national security across Europe, with the situation particularly acute in the UK, which produced only a third of the calories consumed by its citizens and was heavily reliant on lamb, mutton, beef, wheat and corn from the Río de la Plata and Patagonia. This dependency increased significantly during the conflict. Yet there was trouble on the horizon for the Sociedad Explotadora de Tierra del Fuego.

After looking round the museum, I followed a road along the shore of Seno Última Esperanza to Puerto Natales, the second biggest city in the Chilean section of southern Patagonia after Punta Arenas. Although it predated Frigorífico Bories, the town was soon dominated by the plant. By 1919, the 2,000-strong population here and in Puerto Bories was sharply stratified: Sociedad Explotadora de Tierra del Fuego bosses and senior staff, who were predominantly from Britain, Scandinavia and Dalmatia in what is now Croatia, were at the top of the pile; below them was a class of foremen and shepherds, who were mainly British, predominantly Scottish; and at the bottom was a larger group of workers, who mainly came from Chiloé, alongside smaller numbers of Dalmatians.

Workers endured long hours and harsh and often perilous conditions with few rights and little pay, a precarious existence at the whims of a handful of immensely powerful companies and landowners who formed an oligarchy. During this period, there was a burgeoning trade union and anarchist presence in Patagonia's meatpacking plants and *estancias* and growing calls for workers' rights. Globally, revolution was in the air. An uprising was inevitable.

Puerto Natales' small history museum provided a succinct explanation of what happened next. In January 1919, workers at Frigorífico Bories went on strike, demanding a reduction of the working day to eight hours, as had been achieved on *estancias* in the region. They also called for wage increases and the reinstatement of colleagues who they felt had been unfairly dismissed.

Initial negotiations between union leaders and the plant's management were relatively positive, before being fatally undermined. First a painter was fired without being paid. Then, during the negotiations, the British manager of the plant, William Leslie Kidd, shot dead union representative Carlos Viveros from point-blank range. This sparked violent protests by the workers, which in turn prompted a spontaneous uprising among their counterparts in Puerto Natales. Warehouses, commercial properties and businesses were attacked, burned and looted, and there were clashes with the police. Six workers and four police officers were killed, and around twenty people were injured, most of them workers. The local authorities—and Kidd—fled across the border to Argentina, leaving the town in the hands of the Magallanes Workers' Federation and the Red Cross, which prevented the uprising from spiralling further.

THE GOLDEN FLEECE

A few days later, Chilean soldiers arrived and restored the local authority's control over the town. They arrested twenty-seven workers—but no administrative staff or police officers—and took them to Punta Arenas, where they were imprisoned for years awaiting trial. Twenty-three were eventually acquitted, and four were convicted of attacking the police officers.

The revolt on the shores of the Seno Última Esperanza proved a mere precursor to a far larger uprising in the neighbouring Argentine province of Santa Cruz between 1920 and 1922, an event that became known as Patagonia Rebelde or Patagonia Trágica ('Rebel Patagonia' or 'Tragic Patagonia'). As in Chile, the sheep ranches and meatpacking plants in Santa Cruz were largely owned and run by European, and particularly British, interests, including the Sociedad Explotadora de Tierra del Fuego. By contrast, the farm labourers and plant workers were often Chilean immigrants, predominantly from Chiloé, many of whom had fled from Puerto Natales after the 1919 revolt.

After the First World War, wool, mutton and lamb prices plunged across the globe, creating a major problem for a Patagonian economy centred on a single set of products. The result, wrote anarchist journalist, historian and author Osvaldo Bayer in *Rebellion in Patagonia*, was 'unemployment, poverty, repression, depressed wages, economic crisis, resignation among small producers and traders, and panic among large landowners'. These factors combined with longstanding anger over near-feudal working conditions, a buoyant trade unionist movement and increasing anarchist influence to prompt a wave of strikes, boycotts and protests that swelled into a mass uprising.

Eventually, the tension erupted in a series of violent clashes involving the police and armed forces. Workers occupied *estancias*, cut fences and slaughtered or released livestock while holding ranch managers and administrators hostage and killing two police officers. In response, the workers faced violence and repression.

SMALL EARTHQUAKES

Yet by January 1921, the situation had calmed. The new governor of Santa Cruz, Ángel Ignacio Yza, oversaw negotiations between representatives of the workers and the ranchers in which the latter accepted almost all of the former's demands. 'A close reading of the ranchers' offer shows the extent of the strike's success—this agreement was without precedent in Argentina as a whole,' wrote Bayer. To the displeasure of the sheep-ranching elite, Yza also released farm hands who had been arrested.

Strikers returned to work across the province, but anger continued to simmer. Disgruntled ranchers quickly reneged on the agreement, which prompted further strikes, protests and conflict. 'The rich don't waste their time. With an admirable persistence, the press hammers away daily at Governor Yza and President Yrigoyen' with calls for action against the workers, wrote Bayer. These demands were echoed by the British embassy in Buenos Aires.

Yrigoyen—the first Argentine president to be elected under universal male suffrage—ultimately sent in the army to 'protect an unjust feudal regime'. Under the command of Lieutenant Colonel Héctor B. Varela, the 10th Cavalry brutally crushed the rebellion; the exact number of workers massacred is not known, but Bayer put the figure at more than 1,500. Varela, who became known as the 'Butcher of Patagonia', was later assassinated in Buenos Aires by a German anarchist, Kurt Gustav Wilckens. Meanwhile, Antonio Soto, one of the main leaders of the uprising, is buried in Punta Arenas's cemetery, a stone's throw from Menéndez and other members of the sheepocracy.

The rebellion and its aftermath remained a powerful and divisive issue in Argentina. During the 1970s, Bayer—who learned about the events from his parents, who lived near the prison in Río Gallegos and heard the cries of the tortured workers—was forced into exile, and a film version of his book was banned.

* * *

THE GOLDEN FLEECE

Puerto Natales is now a traveller hub, the jumping-off point for visits to Parque Nacional Torres del Paine, the biggest tourist attraction in southern Chile. During my visit, a National Geographic cruise ship had recently docked, flotillas of swans and signets glided across the water and statues and sculptures lined the blustery promenade: a giant hand reached out of the pavement, and a pair of flying figures were whipped into the air by the near-constant winds. There was also a cartoonish statue of a Mylodon, a huge prehistoric ground sloth, at the entrance to the town. In 1895, a German merchant and rancher named Hermann Eberhard Schmith unearthed the remains of the 8-foot tall, 3-ton creature in a cave north of Puerto Natales. As well as generating international media attention, the discovery also inspired one of the most influential travel books of the twentieth century. A scrap of the Mylodon's skin found its way to author Bruce Chatwin, whose fascination with the item—which he initially mistook for a fragment of Brontosaurus skin—prompted him to journey to South America and ultimately write *In Patagonia*. The Mylodon has since become a symbol of the town, and its image adorns street signs in the centre.

A few weeks before the start of the peak summer season, the streets were quiet, and it felt like there were more stray dogs than people. A shaggy pack patrolled the main road, ignoring pedestrians but furiously chasing every car that dared drive past. The few travellers who had arrived early were clad, almost uniformly, in branded outdoor gear. There were plenty of hotels, guesthouses, hostels, restaurants and cafés. Shops sold upmarket woollens and handicrafts and hiking, camping and fishing supplies.

But there were also reminders of Puerto Natales' pioneer past. The town retained a makeshift vibe, with no two houses the same: corrugated-iron bungalows with brightly coloured walls and roofs, sturdier brick houses, wooden lodges, converted warehouses, upcycled shipping containers and multi-storey glass-fronted hotels. A mix of the smart and the decrepit.

SMALL EARTHQUAKES

Murals depicting the region's original Tehuelche and Kawésqar inhabitants covered the exterior wall of the football stadium. A series of scenes represented stylised snapshots of their lives before the Spanish colonisation of South America, then capturing and taming wild horses and using them to hunt guanacos, before finally witnessing the arrival of the first bands of European settlers in southern Patagonia. But a separate mural beside a nearby bungalow better captured the trauma, violence and devastation inflicted on Patagonia's Indigenous peoples during the sheep-ranching boom: the head and torso of a young man stared dead ahead, a pained but determined expression in his eyes, with an indistinct creature—probably a sea lion—howling below. The image was pale blue and white, but the paint had peeled in places and fissures and cracks had opened in the wall, giving the sense that the mural was disintegrating before my eyes.

As Chile expanded its control over southern Patagonia, ranchers, settlers and gold miners forcibly displaced the Tehuelche and Kawésqar, dispossessing them of their ancestral lands; the native inhabitants could not claim legal titles over their territories, as the state did not consider them to be citizens with rights. Countless miles of fences were erected across the region, curtailing their nomadic lifestyles and cutting them off from their hunting grounds and the wild animals upon which they relied.

Massacres were commonplace, often carried out by gangs of hired mercenaries known as 'Indian hunters' who used mastiffs to stalk their human prey and were paid by ranchers in pounds sterling. They included Samuel Hyslop, an Englishman who described himself as 'the best Indian hunter in Patagonia' and made horse hobbles from the skins of those he killed. Tehuelche and Kawésqar men, women and children were also corralled into draconian Salesian missions, where diseases brought over by Europeans took a devastating toll. Others were abducted and exhibited in 'zoological' shows for gawpers in North America and Europe.

THE GOLDEN FLEECE

Indigenous societies fractured, hastened by epidemics of diseases brought over from Europe and the spread of alcohol. Many Tehuelche took work on sheep and cattle ranches—heavily influencing gaucho culture in the process—or as horse breeders, which accelerated an assimilation process that helped to erode traditional identities, languages and beliefs. Unlike the first Welsh settlers in Chubut, there was no *Mimosa* waiting to carry them to a promised land.

* * *

I caught a bus to Parque Nacional Torres del Paine to visit Estancia Cerro Guido, a ranch formerly owned by the Sociedad Explotadora de Tierra del Fuego. One of the earliest first-hand, English-language accounts of this part of Patagonia came from Lady Florence Dixie, a Scottish feminist author, travel writer, war correspondent and suffragist who spent six months in the Pampas and Patagonia in an attempt to escape the strictures and sexism of Victorian Britain. Published in 1880, her bestselling account of the journey, *Across Patagonia*, features a memorable description of the approach to the trio of dazzling granite peaks that soar above the landscape:

> A glance showed us that we were in a new country. Before us stretched a picturesque plain, covered with soft green turf, and dotted here and there with clumps of beeches, and crossed in all directions by rippling streams. The background was formed by thickly wooded hills, behind which again towered the Cordilleras—three tall peaks of a reddish hue and in shape the exact facsimiles of Cleopatra's Needle.

Almost 150 years on, Dixie's sense of awe is echoed by the hundreds of thousands of people who visit Torres del Paine every year to trek, kayak, horse-ride and simply marvel at the landscapes.

The UNESCO World Heritage Site is bordered by Estancia Cerro Guido, a working ranch spanning 100,000 hectares and boasting 16,000 sheep. I spent a day on the site with puma tracker Ricardo Muza. As we gazed up at the ragged Condoreras ridge, he explained that during the age of the 'golden fleece', Patagonia's ever-expanding ranchers came into conflict with the native wildlife, as well as Indigenous peoples. Guanacos—the traditional prey of Patagonia's apex predator, the puma—were hunted or driven off to prevent them from competing with the livestock for grazing land. As a result, the big cats began to prey on sheep and cows, which were easier to hunt than the more robust camelids. In response, ranches employed hunters known as *leoneros* to kill the pumas.

A century on, the sheep-ranching heyday is long gone, thanks, largely, to the opening of the Panama Canal, which reduced trade along the Strait of Magellan, and the development of synthetic fibres. But it remains central to the economy and culture of southern Chile. The day-to-day work of *baqueanos*—the local equivalents of gauchos—has changed relatively little over the past century, and puma hunting remains common, even though it has been illegal in Chile since the 1980s. According to estimates, *leoneros* kill as many as 100 pumas a year, for which they are paid $200–400 per animal.

On a scrubby plateau, we met Pía Vergara, executive director of the Cerro Guido Conservation Foundation and a photographer who has worked with the 'ghost cats' for more than twenty years. She explained that pumas were hunted on Estancia Cerro Guido, too, until the owners decided to dramatically shift course in 2019. 'They are very visionary—they know the world is changing and I was like a mosquito in their ears, buzzing away for them to do something,' she said as we hiked to the top of the Condoreras. 'I presented the project and they said, "Okay, let's go. We will try it for one year and see what happens." The goal of the foundation is to protect the region's natural and cultural heritage, promoting harmonious coexistence.'

* * *

THE GOLDEN FLEECE

Back in Punta Arenas on a typically subdued Sunday morning in Patagonia. Closed shops, empty streets. The only sound of life came from the Anglican church whose service was delivered to a dwindling congregation. Around the corner, I found a kitsch house that looked like a mini castle: dull red brickwork, angular turret, flag-less flagpole and, above the front door, narrow windows that looked as if they shielded archers, ready to unleash a hail of arrows on anyone who dared to enter. The green wrought-iron gate had an 'M' monogram and led into an unkempt garden carpeted with dandelions, a ubiquitous presence in southern Patagonia. A graffitied blue plaque on the front wall described the style as 'Neoclassical architecture with elements of ... English Neo-Medieval.'

Known as Chalet Milward, the house was built in 1924 for Captain Charles Amherst Milward, the cousin of Bruce Chatwin's grandmother. Commonly known as Charley, the merchant seaman was shipwrecked in the Strait of Magellan in 1898 while captaining a New Zealand Shipping Company steamer on the Wellington–London route. Instead of returning home to the UK, he decided to settle in Punta Arenas and over the next twenty years was appointed British consul, became the director of a bank, launched a shipping firm and owned an iron and bronze foundry. Milward was also the source of the scrap of Mylodon skin that inspired Chatwin to make his pilgrimage to South America in the first place. '*In Patagonia* is full of life,' said John Rees, a later British consul in Punta Arenas. 'Chatwin helped to open up Patagonia to the world.'

In the book, the author compared Chalet Milward to a 'Victorian parsonage'. The house is now the office of the *El Pingüino* newspaper and closed to the public, but I knocked anyway. The secretary was reluctant to let me in: the journalists were working, she explained, and must not be disturbed by tourists wandering around. She only relented when I showed her my

British press card, though she insisted that I stick to the ground-floor rooms. Inevitably, I was underwhelmed. The period features had been stripped out and replaced with laminate flooring, office furniture, shelves creaking with ring-binders of past editions of the paper, a scuffed coffee table and net curtains. Only the fireplace looked original. The journalists were also conspicuous by their absence. I asked the secretary if she knew anything about Chatwin, but she said she hadn't heard of him. 'The explorer Ernest Shackleton stayed here though,' she added, as I prepared to leave.

The sheep-ranching boom in Patagonia coincided with the 'heroic age' of Antarctic exploration, and, as the key port on the Strait of Magellan, Punta Arenas was a regular stop-off for the likes of Robert Falcon Scott and Roald Amundsen. But the city is most closely associated with Shackleton. When the explorer arrived in the winter of 1916, he stayed with Milward while plotting the rescue of his crew, who were stranded in perilous conditions off the coast of Antarctica. It was an extremely stressful period for Shackleton, and, reputedly, one evening it got to him. While drinking whiskey and cleaning his revolver, he accidentally fired a shot that grazed Milward's ear, hit a painting and embedded a bullet in the wall.

There are links to Shackleton throughout Punta Arenas, most notably on the waterfront. Beyond a set of old warehouses, some seemingly abandoned, others converted into restaurants, the Costanera ran along the shore of the Strait of Magellan. The scent of barbecued lamb drifted over, and gulls swarmed a 'PUNTA ARENAS' sign before settling on a half-rotten dock. Near the port, the naval HQ and the incongruously glitzy Hotel Dreams and Casino—a cylinder of shimmering blue glass—was the freshly painted prow of a ship, the *Yelcho*. Alongside it was a statue of Captain Luis Pardo, arm outstretched, pointing to safety. A Chilean family posed for photos with him, taking it in turns to touch his outstretched finger.

THE GOLDEN FLEECE

Together, Shackleton, Pardo and the *Yelcho* were involved in the greatest escape in polar history, an epic journey across some of the roughest seas on earth to what is now the British Overseas Territory of South Georgia. At the time, the island was flourishing off the back of a grisly trade: whaling.

5

'TWO BALD MEN FIGHTING OVER A COMB'
FALKLAND ISLANDS AND SOUTH GEORGIA

As I stepped warily out of the boat into the fizzing surf at Stromness Bay, expedition leader Nate Small reiterated his warning: 'Stay well away from the building—it's filled with asbestos and the roof could literally blow off.'

My immediate concern, though, were the packs of truculent fur seals spread across the black pebble beach. They were interspersed with gigantic elephant seals, reclining like Jabba the Hutt. Surrounded by their harems, the dominant male 'beachmasters' mostly laid motionless, rousing from their slumber from time to time to issue a series of bone-shuddering bellows, honks and burps. The largest ones occasionally heaved themselves on to a much smaller female for a spot of low-energy copulation; the most energy they expended was on fights with perceived rivals, though these rarely got beyond a surprisingly quick mock-charge and a bout of snarling. Wide-eyed elephant seal pups sunned themselves and, unlike the temperamental fur seals, were friendly and curious. Nevertheless, I picked a careful path between them, keeping my head on a swivel.

SMALL EARTHQUAKES

At the southern edge of the bay, hard against a slate-grey cliff and surrounded by boggy grass and mounds of greeny-yellow moss, stood a set of dilapidated, heavily rusted buildings. Large sections of the corrugated-iron roofs and walls were missing, and those that remained rattled incessantly in the gale-force wind. Six hundred feet from the site, I stopped at an 'Asbestos—Keep Out' sign and peered through the encroaching mist. A pair of king penguins—bigger than their Magellanic cousins in northeast Patagonia, with orange plumage on their chests and heads—studiously ignored the warning. Instead, they picked their way through the jumble of scrap metal outside the buildings: propellors, cables, oil drums, pipes, cylindrical cannisters, all ochre with rust. It looked as if a hurricane had just whipped through the bay.

As my fingers and toes grew numb from the sub-zero temperatures, I struggled to picture the ruined site as a thriving community, yet just over a century ago Stromness Bay buzzed with activity as part of an immensely profitable—and savage—industry that transformed the distant island of South Georgia into the whaling capital of the South Atlantic. It also featured prominently in an epic feat of Antarctic exploration.

* * *

Some 800 miles from its nearest inhabited neighbour, the Falkland Islands, South Georgia is one of the most isolated places on the planet. An inhospitable realm of fjords, mountains and glaciers, the sub-Antarctic island covers 1,450 square miles—less than a fifth of the size of Wales. Only accessible by sea, it is half covered by ice, though the glaciers are now retreating drastically as the climate emergency intensifies. The vast majority of visitors—around 10,000 a year before the COVID-19 pandemic—arrive on an Antarctic cruise.

The fortunes of South Georgia and the Falklands have long been entangled. Both are British Overseas Territories (South

'TWO BALD MEN FIGHTING OVER A COMB'

Georgia forms one collectively with the South Sandwich Islands, an archipelago 470 miles to the southeast), a reminder that despite their size and remoteness these South Atlantic islands remain of geopolitical importance. Their status is, of course, contested by Argentina, a disagreement that reached its height in the ten-week Falklands War of 1982. The conflict continues to cast a long shadow, warping outside perceptions of the islands and obscuring their remarkable histories.

I visited in 2018 on the *Hebridean Sky*, which departed from Puerto Madryn in early November, springtime in the southern hemisphere and the start of the short Antarctic cruise season. Beyond the Golfo Nuevo, where a few straggling southern right whales, mainly mothers and young calves, were starting their journey south, a two-day sail took us across more than 300 miles of the Atlantic Ocean to West Point, one of the 780 islands that make up the Falklands.

The first people to discover the archipelago were probably members of Yagán communities in Tierra del Fuego. These expert seafarers may have introduced the wolf-like warrah, the only mammal on the islands at the time of European contact (the canine was driven to extinction in the 1870s). Centuries later, the first Europeans to spot the Falklands are believed to be Portuguese sailors around 1518–19, though their identities have since been lost to history. The first recorded sighting was by John Davis, captain of the *Desire*, which was part of the fleet of privateer-pirate Thomas Cavendish's final voyage. On 9 August 1592, having been thwarted in his attempts to reach the Strait of Magellan, a fierce storm drove Davis west towards 'certain isles never before discovered by any known relation, lying fifty leagues or better from the shore East and Northerly from the Straits in which place unless it pleased God of his wonderful mercy to have ceased the winde we must of necessity have perished'. His ship is name-checked in the motto on the Falklands' coat of arms: 'Desire the Right.'

SMALL EARTHQUAKES

Six years later, Dutchman Sebald de Weerdt also sighted the archipelago, naming a northwestern chain of islands the Sebaldines (they are now called the Jason Islands), but it was almost a century before Englishman John Strong, captain of the *Welfare*, made the first recorded landing in 1690. He named the waterway between the two main islands after one of the sponsors of his expedition, the Royal Naval treasurer Viscount Falkland, whose title came from a former royal burgh in Fife. Over the following decades, the archipelago was visited by assorted mariners, including British privateer-pirates William Dampier and Woodes Rogers, as well as Lord Anson, who called for the foundation of a naval base on the islands to aid British ships travelling to the Pacific through the Strait of Magellan.

But the first permanent settlement on the archipelago (other than, perhaps, those established by the Yagán centuries earlier) was French. In 1764, Louis-Antoine de Bougainville, who swapped a career in the army for one in the navy, claimed the islands for Louis XV, founded Fort St Louis (later Port Louis) on what is now East Falkland and introduced cattle. He named the archipelago Îles Malouines, after St Malo, his port of departure. A year later, unaware of de Bougainville's actions, Royal Naval officer John Byron—whose experience of being shipwrecked in Patagonia two decades earlier would help to inspire his grandson, Lord Byron, to write the poem 'Don Juan'—arrived to claim the islands, which he called the Falklands, for Britain. In 1766, another Royal Naval officer, Captain John McBride, founded a naval garrison and settlement at Port Egmont on Saunders Island, off West Falkland. A few months later, he discovered the French presence at Fort St Louis.

The following year, the Spanish arrived on the scene and further muddied the waters. After some diplomatic wrangling, de Bougainville was forced to sell Fort St Louis to the Spanish, who renamed the settlement Puerto Soledad and Îles Malouines as

'TWO BALD MEN FIGHTING OVER A COMB'

Islas Malvinas. The fledgling British and Spanish presences existed in isolation until 1770, when a confrontation broke out at Port Egmont. It quickly became clear that the British were heavily outgunned. 'The Spaniards had sixteen hundred men, five frigates, and a formidable train of artillery [which] convinced the English that resistance from one sloop and a wooden blockhouse would be worse than futile,' wrote historian Vera Brown Holmes in *Anglo-Spanish Relations in America in the Closing Years of the Colonial Era (1763–1774)*. Perfunctory shots were exchanged before the British beat a hasty retreat.

Although a round of British–Spanish–French diplomatic talks restored Port Egmont to Britain the following year, it was a short-lived reprieve. In 1774, once the furore had died down and the onerous financial implications of maintaining an armed presence on these faraway islands became clear, the British abandoned Port Egmont. They left behind only a Union flag and a lead plaque attached to the blockhouse door that read: 'Be it known to all nations that Falkland's islands with this fort, the storehouses, wharfs and harbours, bays and creeks thereunto belonging are the sole right and property of his most sacred majesty, George the Third, King of Great Britain.'

* * *

Saunders Island is now colonised by penguins. We landed at the Neck, a narrow strip of sandy beach connecting green, treeless hills grazed by sheep. Port Egmont, today just a collection of collapsed stone walls with an information board and a flagpole, lies some 6 miles to the southeast. Saunders Island is home to four species of penguin—rockhopper, gentoo, Magellanic and king—and while the passengers of the *Hebridean Sky* were firmly instructed to keep well away, the birds themselves were under no such restrictions. Nosy and fearless, they shuffled up to us inquisitively, cocking their heads at the strange creatures who had appeared within their midst, each swaddled in matching red jackets and heavy-duty, fleece-lined boots.

'The penguins come here to breed in huge numbers, and you get to see them nesting, protecting their eggs and courting,' said Marty Garwood, the onboard ornithologist and former head penguin keeper at Sydney Aquarium. 'There are few land-based predators here, so the birds are very curious of humans. Sometimes they even peck at you to see if there's something tasty to eat.' On several occasions, as I lined-up to take a photo, I heard a rustle behind me and spun round to find myself face-to-face with a curious-looking penguin. At one point, a Magellanic wandered through my legs.

It was the start of the nesting season, and while the penguins kept beady eyes out for potential predators, there were moments of tragedy. I watched with horror as a muscular, gull-like skua swooped in and snatched away an egg, leaving the mother distraught. Meanwhile, another penguin was undergoing what Garwood described as its annual 'catastrophic moult': midway through this routine but rather unsettling process, the bird's body was a patchwork of bald patches and unruly tufts of new feathers. To take my mind off it, I wandered to the beach, where penguins with fully intact plumage 'porpoised' through the surf, skimming the surface as if they were dolphins.

The day started on West Point Island, home to Jackie and Allan White's farm. Their weekly schedule was chalked up on a blackboard in the kitchen—Monday: Check for new lambs. Tuesday and Wednesday: Prepare tea and cakes for hundreds of cruise passengers. Thursday: Kill mutton. Friday and Saturday: Host hundreds more cruise passengers. Sunday: Move the ewes. The Whites took their hosting duties seriously, greeting the passengers of the *Hebridean Sky* with a table heaving with homemade cakes, tarts, biscuits and pastries—twenty-six varieties in total, from scones to cinnamon rolls—as well as an endless supply of tea and coffee.

'TWO BALD MEN FIGHTING OVER A COMB'

At the northwestern tip of the Falklands, West Point was vaguely reminiscent of the Scottish Highlands. Beyond the Whites' picket-fenced, weather-boarded homestead was a landscape of mist-swirled hills, low scrubs and vivid patches of canary-yellow gorse. Although the Falklands remain synonymous with the 1982 war, West Point offered a different perspective. The island's staggering array of birdlife has made it a regular stop on cruise ships bound for Antarctica. There are huge rockhopper penguin and black-browed albatross breeding sites, alongside 800 sheep, 200 cows and two humans, the Whites.

A twenty-minute walk from the homestead took me to a precipitous sandstone cliff rising out of the choppy South Atlantic. Encircled by thickets of grass and slicks of sticky mud, hundreds of rockhoppers and albatrosses issued a racket of hoots, quacks, sheep-like bleats and coos. The rockhoppers lived up to their name, hopping across the terrain with surprising ease, periodically squawking at rivals or pausing to preen themselves in front of a panoply of top-of-the-range camera lenses. The albatrosses were more sedate: most sat quietly on their nests, but a few stragglers engaged in complex mating rituals, elegantly mirroring each other's movements.

In terms of wildlife, West Point is emblematic of the Falklands as a whole. The archipelago is a hotspot for birdlife, home to around 70 per cent of the world's black-browed albatrosses, alongside hundreds of thousands of penguins from five different species. There are also endemic birds such as the flightless steamer duck, plus sea lions, seals, dolphins and several whale species, including orcas, in the surrounding waters.

* * *

Sovereignty disputes over the Falklands persisted as the countries of South America began to throw off their colonial shackles in the early nineteenth century. In 1811, the Spanish withdrew their settlers from Puerto Soledad, leaving behind a plaque asserting their claim, just as the British had done four decades earlier.

After winning independence in 1816, the United Provinces of the Río de la Plata—a short-lived entity spanning much of modern-day Argentina, Uruguay, Bolivia and Peru—took on its former coloniser's claim to the islands. The following decade saw an attempt to seize the archipelago by Connecticut-born privateer David Jewett, acting on behalf of the authorities in Buenos Aires, as well as a failed cattle-ranching venture and regular visits from an eclectic cast of whalers, sealers and fishers. But the next meaningful development took place in 1828. Having sought permission from both the United Provinces of the Río de la Plata and the British authorities, Luis Vernet, a Franco-German merchant who emigrated to Buenos Aires, founded a new settlement at Puerto Soledad. The United Provinces of the Río de la Plata later appointed him commander of the islands and Tierra del Fuego (which remained under the control of its Indigenous inhabitants at this point). But Vernet's attempts to curb visiting seal hunters—which would allow him to exploit the creatures himself—drew the ire of the United States. In 1831, the warship *Lexington* attacked the settlement in retaliation for the arrest of US sealers, prompting many of the settlers to leave for Montevideo.

The following year, the United Provinces of the Río de la Plata appointed Esteban Mestivier as governor of the islands, only for him to be killed in a mutiny a month after his arrival. These events shook Britain into action. A pair of Royal Navy warships were dispatched to restate its claim to the Falklands, and, in early 1833, the last remaining officials from the Argentine Confederation—which had emerged from the recent break-up of the United Provinces of the Río de la Plata—were expelled.

A contemporaneous account of this period is provided by Charles Darwin, who arrived on the *Beagle* in March 1833. His first impressions of the Falklands were not positive. More than

'TWO BALD MEN FIGHTING OVER A COMB'

half of the small multinational population of these 'miserable islands' was made up of 'runaway rebels and murderers'. Darwin was similarly unimpressed with the terrain, which he described in *The Voyage of the Beagle* as uninteresting and possessing a 'desolate and wretched aspect'. Everywhere, he continued, was 'covered by a peaty soil and wiry grass, of one monotonous brown colour'. Exploring the islands, Darwin encountered a few gauchos who pursued wild cattle—the descendants of animals introduced by the French in the 1760s—that resembled 'Grecian marble sculptures', a rare instance of praise from the naturalist.

Despite the British actions, the islands remained lawless. Five months after Darwin's visit, a band of gauchos killed six settlers in a payment dispute, prompting the rest of the community to flee temporarily to an island in Berkeley Sound before the Royal Navy arrived to arrest the culprits and restore order. In 1842, the Falklands' first civilian lieutenant governor, Richard Clement Moody, arrived on the archipelago, and a new capital, Stanley, was founded on the northeast coast of East Falkland.

* * *

Today, Stanley is home to almost three-quarters of the islands' 3,500-strong population. It is a neat-and-tidy town with a mix of smart, modern weatherboarded homes with daffodil-filled gardens and semi-detached Victorian houses that would not look out place in the UK, save for their bright corrugated-iron roofs. Alongside the requisite red mailboxes, a double-decker London bus—a number 22, which once plied the route between Putney and Oxford Circus—was parked near the tourist office, used by a local travel agency to ferry visitors around.

There were several pubs, including the Globe Tavern, which had a dartboard, fish and chips on the menu and Premier League football on the TV, albeit with Spanish-language commentary courtesy of Fox Deportes. The jawbones of a pair of blue whales formed an arch outside the cathedral, souvenir shops sold penguin-related memorabilia and bumper stickers read 'Falklands—British to the Core.'

To escape the ferocious wind, I popped into the Historic Dockyard Museum, which traces the past and the future of the Falklands. Alongside displays on the archipelago's links to the First and Second World Wars, and the 1982 conflict with Argentina, there was a recreation of a turn-of-the-twentieth-century general store, complete with tins of boiled mutton and boxes of Huntley & Palmers biscuits. There were stories of shipwrecks, vintage sheep-shearing equipment and a gruesome-looking dental chair with a foot-pump-powered drill that was once flown from farm to farm.

In the museum grounds, a gregarious white-haired man with a long beard and a blue fleece called out to me: 'I sell coins and stamps and answer difficult questions.' Turning down the BBC World Service in his one-room souvenir shop, Phil Middleton explained that he had originally moved to the Falklands from the UK in the late 1970s to work as a teacher before deciding to stay. Now a tour guide, he was keen to challenge stereotypes and prejudices about the islands:

> There's an attitude among certain types of British tourists who say things like, 'This is like Britain after the Second World War.' It's not. The biggest misconception is that the Falklands are a little part of Britain. We're a British Overseas Territory. We're Falkland Islanders. There's a strong local identity. We're a small, forward-looking, progressive community.

The Falklands are self-governing, apart from defence, which is controlled and funded by the UK. They are also economically self-sufficient, thanks primarily to the strength of the local commercial fishing industry—as in Patagonia, the age of the golden fleece is long gone, but there are still half a million sheep on the

'TWO BALD MEN FIGHTING OVER A COMB'

islands, as well as more than 3,000 cattle. The Falklands are also much more cosmopolitan than might be expected, currently home to around sixty nationalities. While most are of British descent, there are also significant Chilean, Santa Helenian, Filipino and South African communities, as well as people from as far away as Nepal and Zimbabwe.

'Some people still think we're living like we were during the war in 1982,' added Middleton. 'We're not—we've moved on.'

* * *

Yet even a short visit to the Falklands reminds you that the war continues to cast a long shadow over the islands. Many tourists still head straight to the war cemeteries or battlefield sites such as Goose Green, while Britain maintains a major military presence, with a permanent military base, RAF Mount Pleasant, staffed by up to 1,700 military and civilian personnel.

Jorge Luis Borges famously compared the seventy-four-day conflict to 'a war between two bald men fighting over a comb'. Having established a presence on the South Sandwich Islands in 1976, Argentina's military dictatorship, led by General Leopoldo Galtieri, turned its focus to the Falklands. Abandoning longstanding negotiations with Britain over the sovereignty of the islands, Argentine forces seized control of the Falklands, as well as South Georgia, in early April 1982. Quickly subduing a small contingent of Royal Marines, they repatriated the British governor and deported or detained many islanders.

In response, a British military task force featuring 127 warships, submarines and merchant vessels sailed to the South Atlantic. After weeks of fierce fighting, Argentine forces surrendered on 14 June. During the conflict, 907 people were killed: 649 Argentines, 255 Britons and three Falkland Islanders. The most notorious incident was the British sinking of the *Belgrano*, even though the warship was outside Britain's 200-mile 'total exclusion zone' around the Falklands and heading away from the islands. The attack killed 323 Argentines and has been called a war crime.

The conflict was a huge boost for the Thatcher government and helped to topple the junta, which had briefly ridden a wave of patriotic fervour. Since seizing power in a coup in 1976, it had kidnapped, tortured and 'disappeared' 30,000 people while overseeing an economic collapse and now a military disaster. In 1983, constitutional elections were held, and democracy finally returned.

The Falklands remain a potent issue in Argentina. There is widespread public support for the country's claim to 'Las Malvinas', and the issue is often whipped up at times of political and economic crisis. Countless monuments and signs assert Argentine sovereignty over the archipelago. There's even a bus company named 'Malvinas Argentinas'. There are also periodic stunts—a football team standing behind a banner on the islands, a 50-peso note restating Argentina's 'undying claim'. When Argentines have raised the issue with me in the past, they were often disappointed to hear the Falklands are not a big deal in Britain today and that, in fact, most people would struggle to place the islands on a map.

Anglo-Argentine relations are now cordial, but few people in Stanley were optimistic that the situation with their neighbour would improve any time soon. Argentine veterans and their families are allowed to visit graves at the Argentine military cemetery on East Falkland, where 237 soldiers are buried, though the subsequent social media posts featuring photos of Argentine flags and the like inevitably raise tensions with islanders. 'Argentina is a pain in the butt,' one resident told me.

Asking to speak off the record, she also criticised Brexit for damaging the local fishing industry, which exported much of its catch—particularly squid—to the Eurozone, and expressed concerns over plans for oil extraction. Like most locals I met, she said she would support independence if it was economically viable but did not think it was a realistic prospect any time soon.

'TWO BALD MEN FIGHTING OVER A COMB'

The Falkland Islands government has refused UK requests to ratify the Paris Agreement on climate change and is set to give the go-ahead for a company named Rockhopper Exploration to push ahead with the controversial exploitation of the offshore Sea Lion basin, which is estimated to hold in excess of 800 million barrels of oil, 'making it larger than any North Sea project', according to the *Telegraph*. The fate of the archipelago's fragile ecosystems—not least its actual rockhoppers and sea lions—remains in doubt.

In the meantime, as word spreads about the wildlife-spotting possibilities, tourist numbers are increasing: cruise ships regularly call in during the summer months, and there are flights from RAF Brize Norton in the UK and Santiago and Punta Arenas in Chile. 'It's only when you come with an open mind,' said Middleton, as I left his shop, 'that you can really understand what this place is about.'

* * *

If the Falklands are remote, South Georgia is positively isolated. A two-day sail from Stanley took the *Hebridean Sky* southeast across the South Atlantic to a starkly beautiful, ice-covered, windblasted island riven with more than a dozen mountains taller than Ben Nevis. Buffeted by 75-knot gales and tempestuous seas that confined a third of the passengers to their cabins and left the dining hall and lounges virtually deserted, we arrived in King Edward Cove on the north coast of South Georgia, ominously dotted with icebergs and shipwrecks. On the shore, backed by a massif of forbidding peaks and partially obscured by a curtain of icy drizzle, I could just about make out the semi-collapsed settlement of Grytviken, a relic from a period in which this distant, uncompromising island played a key role in the global economy.

The first sighting of South Georgia is generally considered to have been in 1675. On his journey back from Peru, Antoine de la Roché, a merchant born in London to a French Huguenot father and an English mother, was blown off course after rounding Cape Horn and spotted an island in the distance with a range of ice-clad mountains. Doubt has since been cast on the accuracy of his account, and some academics have even questioned whether he existed at all, but James Cook's arrival a century later is not in dispute.

In 1775, Cook was sailing home after an unsuccessful attempt to find a hitherto 'undiscovered' southern continent—Terra Australis, aka Antarctica—the existence of which was much speculated upon in Europe at the time (given their expert maritime skills and extensive voyages, it is possible the Yagán of this period were aware of this ice-bound landmass to the south of Tierra del Fuego). Commanding HMS *Resolution*, he made the first landing on South Georgia on 17 January, at what is now Possession Bay on the northwest coast and claimed the uninhabited 'island of ice' for Britain. His accounts of the huge populations of Antarctic fur seals soon aroused attention.

In 1786, the first British sealing vessel, the *Lord Hawkesbury*, collected a cargo of seal pelts from South Georgia. A host of British and American sealers swiftly followed suit. Within fifty years of Cook's landing, an estimated 1.2 million fur seals had been killed in and around South Georgia. By the end of the nineteenth century, the species had been hunted to the verge of extinction. As a result, sealing collapsed in this part of the world, only to be replaced by a similarly bloody, and even more profitable, industry.

* * *

Today, Grytviken is the site of the main settlement on South Georgia, home to the roughly fifteen to thirty people who live on the island at any one time. They are mostly British Antarctic Survey (BAS) scientists and government officials, who carry out immigration formalities and biosecurity checks on all visitors. Alongside a BAS station, there is a small museum and post office (delivery time to the UK: six weeks). During the early stages of the Falklands War, there was fighting in Grytviken, with Argentine forces briefly seizing control of the island. An Argentine submariner who died during the conflict, Felix Artuso, is buried at the cemetery, a spray of plastic flowers laid on his grave.

Grytviken dates back to 1902 and a Norwegian polar explorer named Carl Anton Larsen, who had previously found fame for discovering the first fossils of petrified wood on Antarctica; he was also the first person to ski on the continent, traversing the ice shelf that now bears his surname. Larsen arrived in King Edward Cove, a beautiful natural harbour, in fair weather at least. 'He moored not far off from where your ship is today,' explained Finlay Raffle, a curator at the South Georgia Museum. 'The only difference was when he looked out over the water he saw hundreds of whales in this bay alone.' During this period, the waters surrounding South Georgia were home to some of the densest populations of large whales in the world, thanks largely to the abundant supplies of krill.

On the shore, Larsen found some old try-pots—items used by sealers to render oil from blubber—and named the area Grytviken ('Pot Cove' in Norwegian). He also sensed a business opportunity at hand. Two years later, Larsen founded South Georgia's first whaling station on the site, at a time when the industry in the northern hemisphere was in sharp decline due to the devastation of whale populations from over-hunting. In less than a decade, six more whaling stations had been set up on the island: Husvik, Leith, Prince Olav, Ocean Harbour, Godthul and Stromness, their names betraying the strong British (especially Scottish) and Scandinavian connections to the industry.

Raffle guided me through a decaying industrialised landscape. A flotilla of abandoned ships and boats lay beached or semi-submerged, jutting into the air at erratic angles, assailed by the tide. Inland, half-obscured by a shroud of rust, was a collection of warehouses, chimneys, towers, tanks, pipes and power plants, alongside large cookers for bone and blubber, one of which had a 24-tonne capacity. Silvery-grey fur seals slumbered amid the machinery, and fragments of whale bone crunched underfoot as we trudged across the muddy terrain.

After the founding of Grytviken, South Georgia quickly developed into the hub of industrial, land-based whaling in the southern hemisphere. Raffle pointed out the *Petrel*, a steam-powered vessel with a reinforced hull and cartoonishly large harpoon gun that could capture up to fourteen whales per voyage. With populations of the heavily hunted southern right whales already at low levels at this point due to commercial hunting off the coasts of the Falklands and Patagonia, the whalers focused on the most valuable and easiest-to-catch species, driving them to virtual extinction before moving on to the next: first humpbacks and then, in succession, blue, fin, sei and sperm whales.

The harpooned cetaceans were brought back to Grytviken and winched on to a grisly slipway named a 'flensing plan'. They included the longest whale ever recorded: a female blue whale measuring 110 feet, which was landed in 1909. 'The flensing plan was very slippery with all the blood and oil, so the men wore boots with nails in them so they could grip properly,' said Raffle. 'They had a flensing knife—a long, almost hockey stick with a sharp, curved blade, which they used to cut the blubber away.' A whale could be processed in as little as twenty minutes.

In the early days, the whalers focused only on the blubber, but regulations were later introduced obliging them to use the entire carcass, as testified by the presence of a set of fearsome rotating blades. Whale products were in high demand during this period. The meat and bonemeal were used as fertiliser and as livestock feed and supplements, but the oil was a far more valuable com-

'TWO BALD MEN FIGHTING OVER A COMB'

modity. 'The best oils went into food products like margarine and ice cream,' said Raffle. 'The second grade went into soap and cosmetics, and the worst was used in industrial processes.' Like the meat-processing plants in Fray Bentos and Patagonia, the whaling industry benefitted from the outbreak of the First World War. The conflict drove demand for whale oil, which provided glycerol, vital both for the manufacture of explosives and in high-quality lubricants for arms such as rifles and military equipment such as chronometers.

At its height, the industry, driven by British companies and investment, was staggeringly profitable: an oil boom crossed with a gold rush. For example, Christian Salvesen, an Edinburgh-based firm that built and owned Leith, the largest of South Georgia's whaling stations, and operated a fleet of factory ships, made 'the equivalent [of] £100m a year in profit in today's money', according to a BBC report.

While the overwhelming majority of the workforce at Grytviken were from Scandinavia, a large proportion of working-class Scots were employed in the industry across the island's whaling stations as a whole. Lured by relatively high wages, the chance to escape poverty and, for many, a sense of adventure, they spent a year or more away from home.

Whalers are not the easiest people for whom to feel sympathy. But the working and living conditions on the South Georgia stations were bleak. At its peak, around 450 men—there were very few women on the island at the time—worked twelve-hour shifts, seven days a week, in temperatures that often plunged well below 10C. There were, however, some distractions from the gory, repetitive toil, including an imposing Neo-Gothic church, though, according to Raffle, the pastor 'was the least employed man on the station'. The station's small cinema, a mire-like football pitch and a rudimentary ski jump—now just a few split timbers sticking out of the hillside—received far more use, as did the shop, which was known as the 'slop chest'. 'Tobacco was the most popular item, but the men also bought lots of cologne,' said Raffle. 'Larsen didn't allow alcohol, so they drank cologne instead. They also had illicit stills, and even got boot polish, squeezed it through bread, and then drank the drippings, which apparently also had alcohol. Anything to pass the time.'

* * *

As the 1920s drew to a close, South Georgia's shore-based whaling stations began to decline as the industry shifted to pelagic factory ships, which essentially functioned as floating whaling stations and could operate farther out to sea than previous vessels. Predictably, this period saw a dramatic collapse in whale populations, despite efforts by the government of the Falkland Islands to regulate the industry on South Georgia, protect stocks and limit over-exploitation, including by outlawing the killing of mothers with calves. Yet the factory ships ultimately proved to be too ruthlessly efficient for their own good: a glut of whale oil flooded on to the market, and prices plummeted.

Whaling persisted on South Georgia for several decades, but one by one the stations closed. When the final station, Leith, stopped operating in 1965, there were simply not enough whales left to make the industry viable. At the same time, advances in petrochemicals began to provide cheaper alternatives to whale-based products. Between the opening of Grytviken in 1904 and 1965, a staggering 175,250 whales were processed on South Georgia. If you take the Southern Ocean as a whole and include the activity of factory ships, almost 1.5 million baleen whales were killed during the twentieth century.

Whale populations have never recovered from their exploitation in the nineteenth and twentieth centuries. Figures from the International Whaling Commission (IWC), which was established in 1946 and enacted a moratorium on commercial whaling in

'TWO BALD MEN FIGHTING OVER A COMB'

1986, make for depressing reading. Antarctic blue whale numbers have fallen from as many as 200,000–300,000 before the advent of commercial whaling to 2,000-plus today. The IWC noted a large fall in the southern right whale population, once estimated at 70,000–100,000 but now only around 14,000, according to the last survey. Meanwhile, population models suggest there are currently some 96,000 humpbacks in the southern hemisphere, though this is also far lower than the pre-whaling era.

In 2018, pro-whaling countries—including Norway, Iceland and Russia—defeated an IWC proposal to create a whale sanctuary in the South Atlantic. The same year, Japan announced it would resume commercial whaling for the first time in decades.

* * *

Despite its history, South Georgia has developed into an unlikely conservation success story in recent decades. BAS bird ecologist Dr Norman Ratcliffe has described the island as 'the Alps with Serengeti-style wildlife around it'. His organisation carried out the first comprehensive survey of the island in 2011 and found a remarkable 1,445 different species. The following year, one of the world's largest marine reserves was created to protect the nutrient-rich waters around it and the neighbouring South Sandwich Islands. Spanning almost 500,000 square miles, the reserve is more than five times the size of the UK.

After being decimated in the nineteenth century, seal numbers have bounced back. South Georgia is now home to around 5 million of the mammals, including some 98 per cent of the world's Antarctic fur seals and roughly half of its elephant seals. In 2018, following a pioneering £7.5-million eradication programme, South Georgia was declared free of rodents, the ancestors of which stowed away on sealing and whaling vessels and ravaged the native wildlife. This will help to protect the 65 million seabirds of thirty different species found on the island, including the endemic South Georgia pipit, the world's only sub-Antarctic songbird.

SMALL EARTHQUAKES

South Georgia's four penguin species were once hunted for their oil, but the island is now a globally important habitat for these charismatic birds, home to 3 million in total. During my visit, I spent a morning in St Andrews Bay, a sweeping beach enclosed by snow-streaked mountains, observing a 400,000-strong colony of king penguins. Pungent fishy stench and abundant guano aside, it was a magical experience. Amid the penguins' squeals and yelps and the deep bellows of the seals on the beach, the delicate, haunting voice of a single pipit cut through, a piercing, melancholic contrast. Later in the day, we navigated a tract of shallow, rocky waters to land on a pebble beach at Prion Island, an important breeding site for the wandering albatross, which have the longest wingspan of any bird—up to 11 feet. It was nesting season, and a trio of fluffy chicks—one of the guides compared them to sheep with wings—rested on tussocks of grass while their parents spent the day hunting for squid. South Georgia is also an internationally important breeding site for black-browed and grey-headed albatrosses.

While numbers remain far lower than before the start of commercial whaling in South Georgia, there are indications that some whale populations in the region may be making a comeback. A BAS study published in 2020 reported that critically endangered blue whales, driven to the brink of extinction in the twentieth century, had made a return, with fifty-eight annual sightings. Southern right and humpback whales are also increasingly spotted in the area. I spent hours on the deck of the *Hebridean Sky* peering through snow flurries at humpback whale flukes amid walnut whip-shaped icebergs in the seas around South Georgia, warming my hands with glasses of hot ginger-spiced apple juice.

'When you walk about these stations all you see are these rusting boilers, blubber cookers and bone saws,' said Seb Coulthard, an expedition guide and historian on the *Hebridean Sky*. 'It's a

'TWO BALD MEN FIGHTING OVER A COMB'

bittersweet irony in that it was a terrible, brutal industry, yet nature took its sweet revenge by reclaiming it. It's a reminder that nature doesn't need human beings; we need nature.'

It's tempting to end the story there: the transformation of the epicentre of exploitative industries that decimated wildlife into a biodiverse haven. But that wouldn't be entirely accurate.

Despite South Georgia's remoteness, the outside world takes its toll. In 2024, an outbreak of High Pathogenic Avian Influenza, commonly known as avian flu, hit the bird and mammal populations here and in the Falklands; wandering albatrosses, penguins and elephant seals were among the species affected. There are also concerns about commercial fishing, which developed at scale here in the 1960s.

The impact of the climate emergency is clear to see, too. Around half of South Georgia is permanently covered by ice, but all of its glaciers are now in retreat as global temperatures climb. On our final day, we moored in Gold Harbour at the southwest tip of the island. Piloting a boat through light but persistent snow, expedition guide and biologist Annette Bombosch explained that the bay's name came from a band of German explorers who spotted something glittering on the jagged black rocks; it turned out to be fool's gold, but the soubriquet stuck. We circled the coast, avoiding the clogging kelp strands, which swirled like super-sized tagliatelle in a bubbling pan. A solitary caramel-blond fur seal reclined on an outcrop, and giant petrels, kelp gulls and skuas prowled overhead.

After landing on the beach, I avoided the 3-tonne elephant seals and peered up at the huge Bertrab Glacier. It was a gaping blue-white band of ice, winding its way through the black mountain slopes. From one end, a thin waterfall trickled down to the beach. Bertrab may have looked impressive to my untrained eye, but less than forty years ago it stretched all the way to the sea. Since then, it has steadily shrunk back from the water line, across the beach and up towards the mountain, leaving behind a lake and a mass of bare black rock, free of plant life. It was a troubling sight. 'It's receded right back,' said expedition guide Bob Gilmore. 'That's essentially what we see across South Georgia.'

* * *

The *Hebridean Sky* continued south across the Scotia Sea until we reached Elephant Island at the eastern end of the South Shetlands. Obscured by mist, lashed by waves, the narrow stretch of beach known as Point Wild was backed by barely visible snow-draped cliffs and crystalline glaciers. A large tabular iceberg lingered offshore. Although a rookery of chinstrap penguins appeared happy enough, it looked a profoundly inhospitable place. Yet this was the site where the shipwrecked crew of Shackleton's ill-fated Imperial Trans-Antarctic Expedition camped out for four and a half months, hoping against all sense of rationality that they would be rescued.

When he set off in August 1914, days after the outbreak of the First World War, the Anglo-Irish polar explorer aimed to complete the first land crossing of Antarctica. En route south, he ignored warnings from South Georgia's whalers about record levels of sea ice. Sure enough, after departing the island, his ship, the *Endurance*, subsequently got trapped in pack ice in the Weddell Sea, drifting for ten months before being abandoned in October 1915. Shackleton ordered the twenty-seven-strong crew to leave behind all of their personal possessions apart from photographer Frank Hurley's photos and meteorologist Leonard Hussey's banjo. The wreck sank the following month, while the 'Boss' and his men were forced to survive in makeshift camps on the ice floes.

In early April 1916, they sailed for six days in three small lifeboats through treacherous waters to Elephant Island, whose inhospitable terrain at least provided the reassurance of solid

'TWO BALD MEN FIGHTING OVER A COMB'

ground beneath their feet. But the chance of rescue was slim to none this far off commercial shipping routes, so, after setting up camp at Point Wild, Shackleton and five companions—Captain Frank Worsley, second officer Tom Crean, carpenter Chippy McNeish, and seamen Timothy McCarthy and John Vincent—set off on an even riskier voyage to South Georgia, whose whaling stations offered potential salvation. Their 800-mile crossing in the *James Caird* is widely regarded as among the most daring feats in polar exploration.

The *Hebridean Sky*'s Coulthard had taken part in a 2013 recreation of the journey in a replica boat, using only the equipment, clothing and techniques available to Shackleton. He described heavy snow, ice choking the sails and 'fairly squalid conditions' in the cramped living space. 'The greatest challenge was the Southern Ocean,' he wrote in an article for the website Ends of the Earth. 'Waves crashed around us all the time and on a couple of occasions we thought the boat would get swamped ... To this day I am still at a loss for an explanation as to how [the boat] survived.'

Miraculously, after a tumultuous fifteen-day voyage, the *James Caird* safely reached the south coast of South Georgia on 10 May. But the ordeal was far from over. This part of the island was uninhabited, so Shackleton, Worsley and Crean were forced to embark on a 32-mile, life-or-death trek from King Haakon Bay across the uncharted mountainous interior of the island to Stromness Bay. Their unexpected arrival at the whaling station caused surprise and bafflement. Thoralf Sørlle, the Norwegian manager, had met Shackleton before but did not recognise him in his bedraggled state, as one of the whalers present later recounted: 'Sørlle asked: "Who the hell are you?" and [the] terrible bearded man in the centre of the three say very quietly: "My name is Shackleton." Me—I turn away and weep. I think manager weep too.'

SMALL EARTHQUAKES

While recuperating, Shackleton plotted the rescue of his twenty-two comrades, who remained stranded on fog-bound, snow-covered Elephant Island under the command of the Boss's deputy, Frank Wild. Desperate attempts by the whalers and a Uruguayan vessel were thwarted by the ice, but Shackleton refused to give up, travelling to Punta Arenas to seek help from the city's British community and the Chilean authorities. Finally, a Scottish-built Chilean naval tug, the *Yelcho*, under the command of Captain Luis Pardo, found a way through gales and perilous waves, reaching Elephant Island on 30 August 1916, as the stranded men tucked into a meal of boiled seal. When he realised all twenty-two had survived against the odds, Shackleton broke down in tears.

After returning to the UK, he made unsuccessful attempts to persuade the Chilean and Argentine governments to join the war on the side of the Allies. Many of his crew served in the Royal Navy during the conflict, with several ending up badly wounded or losing their lives. As for Pardo, he refused a £25,000 reward from the British government for his efforts, as he had 'simply done his duty'. He later became the Chilean consul to Liverpool.

Shackleton never stopped dreaming of Antarctica. In 1922, at the start of his fourth expedition, he died after suffering a heart attack in Grytviken. Six men from the Shetland Islands employed by the Leith whaling station acted as the pallbearers at his funeral, which took place at the settlement's church, after which the Boss was 'carried over piles of whalebones and many small mountain streams to the little cemetery on the hill' to be buried alongside whalers and sealers, reported the *Times*. A century on, passengers on Antarctic cruises now stop to pay their respects, often raising a toast of Shackleton-brand whiskey. Shackleton's gravestone features a nine-pointed star, an emblem closely associated with his family, and a line from Robert Browning's poem 'The Statue and the Bust': 'I hold that a man should strive to the uttermost for his life's set prize.'

'TWO BALD MEN FIGHTING OVER A COMB'

The nearby museum has a replica of the *James Caird*—the original is now at Dulwich College, Shackleton's old school, a mile and a half from where I grew up in South London. Meanwhile, the wreck of the *Endurance*, lost for more than a century, was finally discovered on the bed of the Weddell Sea in 2022. Some 10,000 feet below the surface, the ship was upright and remarkably intact given its ordeal. Its name was still visible on the stern, while a digital scan revealed the presence of dinner plates, a flare gun and even a boot, which may have belonged to Wild, whose ashes were buried alongside Shackleton in 2011.

* * *

The Falkland Islands and South Georgia remain a political flashpoint between Britain and Argentina. After finally agreeing to relinquish sovereignty over the British Overseas Territory of the Chagos Islands in 2024, the UK government was keen to insist that it would not be pursuing a similar policy in the South Atlantic. Welcoming the Chagos decision, Argentina's foreign minister, Diana Mondino, promised that with 'concrete actions and not empty rhetoric, we will recover full sovereignty over our Malvinas Islands'.

Beyond the pantomime sabre-rattling, there was little discussion of the wider history of the Falklands and South Georgia. Although uninhabited at the time of European contact, the islands have long been entwined with colonisation, geopolitical ambitions and resource extraction in southern South America. As well as providing the impetus for Patagonia's sheep-ranching revolution, the Falklands were also the base for a group of Anglican missionaries who would have an equally significant impact on Tierra del Fuego.

6

END OF THE WORLD

TIERRA DEL FUEGO

The trail to the summit of Cerro Bandera—'Flag Hill'—rose steeply through a forest of southern beeches studded with clumps of orange fungi the size and shape of golf balls. Their branches were miniature ecosystems, blanketed with tiny bryophytes—a group of plants that includes mosses, liverworts and hornworts—and draped with a wispy lichen known as old man's beard, which rippled as I hiked past. Sinuous roots and freshly fallen trunks crisscrossed the path, while an ominous creaking rang out as the canopy shook violently in the wind. The pneumatic tapping of a Magellanic woodpecker periodically sounded above the din, though its crimson head remained hidden from view. As I climbed, the forest began to thin out—the trees increasingly stunted and bowed over, as if paying their respects—before disappearing completely at the summit, replaced by a barren, stony expanse dusted with snow, racked by gales and utterly deserted.

Puffing from the forty-minute hike, I sheltered behind a half-collapsed cairn and watched a faded Chilean flag thrash at its pole like a fish on a hook. Nearby, a stream of snowmelt trickled over the terrain, which was chequered with cushion plants—slow-growing, snooker-baize-green hummocks—one of the few species hardy enough to survive in the sub-polar tundra. Occasionally, the wind dropped for a few moments, leaving behind a silence so perfect it felt all-consuming.

After catching my breath and slipping on an extra base layer and woollen hat to stave off the biting cold, I trudged to an exposed ridge offering 360-degree views. When I was stuck at home in South London during the long, claustrophobic COVID-19 lockdowns, this was the place I daydreamed of the most, a landscape symbolic of space and freedom. To the south, beyond a glacial lake, rose the Dientes de Navarino, a range of fang-like mountains streaked with snow, the last gasp of the Andes. Aside from a few Chilean naval officers on Cape Horn and a handful of scientists at Antarctic research stations, there was no one between me and the South Pole.

To the north lay the navy-blue Beagle Channel and, on its near shoreline, the glinting rooftops of Puerto Williams, the southernmost city on earth and a place that provides an etymological hint at the deep British connections with this far-flung region.

* * *

Beneath Patagonia, across the Strait of Magellan, South America crumbles into a labyrinth of sparsely populated islands, rocky outcrops and serpentine channels before dissolving completely into the Southern Ocean. Divided unevenly between Chile and Argentina, Tierra del Fuego is one of the world's last surviving wildernesses, a realm of shimmering glaciers, jagged massifs, evergreen forests and meandering coastlines.

According to the oral traditions of the Selk'nam (also known as the Ona), one of the Indigenous peoples who inhabited the archipelago for 10,000 years before the arrival of Europeans, the topography was created by the slingshot of a young man named

END OF THE WORLD

Táyin. After decapitating a 'powerful woman' who had covered the lagoons, lakes and wells with fur to prevent people drinking from them, Táyin 'grabbed stones, and with his sling hurled them in all directions. Where the stones landed there appeared large cracks in the ground which filled up with water.' According to the legend, which was recorded by Austrian priest and anthropologist Martín Gusinde in the early twentieth century, this formed the waterways now known as the Strait of Magellan and, to the south, the Beagle Channel, both of which connect the Atlantic with the Pacific.

Tierra del Fuego's poetic modern name was inspired by the shoreline bonfires of the Selk'nam, which were spotted by Portuguese explorer Ferdinand Magellan in 1520 as he attempted to complete the first circumnavigation of the globe. A form of long-distance communication, the blazes were probably lit to signal the arrival of a vessel far larger than the canoes typically found in the region and filled with unkempt strangers babbling away in an unintelligible tongue. Magellan originally called the archipelago Tierra de Humo—'Land of Smoke'—a name later refined by his royal patron, Charles V, Holy Roman emperor, who reputedly reasoned that where there's smoke, there's fire, hence Tierra del Fuego—'Land of Fire'.

* * *

A motley cast of European navigators, explorers and sailors followed in Magellan's wake, including the privateer-pirate—and slave trader—Francis Drake, whose exploits along South America's coastline are among the UK's earliest, and most notorious, links with the continent. Frustratingly, we only have European accounts—sometimes judiciously edited many years after the fact—of these voyages, while the voices of Indigenous peoples such as the Selk'nam are largely absent. This is a common problem, as historian Caroline Dodds Pennock noted in *On Savage Shores*:

SMALL EARTHQUAKES

Indigenous peoples have 'tended to be seen as objects: of curiosity, of desire, of greed, of prejudice, of ambition. They have become ciphers for European ideas and aspirations, rather than actors at the centre of their own story.'

This is evident in the account of Drake's inadvertent circumnavigation of the globe, during which he became the first Briton to sail along the Strait of Magellan in 1578. There is a revealing description of the sixteen-day journey in *The World Encompassed by Sir Francis Drake*, the publication of which was delayed until 1628, such was the sensitive nature of its contents. On entering the strait from the Atlantic, the *Golden Hind* (originally the *Pelican*) and companion ship the *Marigold* found 'no Continent ... but broken islands and large passages amongst them'. The area was filled with 'strange birds'—penguins—which aroused great curiosity among the crew. In one of the first English colonial claims in the Americas, Drake took 'possession' of an island and dubbed it 'Elizabeth Land'. Now part of Chile and known as Isla Isabel, it was where Henry Reynard launched Patagonia's sheep-ranching boom.

Drake then landed on two neighbouring islands, where 'such was the infinite resort of these birds ... that in the space of 1 day we killed no lesse than 3,000'. Fortunately, he left before causing even more damage: now called Marta and Magdalena, the islands are today a wildlife reserve and an important Magellanic penguin nesting site.

Drake also traded with Indigenous peoples. Near the western edge of the strait, he met a canoe of 'most comely proportion and excellent workmanship', probably from a Kawésqar (also known as Alacaluf or Halakwulup) or Yagán (Yaghan or Yámana) community, which were part of predominantly nomadic, seafaring societies in southern Patagonia and southern Tierra del Fuego, respectively:

> The people are of a mean stature, but well set and compact ... they have great pleasure in painting their faces ... Within the said Iland

they had a house of meane building, of certaine poles, and couered with skinnes of beasts, having therein fire, water, and such meate, as commonly they can come by, as seales, mussells, and such like ... Their working tooles ... are knives made of most huge and monstrous mussell shells.

After reaching the Pacific, Drake attempted to head north with the aim of plundering Spanish treasure. But he was caught in a mighty storm: the *Marigold* sank, and the *Golden Hind* was pushed south to the 'uttermost cape ... without which there is no maine nor Iland to be seene to the Southwards, but that the Atlanticke Ocean and the South Sea [Pacific], meete'.

Drake is unlikely to have made it as far south as Cape Horn—the continent's southernmost headland—as is often claimed, but he inadvertently discovered something the Yagán had long known: Tierra del Fuego was an archipelago, not the northern tip of another continent, as commonly thought in Europe at the time, and thus it was possible to sail around the bottom of it through the notoriously rough waters of what became known as the Drake Passage.

* * *

Drake's exploits spurred increased European interest in Tierra del Fuego in the seventeenth and eighteenth centuries, including a 1624 Dutch-led expedition by Jacques L'Hermite—whose unfounded claims of cannibalism against the Yagán would prove stubbornly persistent—and James Cook's 1768–71 *Endeavour* voyage, which rounded Cape Horn. There were also less-documented but equally impactful visits by whalers, sealers and sea lion hunters from Britain, Scandinavia, North America and beyond. They came into direct conflict with the Yagán, who depended on marine mammals for food and fuel and had no resistance to the diseases brought over by the Europeans.

From a British perspective, the most consequential voyage took place in the early nineteenth century. In 1826, the Royal

SMALL EARTHQUAKES

Navy dispatched Australian-born Captain Phillip Parker King on HMS *Adventure* on a hydrographic expedition. He was accompanied by Lieutenant Pringle Stokes, who commanded the smaller HMS *Beagle* on its maiden voyage. Their aim was to survey the coast of southern South America, a long loop stretching from the Uruguayan capital Montevideo to the Chilean archipelago of Chiloé, though the authorities in Buenos Aires and Santiago rightly suspected that the expedition was linked to Britain's expanding imperial and trading ambitions.

Born in Surrey, Stokes had served in the navy for more than two decades, having joined at the age of twelve, but the expedition took a heavy toll on him. As it progressed, his mental health deteriorated as despair over surveying errors combined with tempestuous winter weather, the deaths of crewmen and what he saw as the harsh landscapes of southern Patagonia and Tierra del Fuego. In his journal, he wrote of 'lofty, bleak and barren heights that surround the inhospitable shores', scenes of 'dreariness and utter desolation' and, quoting Scottish poet James Thomson's *The Seasons*, a climate in which 'the soul of the man dies'.

On 1 August 1828, while navigating the Strait of Magellan, Stokes locked himself in his cabin and attempted to commit suicide by shooting himself in the head with a pistol. The bullet lodged itself in his skull, but, despite heavy blood loss, he remained conscious for eleven agonising days before gangrene eventually reached his brain. Stokes was buried on the north shore of the Strait of Magellan, near the abandoned Spanish settlement of Port Famine. His grave lies in the small 'English Cemetery', marked with a slender white cross and an inscription that notes he died 'from the effects of the anxieties and hardships incurred while surveying the western shores of Tierra del Fuego'.

Stokes' death shifted the course of history. The captaincy of the *Beagle* was handed to a twenty-three-year-old officer from an aristocratic family from Suffolk: Robert FitzRoy. Previously a

END OF THE WORLD

Royal Navy flag lieutenant in South America, FitzRoy completed the expedition's cartographic mission over the next two years, a period documented in *Narrative of the Surveying Voyages of His Majesty's Ships Adventure and Beagle*.

On 19 December 1829, FitzRoy anchored in a Strait of Magellan bay that was home to a Kawésqar community. From their 'unwillingness to part with furs or skins, unless for serviceable articles, such as knives ... [they] appeared to have had dealings with Europeans: beads and trinkets they did not value. They had, in the canoe, many eggs, and dead birds.' Two days later, FitzRoy dispatched a small team in a whaleboat, an open-topped, narrow-hulled vessel. But they got into difficulties in a storm, and some 'Fuegians took advantage of [their] weak state to beat the coxswain and take away some of his clothes.'

In response, FitzRoy approached the Kawésqar settlement, only to be driven back by a twenty-strong group wielding 'clubs, spears, swords'. Their hostility was understandable, as even FitzRoy—who was far from sympathetic towards the plight of the Indigenous peoples of South America—appeared to note: 'By the visits of [sealing] vessels, I suppose, they have been taught to hide their furs and other skins, and have learned the effects of fire-arms.'

The next encounter was even more eventful. On 5 February 1830, FitzRoy learned that one of his whaleboats had been stolen while moored overnight in an area known as Cape Desolation, forcing its three-man crew to flee in a cobbled-together canoe resembling a 'large basket'. A search party found the whaleboat's mast on a nearby island, which only sharpened FitzRoy's determination to 'chase the thieves'. He scoured the area, questioning and searching any Indigenous person he came across—communicating through gesture, as neither spoke the other's language—and forcing some to act as guides. Several other items from the whaleboat were discovered—a torn sail, an oar fashioned into a seal club, an axe and a tool bag.

SMALL EARTHQUAKES

Finally, on 12 February, the suspected thieves were spotted in a cove. After arming themselves with a 'pistol or gun, a cutlass, and a piece of rope to secure a prisoner', a party from the *Beagle* launched an attack. In the ensuing chaos, a crewman named Elsmore fell over while jumping across a stream and was attacked and almost killed. One of the culprits was subsequently shot dead, but most of the Kawésqar escaped, save for a small group—two men, three women and six children—who were taken prisoner.

Although FitzRoy expressed regret for the killings, he continued to search furiously for the whaleboat, using some of the 'prisoners as guides, and leaving the rest on board [the *Beagle*] to ensure the former remaining, and not deceiving us'. It proved a futile and frustrating experience, which the captain blamed on the language barrier:

> I became convinced that so long as we were ignorant of the Fuegian language, and the natives were equally ignorant of ours, we should never know much about them, or the interior of their country; nor would there be the slightest chance of their being raised one step above the low place which they then held in our estimation.

His solution to the problem was to kidnap four Indigenous youngsters.

* * *

On 23 February, FitzRoy discovered the prisoners had escaped by clambering overboard and swimming to shore. Yet presumably because of the treacherous conditions in the strait, three young children had been left on the *Beagle*. He returned two of them to Kawésqar communities but decided to keep the third, a 'happy and healthy' girl of around eight named Yokcushlu, 'as a hostage for the stolen boat, and [to] try to teach her English'. She was renamed 'Fuegia Basket', after the rickety vessel built by the whaleboat's crew.

END OF THE WORLD

On 3 March, a canoe approached the *Beagle*, and FitzRoy spotted an opportunity to kidnap a young man called El'leparu, reasoning that he could also be trained to work as an interpreter. El'leparu was dubbed 'York Minster' after a nearby landmark, a rocky cliff that had been named by James Cook. 'Fuegia, cleaned and dressed, was much improved in appearance: she was already a pet on the lower deck, and appeared to be quite contented. York Minster was sullen at first, yet his appetite did not fail ... as soon as he was well cleaned and clothed, and allowed to go about where he liked in the vessel, he became much more cheerful.'

Six days later, the crew seized a man in his early twenties, whose original name was not recorded. Renamed 'Boat Memory', he was apparently 'frightened, but not low-spirited'. While praising the Indigenous people for their strength, courage and hardiness, FitzRoy declared them 'savages', adding: 'Until a mutual understanding can be established, moral fear is the only means by which they can be kept peaceable.'

The *Beagle* continued its journey and, on 14 April, stumbled upon another waterway that cut through Tierra del Fuego, connecting the Atlantic and the Pacific. Known to the Yagán as Onašaga, it was later named the Beagle Channel. The following month, FitzRoy came across a Yagán group who approached in three canoes, 'anxious for barter':

> We gave them a few beads and buttons, for some fish; and, without any previous intention, I told one of the boys in a canoe to come into our boat, and gave the man who was with him a large shining mother-of-pearl button. The boy got into my boat directly, and sat down. Seeing him and his friends seem quite contented, I pulled onwards, and, a light breeze springing up, made sail. Thinking that this accidental occurrence might prove useful to the natives, as well as to ourselves, I determined to take advantage of it.

His name was Orundellico, but the crew called him 'Jemmy Button'.

SMALL EARTHQUAKES

FitzRoy claimed that he only decided to take the four to the UK after they proved to be 'happy and in good health' and because there would be 'various advantages which might result to them and their countrymen, as well as to us, by taking them to England, educating them there as far as might be practicable, and then bringing them back to Tierra del Fuego', where he hoped they would share their new-found knowledge, skills and Christianity with their communities. Yet the fact they were named after objects and landmarks indicates FitzRoy's underlying attitude: the Indigenous peoples of Tierra del Fuego were potentially useful but not quite human.

* * *

Yokcushlu, Orundellico, El'leparu and 'Boat Memory' arrived in Plymouth in October 1830, but examining their time in Britain feels like looking at a painting through frosted glass. We rarely hear their voices in the historical sources and can only guess at the sense of dislocation they must have felt. Although FitzRoy was keen to present it as a 'civilising' mission, contemporary newspaper reports quoted in Nick Hazelwood's *Savage: The Life and Times of Jemmy Button* described the four as being 'kidnapped', though the use of the phrases 'lowest of mankind' and 'without a doubt, cannibals' also betrays the prevailing prejudices of the time.

Having received their first smallpox vaccination in Montevideo, the four were given a second dose in Plymouth, but 'Boat Memory' still contracted the disease and died on 11 November. 'It may readily be supposed that this was a severe blow to me ... however unintentionally, [I] could not but feel how much I was implicated in shortening his existence,' wrote FitzRoy.

Fortunately, Yokcushlu, Orundellico and El'leparu survived and were transferred by stagecoach to Walthamstow, then a village northeast of London. For the best part of a year, they lived

END OF THE WORLD

with a Mr and Mrs Jenkins, who ran St Mary's, a church school founded by an evangelical preacher. Having failed to find a wealthy benefactor, FitzRoy—somewhat reluctantly—paid for their education himself. He described them as being 'very healthy' and 'no particular trouble' during their time in Walthamstow. Although El'leparu, who was aged around twenty-eight, understandably found it hardest to adapt to his dramatically changed circumstances, 'the two younger ones became great favourites wherever they were known'. Viewed as exotic curiosities, the trio were taken to see friends 'who were anxious to question them', and a phrenologist, who examined them.

In the summer of 1831, they were also invited to a private audience with King William IV and Queen Adelaide. 'His Majesty asked a great deal about their country, as well as themselves,' wrote FitzRoy. Some reports suggest the queen placed her bonnet on Yokcushlu's head and gave her a ring and money to buy a change of clothes.

* * *

Unless you fly, travelling to Tierra del Fuego today still takes time, patience and a degree of luck. My convoluted journey started on a cold, bright morning in Punta Arenas, on the blustery northwest shore of the Strait of Magellan. The half-empty bus bore northeast out of the city, its overactive heater gradually lulling me to sleep.

At Punta Delgada, my fellow passengers and I boarded a ferry, joining an Argentine motorcycle club—leather-clad men in their fifties and sixties riding pristine Triumphs—a squad of teenage Chilean boxers in matching green tracksuits and Nike trainers, and heavily laden lorries that swayed alarmingly as we crossed the aquamarine channel. Twenty minutes later, we reached Isla Grande, the largest island in Tierra del Fuego. The Chilean–Argentine border runs in a straight line from the north of the island to the south, with Chile to the west and Argentina to the east, before making a sharp right turn in the middle of the Beagle Channel. It then meanders west towards the Southern Ocean, with everything to the north in Argentina and everything in the south—notably Isla Navarino and Cape Horn—in Chile.

The bus headed south into a landscape that resembled the gently undulating steppe that spans much of Patagonia: solitary *estancias* with red-roofed homesteads, flocks of sheep, shallow grey lakes, banks of white clouds that felt close enough to touch and families of guanacos. Occasionally, a 4X4 rumbled past, triggering a mini dust tornado. At the village of Cerro Sombrero—'Hat Hill'—the bus driver halted outside a grocery store and unloaded boxes of powdered soup and Nestlé chocolate while being studied intently by a suspicious dachshund. Farther on, beyond a guanaco carcass picked clean by turkey vultures, we pulled on to a bumpy, unpaved stretch that led to the San Sebastián border post, making slow, uncomfortable progress.

After a perfunctory passport check, we entered Argentina and re-joined a paved road, alongside which ran a rust-red pipeline and the occasional nodding donkey pump. Bearing south along Ruta Nacional 3, the final leg of the Pan-American Highway, we passed *estancias* and a Salesian mission before arriving in Río Grande, where we bolted down a late lunch of crustless *sándwiches de miga* and dulce de leche pastries. The second-biggest city in Tierra del Fuego was filled with boxy homes, a rugby and hockey club, and a John Deere tractor warehouse. A monument featuring a giant fish declared the city to be the 'International Capital of the Trout', and a large sign stated 'Las Malvinas are Argentine.'

South of the river that gave Río Grande its name, the weather and landscape shifted: rainclouds gathered, and the Andes reappeared in the distance, with sparse forests by the roadside and denser ones farther back replacing the treeless expanse of northern Isla Grande. After a brief stop in Tolhuin, a rustic town with wood-panelled shops selling wheels of cheese and locally brewed beer, we traced the shoreline of placid Lago Fagnano, which stretches west into Chile and is known to the Selk'nam as Kami.

From there, we zigzagged over a mountain pass lightly dusted with snow before arriving in the city of Ushuaia in the early evening. Gathering up my backpack, I trudged along the waterfront in search of a taxi, passing a sign that declared I had reached the 'Fin del Mundo'—the 'End of the World.'

* * *

Kitted out with clothes, tools, crockery and books donated by the local community in Walthamstow, Yokcushlu, Orundellico and El'leparu returned to Tierra del Fuego on the second voyage of the *Beagle*, which departed from Plymouth in December 1831. They were accompanied by a young missionary, Richard Matthews, who provided religious instruction during the voyage and hoped to launch a Christian outpost in the region.

Anxious to avoid the fate of his predecessor, Captain Stokes, FitzRoy also sought out an educated gentleman whose company could help him stave off loneliness and despair on the five-year expedition, which aimed to complete the surveying work of the *Beagle*'s maiden voyage and gather chronometrical measurements. As a result, a twenty-two-year-old Charles Darwin, freshly graduated from Cambridge University with aspirations of becoming a parson, was hired as the ship's naturalist, with earth-shaking consequences for humanity. (FitzRoy, who probably suffered from depression, ultimately died by suicide in South London in 1865.)

Darwin's experiences on the *Beagle* are well documented—not least by himself in *The Voyage of the Beagle*, published in 1839—but his accounts of Tierra del Fuego are often overlooked. He described his arrival in December 1832 in terms that have become familiar to the point of cliché in outsider accounts ever since: the landscape is 'rugged' and 'inhospitable', a 'savage land' with 'gloomy' forests and a 'wretched' climate in which 'gale succeeds gale with rain, hail and sleet' and 'Death, instead of Life, seemed the predominant spirit.' At times, the naturalist resembles the kind of travel writer who grumpily delights in the discomfort and disappointments he—and it generally is a 'he'—encounters in some far-off land.

Darwin's descriptions of the first Indigenous people he meets are similarly disparaging: 'I could not have believed how wide was the difference between savage and civilised man: it is greater than between a wild and domesticated animal, inasmuch as in man there is a greater power of improvement.' Their black-painted faces reminded him of 'devils', their countenances were 'distrustful, surprised, and startled', and their language was 'hoarse, guttural, and clicking sounds'. Nevertheless, unlike many of his peers, Darwin did not view them as a separate species, and these encounters had a lasting impact on him, helping to shape the arguments he made in 1871's *The Descent of Man, and Selection in Relation to Sex*.

He was more positive about Yokcushlu, Orundellico and El'leparu. Yokcushlu was 'nice, modest, reserved', a quick learner who picked up some Spanish and Portuguese on board. El'leparu was 'reserved, taciturn, morose' but also 'violently passionate' with a 'good intellect', affectionate towards his friends and 'determined to marry' Yokcushlu in the future. But Darwin was most effusive about Orundellico, a 'universal favourite' on board. His account provides a rare—if fleeting—glimpse of Orundellico's personality:

> He was merry and often laughed, and was remarkably sympathetic with anyone in pain: when the water was rough, I was often a little seasick, and he used to come and say in a plaintive voice, 'Poor, poor fellow!' but the notion, after his aquatic life, of a man being seasick was too ludicrous, and he was generally obliged to turn on one side

to hide a smile or laugh ... He was of a patriotic disposition; and he liked to praise his own tribe and country.

Darwin also noted that Orundellico 'stoutly declared there was no devil in his land', which could be read as a subtle rejection of the Christian notion of good and evil, a simple binary that did not fit into the Yagán belief system.

* * *

As the *Beagle* travelled through Tierra del Fuego, Darwin explored the landscapes, collected specimens and made detailed notes on the climate, topography and flora and fauna. After rounding Cape Horn, the ship anchored nearby at a 'snug little harbour' on Christmas Eve, where he mused that the archipelago could be considered 'the extremity of the submerged chain of mountains'.

There were more negative portrayals of the Indigenous peoples—probably members of Yagán communities—he encountered: 'Viewing such men, one can hardly make oneself believe that they are fellow-creatures, and inhabitants of the same world.' Damagingly, he also repeated the unfounded slur that the Yagán practised cannibalism, of which tall tales had long swirled among European sailors. 'The different tribes when at war are cannibals ... [and] when pressed in winter by hunger, they kill and devour their old women,' he wrote, referring both to a story he had heard from a British sealer and the responses of Orundellico, Yokcushlu and El'leparu when asked about the practice.

As author Lucas Bridges, who spent most of his life living and working with the Yagán and Selk'nam, noted in the 1940s, there was, in fact, no evidence of cannibalism. Orundellico, Yokcushlu and El'leparu probably gave the responses they felt were 'expected or desired', with positive responses always easier to give than negative ones. Moreover, their English-language skills were relatively limited, and Orundellico and Yokcushlu were still just children.

SMALL EARTHQUAKES

During periods of famine, the Yagán sometimes resorted to eating their leather moccasins, yet eating vultures remained taboo, even in extremis, as the birds might have fed on a human corpse, wrote Bridges. As well as incorrectly maligning the Yagán as cannibals, Darwin also missed the richness and complexity of their language, social customs and beliefs, not to mention the hardiness, resilience and ingenuity required to live in this 'wretched' environment.

Although the naturalist despaired at the 'broken mass of wild rocks, lofty hills and useless forests', there were also flickers of the ideas that would transform our understanding of humanity:

> What could have tempted, or what change compelled a tribe of men to leave the fine regions of the north, to travel down the Cordillera or backbone of America, to invent and build canoes, which are not used by the tribes of Chile, Peru, and Brazil, and then enter one of the most inhospitable countries within the limits of the globe? Although such reflections must at first seize on the mind, yet we may feel sure that they are partly erroneous. There is no reason to believe that the Fuegians decrease in number; therefore we must suppose that they enjoy a sufficient share of happiness, of whatever kind it may be, to make life worth having. Nature by making habit omnipotent, and its effects hereditary, has fitted the Fuegian to the climate and the productions of this miserable country.

In early 1833, the *Beagle* sailed through stormy weather to drop off the three abductees, starting with Orundellico. On 15 January, three whaleboats and a three-masted vessel known as a yawl were despatched along the Beagle Channel, which Darwin compared to Loch Ness. After passing the future sites of Puerto Williams and Ushuaia, they made camp on the 22nd on Isla Navarino, near the entrance to Ponsonby Sound. The next day, they were greeted by members of Orundellico's tribe, who informed him his father had died.

END OF THE WORLD

Guided by Orundellico, the *Beagle* party sailed round to Bahía Wulaia, a 'pretty cove ... surrounded by islets ... and bordered by some acres of good sloping land', where Orundellico found more members of his community. FitzRoy originally planned to take Yokcushlu and El'leparu farther west, but they asked to stay with Orundellico. Over the next five days, the crew constructed 'three large wigwams', dug gardens and sowed crops for the trio. When Orundellico's mother and brothers arrived, Darwin complained the meeting was 'less interesting than between a horse, turned out into a field, when he joins an old companion' due to a supposed lack of affection, despite going on to write: '[His] mother had been inconsolable for the loss of Jemmy, and had searched everywhere for him, thinking he might have been left after having been taken in the boat.'

As they settled into Bahía Wulaia, a group of 120 Yagán gradually arrived to observe the proceedings, before every woman and child suddenly disappeared on the 27th, spooked, perhaps, by the crew cleaning and firing their muskets. Fearing conflict, FitzRoy decided to spend the night on the boats, which were moored nearby, though Matthews insisted on staying with Orundellico, Yokcushlu and El'leparu. Ultimately, the night passed without incident, so FitzRoy embarked on a surveying trip into the western Beagle Channel, including the shores of what is now Parque Nacional Alberto de Agostini. Spouting whales appeared, and the ever-changeable weather became 'over-poweringly hot', brightening Darwin's mood and appreciation of the landscape of 'magnificent glaciers extend[ing] from the mountain-side to the water's edge. It is scarcely possible to imagine anything more beautiful than the beryl-blue of these glaciers.'

But on returning to Bahía Wulaia on 6 February, they discovered Matthews, Yokcushlu, El'leparu and Orundellico had been robbed by a group of men armed with 'stones and stakes', who also threatened to strip the missionary and 'pluck all of the hairs off of his face and body'. Unsurprisingly, Matthews returned with FitzRoy and Darwin to the *Beagle*, which sailed on to the Argentine Patagonian coast and the Falkland Islands. Darwin recorded:

> It was quite melancholy leaving the three Fuegians with their savage countrymen, but it was a great comfort that they had no personal fears. York, being a powerful resolute man, was pretty sure to get on well, together with his wife Fuegia. Poor Jemmy looked rather disconsolate, and would then, I have little doubt, have been glad to have returned with us. His own brother had stolen many things from him; and as he remarked, 'what fashion call that': he abused his countrymen, 'all bad men, no *sabe* (know) nothing!' and, though I never heard him swear before, 'damned fools' ... I fear it is more than doubtful, whether their visit [to England] will have been of any use to them.

The *Beagle* returned to Bahía Wulaia on 5 March 1834 amid reports of fighting. Orundellico soon appeared, naked except for a blanket around his waist and paint streaks on his face, but still very much his old self. Over dinner, he explained that he was now married and reconciled with his family and did not want to return to Britain, before distributing presents of otter skins, arrows and spearheads. He had relearned some of the Yagán language, built a canoe and started teaching English to his compatriots. But there had been problems, too. El'leparu had persuaded Orundellico and his mother to move with him and Yokcushlu to his homeland, only to abandon them en route and steal their possessions.

Orundellico lit a signal fire as the *Beagle* set sail. Darwin expressed hopes that some future shipwrecked sailor might be aided by the youngster's descendants, before claiming that the 'perfect equality' within Yagán society had stunted their 'civilization' and declaring: 'I believe, in this extreme part of South America, man exists in a lower state of improvement than in any other part of the world.' (Interestingly, as Pennock notes in *On Savage Shores*, Indigenous peoples from the Americas who travelled to Europe during this period were often shocked by the inequality and poverty they saw in countries such as Britain and France.)

The *Beagle* returned to the Strait of Magellan and eventually anchored at Port Famine, which lived up to its gloomy name. 'I never saw a more cheerless prospect,' wrote Darwin, as he climbed nearby Mount Tarn. Yet when it came to the local kelp, his musings verged on the joyful:

> A great volume might be written, describing the inhabitants of these beds of seaweed ... [If] in any other country a forest was destroyed, I do not believe nearly so many species of animals would perish as would here, from the destruction of the kelp. Amidst the leaves of this plant numerous species of fish live, which nowhere else could find food or shelter; with their destruction the many cormorants and other fishing birds, the otters, seals, and porpoises, would soon perish also; and lastly the Fuegian savage.

The *Beagle* carried the naturalist north along Chile's Patagonian coast towards the Galápagos. Darwin never returned to Tierra del Fuego, but the region left a lasting impression on him: 'The inanimate works of nature—rock, ice, snow, wind, and water—all warring with each other, yet combined against man—here reigned in absolute sovereignty.'

* * *

Although it trades heavily on its isolated location—the 'end of the world' slogan adorns hotels, guesthouses, restaurants, shops, a newspaper, the railway and even a tango club—Ushuaia is a modern and comfortable place. Home to around 80,000 people, out of a total population of 190,000 in Argentine Tierra del Fuego, Ushuaia is a major tourist draw thanks to its role as the key port for cruises to Antarctica. If you discount Puerto Williams—which most locals on this side of Tierra del Fuego do—it is the closest city to the 'white continent', which lies just 620 miles to the south. Buenos Aires, by contrast, is more than 1,850 miles to the north.

In the summer, Ushuaia is thronged with well-heeled cruise passengers, plus a scattering of backpackers. The centre has an ersatz feel, with a jumble of souvenir shops, duty-free outlets, travel agencies and overpriced restaurants with fish tanks of writhing king crabs. During my visit, a pair of Antarctic cruise ships were moored alongside a hulking Russian icebreaker in the busy port.

Indigenous peoples inhabited this area for thousands of years before the arrival of Europeans, and, though often disregarded today, there are plenty of reminders if you care to look. Just west of Ushuaia, Parque Nacional Tierra del Fuego encompasses a swathe of bays, massifs, peat bogs and sub-polar forests, criss-crossed by trails. Most visitors come to hike or birdwatch: there is a surprising array of avian life, including condors, green-backed firecrown hummingbirds and austral parakeets, the southernmost parrot species. The park's ancient sites are easier to spot, yet generally overlooked. Along the coast, I saw scores of middens—piles of mollusc shells discarded by Yagán families hundreds or even thousands of years earlier—and bowl-shaped depressions that once provided shelter from the harsh weather. Now overgrown with grass, they looked like natural features of the landscape.

The Yagán are commonly depicted as nomadic, canoe-based seafarers, as opposed to the predominantly land-based, guanaco-hunting Selk'nam. But while that was certainly the case for long periods, some of the oldest archaeological sites—dating back 7,000–8,000 years—paint a more nuanced, dynamic picture. Alongside seal, sea lion and penguin bones, harpoons and limpet shells, archaeologists have unearthed guanaco skeletons, basalt tools, finely worked jewellery and shards of obsidian that suggest complex trading networks with societies hundreds of miles away in Patagonia.

In the nineteenth century, European visitors had little appreciation of Yagán history. Instead, their views—in this age of empire—were shaped by lurid tales of 'savagery'. That the Yagán were generally scantily clothed at the time of European contact—beyond otter- or seal-skin aprons and shawls—only fed into their exoticisation. For British Anglican missionaries, they also represented an opportunity.

* * *

In 1844 (or possibly 1845; the exact year is unknown), a smartly dressed boy aged two or three was found alone on a bridge in Bristol. He wore clothes embroidered with the letter 'T' and had a religious medal but spoke no English. Bristol was rife with diseases such as cholera, and it was assumed the boy's parents had died. After being taken to an orphanage, he was adopted by Reverend George Pakenham Despard, who named him Thomas Bridges, inspired by his original attire and place of discovery. It was an inauspicious start in life for a man who would have a decisive role in the history of Tierra del Fuego.

Around the same time, the South American Missionary Society was founded in Brighton by Captain Allen Gardiner, a former Royal Navy officer born, appropriately, in a parsonage. Originally known as the Patagonian Missionary Society, the Anglican organisation made several unsuccessful attempts to establish bases in Bolivia, Patagonia and Tierra del Fuego, which still lay beyond the reach of Spanish colonial—and thus papal—power. On 5 December 1850, Gardiner landed on Picton Island, near Isla Navarino, with a small band of missionaries and six months' supplies but quickly realised they were hopelessly out of their depth.

SMALL EARTHQUAKES

The local Yagán communities were understandably unwelcoming, attempts to contact Orundellico floundered, and illness, harsh weather and fishing and hunting struggles took their toll. More seriously, the resupply ship failed to materialise as planned after six months. In his final journal entry on 5 September 1851, Gardiner wrote: 'Great and marvellous are the loving-kindnesses of my Gracious God unto me. He has preserved me hitherto, and for four days, although without bodily food, without any feeling of hunger or thirst.' A South American Missionary Society ship arrived the next month to discover Gardiner and his men had starved to death.

The incident resulted in public criticism of the South American Missionary Society but also renewed support for its efforts. Disheartened but not dissuaded, members developed a revised plan, and, in 1854, a schooner named the *Allen Gardiner* set sail from Bristol, captained by polar explorer William Parker Snow. The expedition aimed to found a mission on the Falkland Islands—then a British Crown colony—to which would be brought 'Fuegian lads, to teach them English, and to learn their language.' After establishing a base on Keppel Island, near West Falkland, Snow made contact with Orundellico in Bahía Wulaia.

Now in his forties, Orundellico's English was rusty, but he was friendly and charming to the missionaries while politely declining their request to join them on the Falklands. In *A Two Years' Cruise off Tierra del Fuego, the Falkland Islands, Patagonia and in the River Plate,* Snow wrote that the meeting persuaded him to break with the South American Missionary Society's plans:

> Jemmy Button has tasted the sweets, or, as they might be to him, the bitters of high civilization ... yet, what was his answer, when I ... asked him if he, or any of his boys, would accompany us only a little way? Why *a positive negative*! and, therefore, if I were to hear of ten or of fifty Fuegian boys as being at the mission station in the Falklands, I would never believe, until I knew that the Fuegians had

learned our language, that those poor lads had gone there as only a religious society ought to let them go, namely, with a full and perfect knowledge of what it was for. Evil must not be done that good *may* perchance, and only perchance, come.

Snow was subsequently sacked after a bitter falling out with Despard, by now the general secretary of the society. In 1856, Despard arrived on Keppel Island with his family, before travelling on to Bahía Wulaia to hold prayer meetings. There he managed to persuade Orundellico to travel to the Falklands mission; we only have Despard's account of the meeting, so it is unclear what prompted Orundellico to change his mind.

Orundellico, his wife and three children arrived on Keppel Island in June 1858 and were later joined by another Yagán group, including a young man named Okokko. Over the following months, Despard attempted to learn 'the Fuegian language' and enlist the Yagáns in his proselytising mission. With the 'advantages of youth, enthusiasm and a quick ear', Bridges, who was then around the age of sixteen, quickly became the most accomplished Yagán speaker among the missionaries. Polite and curious, Orundellico swiftly recovered his English, too, but remained reticent whenever the prospect of committing to the missionary cause was mooted. Okokko, though, was more receptive.

In October 1859, Okokko returned to Bahía Wulaia with a missionary named Garland Phillips and a small crew of sailors. A 'very friendly' welcome was anticipated, but the group failed to return to the Falklands three months later as planned. A search party discovered that Phillips and most of the crew had been 'massacred by the natives' and their ship 'ransacked and plundered', to quote Despard. The missionary party had 'friendly intercourse' with the local Yagáns until canoes from neighbouring islands began to arrive. On Sunday, 6 November, Phillips and most of the crew went ashore for 'public worship' and were 'barbarously murdered; not a hand was raised for their defence, but

SMALL EARTHQUAKES

Okokko was observed ... running up and down the beach in great distress'.

* * *

The South American Missionary Society was nothing if not resolute. Undeterred by this latest disaster, it sent another party to Bahía Wulaia in 1863 made up of Reverend Waite Stirling, superintendent of the Falklands mission, Bridges and Okokko. The latter acted as a go-between, preaching to the local Yagáns in their native tongue and helping to persuade eleven of them to travel to Keppel Island.

The following year, the missionaries returned to drop off Okokko and his wife Camilenna in Bahía Wulaia, as they were keen to set 'an example of Christian civilization'. But when they reached the Wollaston Islands, south of Isla Navarino, they found a grief-stricken Yagán community who said a 'fatal malady' had killed 'large numbers of people', including Orundellico and the family of Camilenna. At Bahía Wulaia, there was more 'mournful news': many of the older and younger members of the community there had been 'swept away' by the sickness.

The susceptibility of Indigenous peoples to diseases such as smallpox and measles was well known at this point, yet Stirling did not speculate on what might have caused the deaths. Instead, he carried out a funeral service for the missionary party killed in Bahía Wulaia in 1859 before settling Okokko and Camilenna in a simple home. Their proselytising proved unpopular, to put it mildly. According to an account by an unnamed Yagán man quoted by Stirling, Okokko was accused of telling lies:

> [As] they had never seen nor heard God, they would not believe him ... [Humankind], and all things had ever been as they are, without beginning, and therefore without a Maker. One man pretended to be Jesus Christ. Some were afraid to be in hell, and wished to become

quiet, as a requisite preparation for heaven: some threatened to kill Okokko, but were afraid to do so.

The house was set on fire, and Okokko and Camilenna fled back to Keppel Island.

Nevertheless, the South American Missionary Society remained steadfast. In 1865, Stirling took four Yagán teenagers—Jack, Uroopa, Sisoy and Orundellico's son Threeboys, whose name was the result of a linguistic mix-up—to Britain for a year of English lessons and Bible study. On the return journey, Uroopa died of consumption, while Threeboys later succumbed to a 'mortal disease'.

The society continued to search for a suitable site for a mission in Tierra del Fuego. In 1868, Okokko and Camilenna settled in a small cove on Isla Navarino, and the following year Stirling was dropped off at a sheltered bay on the opposite shore of the Beagle Channel. Easily accessible and with ample space for farmland, the area was known to the Yagán as Ushuaia, which meant 'inner harbour to the westwards'.

Accompanied by Jack and his wife, plus an Indigenous boy named Mugatella, Stirling lived in a prefabricated house of wood and corrugated iron on the shingle beach. They were soon joined by Okokko and Camilenna, whose home, once again, had been burned down. In his journal, Stirling described himself as 'God's sentinel', who aimed to exercise a 'direct and constant' influence to encourage the local Yagán community to adopt British customs and Christian beliefs. After morning prayers, his days were spent gardening, woodcutting, charcoal burning—'a curious, busy kind of time'.

After seven months, Stirling was summoned away to be consecrated bishop of the Falkland Islands. His replacement was Bridges, who subsequently had an eventful visit to England, lecturing on Tierra del Fuego, becoming a deacon and meeting, courting and swiftly marrying Devon schoolteacher Mary Ann

Varder. Two days after the wedding, they sailed for the Falklands, where their first child, also named Mary, was born. After several brief visits to Tierra del Fuego, the family settled permanently in Ushuaia on 1 October 1871.

* * *

Bridges ran the Ushuaia mission for fifteen years, making it the first sustained European colony in Tierra del Fuego and a catalyst for the region's transformation. As his son, Lucas, recorded, Bridges was 'the leading figure, the judge and law-giver' for the community, which consisted of a few missionary families and a larger group of Yagáns who lived in the area, as well as others from farther afield drawn by curiosity, concern or a desire to trade. Those early years were 'anxious times', but the settlement avoided the violence that had toppled previous attempts to establish a missionary presence.

The Bridges' family home functioned as a 'church, meetinghouse and schoolroom' and was surrounded by huddles of Yagán shelters, wooden structures roofed with turf and sunk into hollows. By the end of 1874, the settlement had grown into a village featuring simple homes with kitchen gardens, a road, animal sheds and pens and fields planted with everything from potatoes, turnips and cabbages to rhubarb, strawberries and gooseberries. Donations were sent from Britain: clothing, 'generally somewhat shop-soiled'; gifts for Yagáns who had helped shipwrecked European sailors, including 'hatchets, fish-hooks and some great slabs of Navy cocoa'; and a new boat for the missionaries.

The Bridges family grew, too. In time, five more children—Thomas Despard, Lucas, Will, Bertha and Alice—were born. Lucas described an adventurous childhood spent playing with his Yagán friends, picking up their language and going sailing, barberry picking and duck hunting. Meanwhile, Mary Ann Bridges' sister, Joanna Varder, emigrated from Devon and became known as Yekadahby, Yagán for 'little mother'.

END OF THE WORLD

In the early 1870s, Yokcushlu visited Ushuaia. Now in her fifties, she was healthy and in good spirits, though pining for her grown-up children, who had left home. El'leparu had been killed in a dispute with another community some years earlier, and Yokcushlu had later remarried a young man. She recalled a few English words but had forgotten—or rejected—her religious instruction. Bridges saw her briefly for the final time a decade later, when she was around sixty-two and nearing the end of a remarkable life.

During this period, the nearest colonial settlement was Punta Arenas, then a penal colony, 370 miles away. But the Ushuaia mission provided a foothold in Tierra del Fuego, and outside interest in the region was growing: Italian, French and German expeditions arrived in succession, alongside regular whaling and sealing vessels. As the Chilean and Argentine governments expanded their control over southern Patagonia, their focus was inevitably drawn south.

In September 1884, four Argentine naval ships arrived unexpectedly in Ushuaia under the command of Colonel Augusto Lasserre. Having recently founded a 'sub-prefecture' and lighthouse on Isla de los Estados at the western tip of the region, Lasserre told the Bridges he now wanted 'to establish a sub-prefecture in Ushuaia and so inaugurate Argentine rule in the most southerly part of their domain'. The Yagán, unsurprisingly, were not consulted.

An inauguration ceremony was held and the Argentine flag raised, accompanied by a twenty-two-gun salvo. Promising 'cordial assistance', Bridges 'spoke for the assembled natives, expressing their allegiance to the country that had taken them under her protection, and their desire for law and order'. In return, Lasserre guaranteed the mission's 'continued independence'. Under the English-educated sub-prefect, Alejandro Virasoro y Calvo, a team of twenty men, including several British sailors, set to work constructing the new Argentine settlement.

But a highly predictable tragedy soon struck. In October, shortly after the Argentine ships had departed, measles swept through Ushuaia, and within days the Yagán 'were dying at such a rate that it was impossible to dig graves fast enough'. The epidemic killed 50 per cent of the local Indigenous population; half of the survivors were left so weak that they died over the following two years. By contrast, the missionaries had already had measles, and their children all survived.

The disaster was a harbinger of even more devastating epidemics and heralded the end of the period of religious colonialism. Bridges realised the mission was 'doomed' and worried about the arrival of a 'very different type' of foreign settler: it was vital, he believed, that the Bible reached the Selk'nam, Yagán, Kawésqar and Haush (or Manek'enk, an Indigenous people from western Isla Grande) before the 'gin-bottle or the rifle'. After failing to persuade the South American Missionary Society to obtain from the Argentine government a 'grant of land on which to settle and succour the natives, employing them in farming and other works', he met with President Julio Argentino Roca—fresh from the 'Conquest of the Desert'—and secured a vote in his favour in congress.

After selecting an area 40 miles east of Ushuaia, Bridges shipped over a 'large wooden-frame house' along with a bull, some pigs, four Romney Marsh rams, two sheep dogs and a supply of bricks, limestone and coal. The first ranch in Tierra del Fuego was originally called Downeast but was later renamed Harberton, after Mary Ann Bridges' home village in Devon. Bridges also resigned from the South American Missionary Society, one of whose angry members compared him to a rat leaving a sinking ship.

* * *

Located on a peninsula jutting out into the Beagle Channel, Estancia Harberton spans 50,000 acres of mountains, lakes, forests, valleys and islands. The homestead still looks much as it did in the late nineteenth century: a set of whitewashed, red-roofed buildings on the shore, flanked by green hills riddled with creeks and overlooked by snow-streaked mountains. After establishing the ranch, the Bridges continued to play a significant role in Tierra del Fuego, helping to encourage the development of the region, offering support to settlers and shipwrecked sailors and, most crucially, providing something of a sanctuary for embattled Indigenous peoples struggling to preserve their way of life.

Still owned by the family, Harberton today offers visitors a striking insight into life at the end of the world. On an icy morning, I was shown round by Juan Balda, a young, fast-talking guide. We started in a neatly tended garden filled with rose bushes, pine and apple trees, Scotch broom and London pride, reminiscent of an English country cottage, at least until I noticed the giant whale jawbone arching over the gate.

The early years at Harberton were brutal, Balda explained. Arriving in April 1887, the Bridges spent twelve months building the homestead, supported by Yagán families, around sixty people in total, who came to live and work on the ranch. They endured severe winters—temperatures here can plunge below 20°C—and backbreaking labour was needed to tame the land. Provisions were expensive and often inaccessible, there were outbreaks of typhoid and other diseases, and treacherous sea conditions meant the *estancia* was cut off for long stretches. But the family slowly prospered, thanks, not least, to the support and expertise of the Yagán.

When finances ran low, Bridges gambled on bringing over more sheep from the Falklands to take advantage of the booming global wool market. The family finances were also boosted by the custom brought by the Tierra del Fuego gold rush, which began in the early 1880s. Deposits were initially discovered in the north, with others later unearthed farther south. Lucas Bridges inadvertently played a major role in this process. After showing Captain Félix Paz, the first governor of Argentine Tierra del Fuego, 'a mass of magnetic iron sand' from Sloggett Bay, 30 miles west of Harberton, a team was sent to investigate, and 'the first gold [was] struck on the south coast of Tierra del Fuego'. Hordes of miners flocked from across Argentina, Chile and Europe, supercharging the process of colonisation and making fortunes for a lucky few.

This came at a grave cost for the Indigenous inhabitants.

* * *

Balda and I climbed a low hill to the family cemetery and a small nature reserve, the latter the first of its kind in Tierra del Fuego. A grey fox scurried away at our approach, and a flock of upland geese glided overhead. Among the native trees and plants were two reconstructed wooden shelters once used by Yagán families. Although he came to the region to proselytise, Thomas Bridges also dedicated himself to studying Indigenous languages and cultures, spending thirty years compiling the first Yagán–English dictionary, which ran to 32,000 words. (The dictionary was later entrusted to a 'brisk young American' surgeon and anthropologist, Dr Frederick A. Cook, who visited Harberton in 1898 after his ship ran aground nearby en route to Antarctica. Cook got the book published but attempted to pass the work off as his own. He also falsely claimed to have been the first man to reach the North Pole and summit Denali, the highest mountain in the United States.)

Lucas Bridges followed in his father's footsteps. Having picked up Yagán as a child, he also learned the Selk'nam language—as well as some Haush—and gained a deeper understanding of their cultures, customs and beliefs than any other outsider. Though paternalistic and not always free of prejudice, he had a strong interest in and respect for Indigenous communities, becoming one of the first Europeans to be initiated into Selk'nam society. He recorded his experiences in *Uttermost Part of the Earth*, which is both a story of adventure and a poignant documentation of cultures on the brink of destruction, of which the gold rush was a driving force. In a situation that paralleled the Wild West, armed miners invaded native lands and displaced, poisoned and massacred Indigenous communities while also introducing diseases such as measles and smallpox.

It became known as the Selk'nam genocide, which continued as sheep farms spread across northern and central Tierra del Fuego. Vast tracts of land were fenced off, further encroaching on the territories of the Selk'nam—who were largely nomadic and had a completely different conception of private property—and the guanacos on which they relied. Many were killed by hunters, who worked for the ranchers and were only paid after showing a severed ear, hand or head as proof of their work. One of the most notorious culprits was Alexander MacLennan, nicknamed the 'Red Pig'. Born in Toronto to Scottish parents who later moved back to the Highlands, he became a baker and joined the army before emigrating to Argentina. MacLennan ended up managing the Primera Argentina ranch of José Menéndez, one of the biggest landowners in southern South America.

Renamed 'Mr McInch' in *Uttermost Part of the Earth*, Lucas Bridges described him as 'unscrupulous, hard-drinking' and a 'sworn and relentless foe' of the Selk'nam. He also recounted a massacre of Selk'nam seal hunters:

> Armed with repeating rifles and eager for excitement, Mr McInch and a band of mounted white men encircled the headland, thereby cutting off the retreat of the luckless sealers ... Mr McInch claimed afterwards that they had shot fourteen. He maintained it was a humanitarian act ... these people could never live alongside the white man ... and that the sooner they were exterminated the better.

SMALL EARTHQUAKES

When MacLennan retired, Menéndez presented him with a gold pocket watch inscribed to my 'good helper'.

Indigenous peoples were also corralled into Salesian missions such as the one I saw near the city of Río Grande. For Lucas Bridges, this was like 'condemning the natives—rightful owners of the land—to a kind of penal servitude'. At the Dawson Island mission, he met Hektliohlh, a Selk'nam man who had previously escaped from detention in Ushuaia. 'Looking with yearning towards the distant mountains of his native land, he said: "*Shouwe t-maten ya*" ("Longing is killing me").'

* * *

As well as facing violence, disease and displacement, the Indigenous peoples of Tierra del Fuego were also made objects of entertainment. A haunting black-and-white photo has survived of a Selk'nam family, four adults and five children, including a baby. They are draped in thick furs, and two carry bows. All stare piercingly at the photographer. Next to them is a white man, similarly unsmiling, wearing a bowler hat, jacket and trousers and holding a thin stick—probably an arrow but closely resembling the kind of pointer used in a lecture hall or cattle auction.

We do not know the names of the Selk'nam, nor the identity of the photographer, but the white man is probably Maurice Maître, a Frenchman or Belgian who kidnapped the family in 1888 and took them to Europe to be exhibited in human zoos, according to priest and anthropologist Martín Gusinde, who published the photo in *The Indians of Tierra del Fuego*. Apparently with the permission of the Chilean authorities, Maître originally abducted eleven members of the family, but two died en route.

He displayed the survivors at the 1889 Exposition Universelle in Paris, where they 'were presented, behind reinforced bars, as "cannibals" to the curious public. At certain times they were thrown raw horse meat; they were deliberately kept dirty and in total abandon so that they would really look like "savages".' Afterwards, they were taken to London to be 'exhibited in the same conditions' at the Royal Aquarium and Winter Garden in Westminster. According to the *Pall Mall Gazette*, quoted by Peter Mason and Christian Báez Allende in their paper 'In Heavy Chains like Bengal Tigers', their 'savage customs were for a time the talk of the town'.

Human zoos were popular in Europe and North America in the nineteenth and early twentieth centuries. (They also appeared in South America. Following a request from the governor of Argentine Tierra del Fuego, Lucas Bridges sent three Selk'nam to an 'exhibition' in Buenos Aires, during which a dog belonging to one of the men contracted rabies and triggered a deadly outbreak back in Tierra del Fuego.)

The exhibitions objectified and exoticised Indigenous peoples, attempting to underline the supposed superiority of 'western civilisation' and feed growing public interest in distant cultures. But there were pockets of opposition, including from the South American Missionary Society, which held urgent talks with the management of the Royal Aquarium and Winter Garden and with Maître, who swiftly fled to Belgium with the family, apart from one woman, who fell ill and died in St George's Hospital.

Maître put the family on display in Brussels, too, before being arrested by the Belgian authorities after an intervention by the British government, following South American Missionary Society pressure. Now numbering just seven, the family were eventually sent to Dover, where they stayed in a workhouse pending repatriation. After some diplomatic wrangling over whether they had been captured in Chilean or Argentine territory, the Chilean government agreed to pay for their return.

On 18 February 1890, six of them set sail from Liverpool bound for Punta Arenas, with two subsequently dying en route.

SMALL EARTHQUAKES

According to Mason and Allende, 'the seventh, a young boy, did not want to go with them and preferred to stay in Europe with Lecourt', a Chilean man who worked with Maître. Apparently, strict 'terms were imposed on this arrangement, stipulating that Lecourt would take care of his charge, not make him work more than he was able, not exhibit him anywhere, and not dispose of him without the written permission of the Consul-General in London'.

* * *

Tierra del Fuego's Indigenous inhabitants are often painted as passive actors, but *Uttermost Part of the Earth* highlights their fierce resistance to the colonisation of their lands. Despite being heavily outgunned, Selk'nam communities fought against displacement and detention, killing many of the 'Indian hunters' in an echo of Yagán resistance to missionary settlements in the previous century. Increasing numbers moved to Harberton, which became a safe haven, and many urged the Bridges to set up another ranch in northern Isla Grande, the Selk'nam's traditional homeland, to help them preserve their culture. This led to the founding of Estancia Viamonte in 1902, near Río Grande.

The same year, the Argentine government expanded its fledgling penal colony in Ushuaia in a bid to cement its hold on the region amid competition from Chile. It transferred a small military prison from Isla de los Estados to a larger site in the town, then home to around 200 civilians. Inspired by the work of British philosopher Jeremy Bentham, the prison was designed as a panopticon so that a single guard could, in theory, observe every inmate. The prisoners were forced to construct their own cells as well as new homes and municipal buildings for Ushuaia's growing population. Dubbed the 'Siberia of the South', the prison hosted a grisly array of characters, including teenage serial killer Cayetano Santos Godino—known as the 'Petiso Orejudo'

END OF THE WORLD

('Big-Eared Short Man')—and anarchist Simón Radowitzky, who killed a Buenos Aires police chief who had brutally repressed protesting workers. There were also political prisoners, especially after a military coup in the 1930s. At its height, the prison held more than 600 people, double its capacity.

The inmates built a railway—the world's southernmost line—to transport timber from the surrounding forests, with the first *Tren de los Presos* (Prisoners' Train) steaming into town in 1909. It was brutal labour, but when I visited the prison—now an atmospheric museum—it soon became clear why the work was preferable to staying in the tiny, comfortless, frigid cells. Inside one of the cells was a quote from a former inmate: 'Labouring is the only way of defeating the prison. I'll go on in the wood. At least I can breathe some air and see the sun.'

The prison eventually closed in 1947, and the railway followed suit five years later, but eight decades on, Ushuaia leans into its penal colony history. Souvenir shops sell an array of prison-related paraphernalia—fridge magnets, T-shirts, mugs, pictures, snow globes, chocolates—interspersed with pseudo-Indigenous items. In 1994, a short section of the railway line was restored, and replica steam locomotives now chug along it to and from the national park. It is an unashamedly touristy experience: one of the kitsch stations en route is manned by staff in yellow-and-blue-striped prisoner garb. When I rode the *Tren del Fin del Mundo*, passengers urged the 'inmates' to pretend to chase them while their friends snapped photos. One tourist went a step further, asking to be mock-throttled as his wife captured the moment for posterity.

* * *

At the start of the First World War, Lucas Bridges enlisted in the British Army, with other members of the family taking responsibility for Harberton and Viamonte. He later married, started a family and moved to South Africa before business troubles drew him back to South America. During this period, the Argentine and Chilean governments steadily developed Tierra del Fuego, particularly after oil was struck in the 1940s: Ushuaia and Río Grande grew in size and significance; Puerto Williams was founded on Isla Navarino; and roads and telephone lines were laid. At the same time, the plight of the Selk'nam, Yagán, Kawésqar and Haush deteriorated further, with settler violence and displacement exacerbated by devastating measles epidemics. When Lucas Bridges published his memoir in 1947, he estimated that the Indigenous population had fallen to the low hundreds, though many others had been assimilated into the Chilean and Argentine states, their cultures repressed, ignored or abandoned. Two years later, Bridges died in Buenos Aires; he was buried alongside his father, Thomas, in the city's British Cemetery.

Meanwhile, Harberton remained a working sheep ranch until the 1990s, when falling wool prices, poaching, wild dog attacks and a harsh winter that wiped out 80 per cent of the livestock prompted a move into tourism. The *estancia* was named a National Historic Monument in 1999, and the old shearing sheds, sawmill, workshops and cattle pens are evocative testaments to its heritage, housing aged tractors, vicious-looking circular saws and a pair of stuffed condors.

While Harberton is rich in history, most visitors now come to see its penguins. Isla Martillo, one of several islands on the ranch, was originally used for grazing, but when the sheep were moved away, Magellanic penguins began to arrive. There are now thousands of breeding pairs, plus smaller numbers of gentoo and king penguins. During the fifteen-minute crossing to the island, the weather turned dramatically, with crisp sunshine replaced by menacing grey skies. The temperature plunged well below zero, and gale-force winds whipped up stinging snow flurries. It was a

Fig. 1: The Palace of Running Waters, Buenos Aires.

Fig. 2: The Torre Monumental (aka the Torre de los Ingleses), Buenos Aires.

Fig. 3: Street art in the Ciudad Vieja, Montevideo.

Fig. 4: The electricity switchboard of the former meatpacking plant at Fray Bentos.

Fig. 5: The caves that sheltered the first Welsh settlers in Patagonia, Puerto Madryn.

Fig. 6: Ty Nain, a Welsh Patagonian tearoom in Gaiman.

Fig. 7: The prow of the *Yelcho* and a statue of Captain Luis Pardo—who rescued Ernest Shackleton's stranded crew—on the waterfront in Punta Arenas.

Fig. 8: Parque Nacional Torres del Paine, Patagonia.

Fig. 9: King penguins on a beach in South Georgia.

Fig. 10: The rusting whaling station at Grytviken, South Georgia.

Fig. 11: A view of the Beagle Channel from Isla Navarino, Tierra del Fuego.

Fig. 12: Estancia Harberton, the oldest ranch in Tierra del Fuego.

Fig. 13: The view from the ruins of Orongo to the islets of Motu Nui and Motu Iti, Rapa Nui.

Fig. 14: The *moai* of Tahai, Rapa Nui.

Fig. 15: Colourful houses in the port-city of Valparaíso.

Fig. 16: The crumbling nitrate town of Santa Laura in the Atacama.

Fig. 17: Humberstone, the best-preserved nitrate town in the Atacama.

Fig. 18: Nitrate King John Thomas North's glasshouse in Avery Hill Park, London.

struggle to stay on my feet, but the skipper, clad in goggles and waterproofs, just grinned: 'Welcome to the backside of the world.' The penguins were perfectly at ease in the conditions, some tending to fluffy black chicks, others incubating eggs. Their chorus of hoots—to guide mates back to the nests—was interrupted periodically by loud sneezes, as they expelled salt ingested during fishing trips.

It was a relief to get back to the mainland and the warmth of the Harberton tearoom. After thawing out my numbed fingers and toes, I chatted with Abby Goodall, the great-great-granddaughter of Thomas Bridges. 'I'm only here because of *Uttermost Part of the Earth*,' she said. In the 1960s, her mother, US botanist Natalie Prosser, was travelling and teaching in Argentina when she read the book and decided to travel down to Harberton. She ended up marrying Thomas Goodall, Lucas Bridges' great-nephew, and founding the *estancia*'s Museo Acatushún, a museum and laboratory dedicated to studying the region's wildlife.

I spent the night in the old foreman's house, warmed by a wood-burning stove and a lamb-and-mushroom hotpot. At 8.30 pm, the snow stopped, and it was brighter than at any time since the morning, the Andes briefly visible before the setting sun obscured them again. As I went to sleep, a distant ship sounded its horn in the Beagle Channel.

The next day, I was dropped off at Ushuaia's port, where a prominent sign featured a crossed-out Union flag and the message: 'The mooring of English pirate ships is banned', a reference to the Falklands/Las Malvinas dispute, the prism through which Argentine–British relations are too often viewed.

* * *

Some 10 miles southwest of Estancia Harberton, across the Beagle Channel and the Argentine–Chilean border, Puerto Williams is a 2,000-strong settlement in the shadow of the

SMALL EARTHQUAKES

Dientes de Navarino range. Founded as a naval base in the 1950s, it is around 1,500 miles south of the Chilean capital, Santiago—roughly the distance between London and Istanbul. There are no road connections with the rest of the continent, so you have to fly or travel by ferry, which is part of the attraction for the few travellers who venture this far south. In a canny bid to boost tourism, the government upgraded Puerto Williams' status from a town in 2019, allowing it to snatch the coveted 'world's southernmost city' title from its far larger rival Ushuaia.

Despite its new billing, the capital of Chile's Antarctic province still looked and felt like a small town on my most recent visit in late 2022. The naval staff live in a grid of identikit houses with white walls, picket fences, neat lawns, Chilean flags and generally a doghouse. Beyond them is a jumble of homes with corrugated-iron roofs, oversized satellite dishes and piles of firewood, interspersed with a few A-frame churches, some simple guesthouses and a dozen shops and restaurants. Stray horses and cows roam the streets, and large netted pots used for catching *centollas*, king crabs that can measure 5 feet or more from tip to tip, are stacked in gardens. Residents leave their homes unlocked, and passers-by invariably say hello.

But Puerto Williams is more cosmopolitan than you might expect. Over several visits, I've met a Colombian cook, a US cultural anthropologist, an Estonian polar researcher, a German visual artist and an Austrian teacher. And despite its remoteness, the city is developing fast: a modern dock has been built to allow larger Antarctic cruise ships to call in, and an eye-catching socio-ecological research centre has recently opened.

There are also numerous reminders of the UK's connections with Tierra del Fuego. Casa Stirling, the first home of Waite Stirling and the Bridges family in Ushuaia, now sits in the grounds of the Museo Territorial Yagan Usi, near a sun-bleached whale skeleton. If you were unaware of its status as the region's oldest surviving European building, the modest bungalow would be easy to overlook, with its mustard-yellow walls of galvanised steel and short stilts that lift it off the ground. Alongside a range of Yagán exhibits, the museum also highlights the story of the man who gave his name to Puerto Williams, naval officer John Williams Wilson, who played a key role in the Chilean colonisation of southwestern Patagonia.

* * *

The Indigenous peoples of Tierra del Fuego have long been spoken about in the past tense. When Cristina Calderón died in 2022 at the age of ninety-three, Spanish newspaper *El País* called her 'the last full-blooded' Yagán and 'the last speaker of [the] Yaghan language', while the *Economist* dubbed her 'the last representative of her world'. These kinds of descriptions have long been attached to her by outsiders. Before she passed away, I was one of a stream of writers and journalists who travelled to Puerto Williams, eager to grab a few moments with her and carelessly write an elegiac piece. By all accounts, 'Grandma Cristina', as she was popularly known, found the process tiresome at best.

On a previous visit in 2017, I met her briefly at her home in Villa Ukika, a Yagán hamlet just east of Puerto Williams founded in the 1960s, after the authorities relocated most of Isla Navarino's Indigenous residents. Now home to around fifty people, it has a community centre and the Kipa-Akar, a traditional-style dwelling selling arts and crafts. As we chatted in her living room, Calderón showed me items she had knitted—socks, gloves, scarves. 'Puerto Williams is a very beautiful place,' she said. 'Now there is lots of work going on, and they are building new things. There's lots of change.'

Named a 'Living Human Treasure' by the Chilean government in 2009, Calderón was a remarkable person, but her death does not mark the extinction of the Yagán culture, as she herself reiterated. Her granddaughter, author Cristina Zárraga, raised this point in her biography, *Cristina Calderón: Memories of My Yagan Grandmother*: 'One day I asked my grandmother if she was the last Yagan. Of course not, she answered me, I'm not the only one nor the last.'

Although long neglected by the Chilean authorities, the community is working hard to revive its culture and language and claim its social, political and economic rights. According to the 2017 census, around 1,600 Chileans identify as Yagán, and they gained a greater public profile in 2019 after leading a high-profile campaign against a controversial plan to open a salmon farm in the Beagle Channel, as attested by murals across Puerto Williams declaring 'No a las Salmoneras.'

Two years later, Calderón's daughter, former city councillor Lidia González Calderón, was elected to represent the Yagán people in a national citizens' assembly tasked with drafting a new Chilean constitution. Members of the community are taking advantage of the rising number of tourists in Puerto Williams, too. On my latest visit, I met a young Yagán man who had recently launched a business offering kayak tours.

A Yagán and Kawésqar delegation also visited the UK in 2022 to examine artefacts taken from Tierra del Fuego by the likes of Cook and FitzRoy with a view to restitution in the future. Now held by institutions such as the British Museum, the British Library and the Pitt Rivers Museum in Oxford, the items included the original version of Thomas Bridges' Yagán–English dictionary, a large Yagán canoe brought over by Stirling, exquisite shell jewellery, finely woven baskets and face and body paint used in religious ceremonies.

The Selk'nam have faced similar challenges. According to the 2017 census, more than 1,100 Chileans identify as Selk'nam (there are also around 1,000 Selk'nam in Argentina). Organisations such as the Corporación Selk'nam helped to block legislation that would have declared the Selk'nam people to be 'extinct' in Chile. In 2023, the Chilean congress finally voted to recognise the Selk'nam as one of the country's eleven original peoples. The same year, a government commission report described the events in Tierra del Fuego in the late nineteenth and early twentieth centuries in unsparing terms: '[The] Chilean state policy of concessions and the introduction of sheep farming produced a veritable genocide of Selk'nam families.'

There is also growing awareness of the Selk'nam genocide in wider Chilean society through films such as *Blanco en blanco* ('White on white') and *Los colonos* ('The settlers'), which dramatise the brutal colonisation of Tierra del Fuego, the realities of which have long been obscured. *Blanco en blanco* was Chile's submission to the 2022 Oscars, while *Los colonos* was acclaimed at the 2023 Cannes Film Festival. 'I love the Selk'nam culture, my family's culture, my culture,' wrote activist Fernanda Olivares Molina, president of the Fundación Hach Saye, which promotes Selk'nam culture and protects Karokynká, the Selk'nam name for Tierra del Fuego. 'My efforts aim to strengthen us, so that all of us Selk'nam who are alive are free to be who we are, without fear of nullification and discrimination.'

* * *

After hiking up to the summit of Cerro Bandera, I spent my final afternoon in Tierra del Fuego travelling to the literal end of the road. The owner of my guesthouse, Maurice Van de Maele, drove me along the Y-905 out of Puerto Williams, the tarmac disappearing at Villa Ukika, replaced by a gravel surface that traced an undulating route over low hills topped with wind-sculpted trees. As we rounded a series of deserted bays, coves, headlands and beaches, there were no other vehicles and few signs of life beyond the odd farm or fisherman's cottage and a pair of turkey vultures gliding overhead.

Along the way, Van de Maele—an anthropologist, polar guide, former director of the Museo Territorial Yagan Usi and head of the local tourism association—showed me ancient sites I would otherwise have missed. There were scores of Yagán middens and the remains of ancient fishing traps: rows of stones ingeniously stretched across narrow inlets that allowed fish to enter at high tide but prevented them from escaping when the tide fell. 'This area is one of the top places in the world for archaeological density,' he said. 'Around 750 [ancient] Yagán sites have been found on just a third of Isla Navarino. There are probably 2,000 sites on the island as a whole.' Despite this richness, there are currently only a few archaeological projects in Tierra del Fuego, as its remoteness, transport challenges and unpredictable climate make digs an expensive endeavour.

As we drove on, fierce winds churned the surface of the Beagle Channel into white peaks that resembled the mountains on the Argentine side of the waterway. Inland lay evergreen beech forests, interspersed with scarlet-flowering Chilean fire bushes. There were also occasional patches of devastation—toppled trunks and crushed branches, stripped of their bark. It looked as if they had been hit by a natural disaster. Some carried the tell-tale char of fires set to clear land for farming and grazing, Van de Maele explained, but others had a more unexpected cause—beavers.

In a reckless bid to develop a fur trade in the 1940s, the Argentine authorities introduced a small group of Canadian beavers to their section of Tierra del Fuego, with disastrous consequences. The industry failed to take off, and, with no natural predators, the rodents quickly spread across the region. Now numbering around 200,000, the beavers are estimated to have damaged 25 per cent of Tierra del Fuego's forest eco-systems.

Nearby, Van de Maele pointed out an old military bunker, a relic of a border dispute between Chile and Argentina over a trio of uninhabited islands—Picton, Lennox and Nueva—just east of Isla Navarino that brought the countries to the brink of war in 1978. Despite fears of an Argentine invasion, mediation by Pope John Paul II ultimately helped to resolve the dispute peacefully, and the islands remain part of Chile. Yet the 'Beagle Conflict' is often cited as one of the reasons Chile backed the UK during the Falklands War.

The gravel road disintegrated into a stony track that beat a sinuous route through grass strewn with abandoned farming equipment before petering out at a pebble beach curled like a comma along the shore of the Beagle Channel. A lonely ranch owned by the navy, Caleta Eugenia is the most southerly place you can drive to in Chile. As we parked, a shaggy border collie bounded over excitedly from a dilapidated homestead, whose corrugated-iron roof rattled violently in the wind. Three king crab fishing boats bobbed offshore, delayed by a brewing storm south in the Drake Passage.

The ranch was home to just two people—a father and son who act as caretakers, raising livestock and selling timber. As we strolled along the beach, scanning the channel for cormorants and petrels, the father emerged for a chat, swapping local gossip with Van de Maele while leading a chestnut horse out to graze. Illuminated by the late afternoon sun, Caleta Eugenia felt like a fitting place to end my journey through Tierra del Fuego, even though it may not remain the end of the road forever. Plans have been mooted to extend the Y-905 a further 12 miles or so to the tiny fishing settlement of Puerto Toro, the southernmost village on earth and currently only reachable by boat.

And perhaps it is a mistake to think of the ranch as a finishing point—from a southern hemisphere perspective, it could just as easily be the start.

* * *

Thousands of miles northwest in the middle of the Pacific, Rapa Nui has a completely different landscape, climate and culture from Tierra del Fuego. Yet there are striking parallels in the history of this tiny island and its deep British connections.

7

STOLEN FRIEND

RAPA NUI

The Te Ara O Te Ao trail ascends through a woodland of papaya, eucalyptus, acacia and cypress trees and across a rippling grassland scattered with purple thistles, red and yellow flowers and prickly bushes. A hidden army of cicadas buzzed like an electric current. I was accompanied for a time by a pair of fearless brown birds, who zipped past like fighter jets before landing at my feet in the hope of receiving a stray crumb. When I stopped to catch my breath and glanced back, I was rewarded with a view of the sweeping Hanga Roa, the miniature capital of Rapa Nui. Eventually, I reached the lip of the cauldron-shaped crater rim of Rano Kau, an extinct, 1,060-foot volcano that dominates the southernmost tip of the island. The trill of a hawk-like caracara sounded overhead until it was muffled by a screeching wind that almost swept me over the precipice and into the flooded caldera below. Clumps of tangled yellow and green reeds floated on the surface of the crater lake, which resembled the map of an unknown planet. Dead ahead, a semi-circular gap in the crater wall—blown out by a prehistoric eruption—provided a picture frame for the navy-blue, white-flecked Pacific.

SMALL EARTHQUAKES

The narrow path around Rano Kau was empty, and the first person I met was working in the small visitor centre at the eastern edge of the summit, which marks the entrance to the ruins of a ceremonial village called Orongo. Inside are rows of low, oval-shaped houses built from basalt blocks, each with a low entrance barely high enough to crawl through. With a volcanic crater behind, sheer cliffs in front and the seemingly endless Pacific beyond, Orongo feels like it sits on the edge of the world. As I soaked up the view, I realised that beyond the island's shoreline, there was no one within 1,200 miles.

For around 150 years, the Te Ara O Te Ao trail was walked by athletic young men during the month-long Tangata Manu, or Birdman, competition. Every spring, the chiefs of Rapa Nui would nominate a contestant, a *hopu manu*, to compete on their behalf, with the victor gaining authority over the island for the coming year. After starting at the foot of the volcano at Mataveri, near where the airport is now located, the contestants would follow the trail to Orongo. They would then scale the craggy, 1,000-foot cliffs, desperately keeping hold amid buffeting winds, before plunging into the churning surf and swimming through the perilous waters to Motu Nui, the largest of three islets strung just over a mile offshore. After setting up camp, the contestants faced a nervous wait until the first sooty tern egg of the season was laid. Whoever claimed this prize signalled back to the crowd of spectators gathered at Orongo, transferring the power to his patron who became the Tangata Manu, the spiritual leader of Rapa Nui, for the next twelve months. Meanwhile, the successful *hopu manu* was left to swim back to the island, transporting the egg in a special pouch fastened to his head.

The contest lasted until 1867, when Catholic missionaries put an end to the practice. At the visitor centre, displays emphasised that Orongo could also disappear, as coastal erosion makes parts of the site unstable. The ruins, they warned, are partially cordoned off and 'at constant risk of being lost forever'. The beautiful petroglyphs adorning the basalt—some depicting the Tangata Manu, others the creator god Make Make—are also under threat, exposed to the elements and gradually wearing away.

Despite Orongo's history, scenery and sheer sense of remoteness, I was most struck by an absence, an empty space in one of the larger buildings that once held Hoa Hakananai'a. One of Rapa Nui's iconic monolithic *moai*, standing more than 8 feet tall and decorated with Tangata Manu symbols—including stylised figures, birds and vulvas—the statue is held at the British Museum. He was the first *moai* I saw in the flesh, a sight that tattooed itself on my brain as a child, helping to fire a life-long love of South America before I was old enough to question why the statue was there in the first place. In the Rapanui language, I later learned, Hoa Hakananai'a means 'lost, hidden or stolen friend'.

* * *

A triangular speck of land less than half the size of the Isle of Wight in the middle of the Pacific, Rapa Nui is the remotest inhabited island on earth. Its nearest inhabited neighbour is Pitcairn, which lies around 1,200 miles to the west—roughly the distance between London and St Petersburg. The Chilean mainland, in turn, lies more than 2,200 miles to the east. Islanders refer to it as Te Pito O Te Henua, the Navel of the World.

Home to some 7,750 people, roughly half of whom are Rapanui and speak a Polynesian-based language of the same name, as well as Spanish, the island was settled between 800 and 1200 CE by adventurous bands of Polynesian navigators—probably from the Marquesas or Gambier archipelagos, which are now part of French Polynesia—who voyaged across thousands of miles of uncharted ocean in double-hulled canoes. In splendid isolation, at the southeastern corner of the Polynesian Triangle, they embarked on an intense bout of statue carving—an expression of their religious beliefs of ancestor worship—that lasted for half a millennium or more. The *moai* represent revered forebears and face inland, watching over the Rapanui and providing protection if needed.

Hoa Hakananai'a mesmerised me as a child, but seeing him in the British Museum was no preparation for the awe of encountering *moai* in situ. During the 2010s, my work on the *Rough Guide to Chile* took me regularly to the island, travelling via five-and-a-half-hour flights from Santiago before being greeted on arrival with leis of pink and white flowers. On my most recent visit, before the COVID-19 pandemic, I watched the sun rise over the coastal site of Ahu Tongariki, whose fifteen giant statues—the biggest of which weighs around 86 tonnes—line up along a 720-foot-long *ahu* or platform, the largest ceremonial structure in Polynesia. In 1960, a tsunami struck Rapa Nui, scattering the *moai* of Ahu Tongariki; they were only restored to their perch in 1995.

A short walk inland took me to the grassy volcanic crater of Rano Raraku, where the vast majority of the 900 or so *moai* still on the island were carved from lapilli tuff, a rock of compacted volcanic ash. According to legend, they walked using their *mana* or spiritual energy—or, more probably, were transported on wooden sledges or rollers—to their respective *ahus* around the island. Today, Rano Raraku has a melancholy air, as if the sculptors have suddenly fled, leaving their inscrutable subjects in the lurch. Around 400 broken and unfinished *moai* remain stranded in the quarry, their immense heads and torsos sprouting from the crater at erratic angles, like daffodils in the spring. Among them is Te Tokanga, the Giant, the largest *moai* ever carved, who reclines on his back. Around 70-feet tall, he weighs roughly 200 tonnes, or about the same as thirty African elephants combined.

North of Rano Raraku is Anakena beach. According to the island's oral traditions, this golden crescent of sand, lapped by turquoise waves and shaded by palm trees, was where the first settlers arrived 1,000 years ago or more.

Unsurprisingly, the *moai* dominate outside perceptions of Rapa Nui, yet they are only one aspect of the islanders' remarkable culture. On the northern edge of Hanga Roa, the Museo Rapa Nui has a small but illuminating collection of exhibits. Alongside a rare female *moai*, pairs of piercing *moai* eyes made from red scoria pupils in discs of white coral and some finely worked obsidian tools used to produce the statues is a carved wooden fish, dark brown in colour and resembling a handleless cricket bat. The surface is covered by lines of glyphs: abstract crosses, circles and lozenges, as well as human-like figures, plants and animals. This is an example of *rongorongo*, the only Indigenous writing system to develop in Oceania prior to the twentieth century. It is also a fascinating, and unresolved, linguistic puzzle.

It is unclear when *rongorongo* developed. Some academics argue it predated European contact, others that it developed in response to exposure to European forms of writing. According to oral traditions, *rongorongo* tablets were carried to the island by the first settlers from Polynesia. Cristián Moreno Pakarati, head of research at the Rapanui Pioneers Society, told me that *rongorongo* was mainly used by the island's elite for religious purposes. 'It was never a script of the common people. Only a handful of wise literate people, according to tradition only men, could interpret the texts.'

But knowledge of the script was lost during turbulence on the island in the nineteenth and early twentieth centuries, although some 'traditions, chants and customs' were noted down by foreign visitors towards the end of this period, according to Steven Roger Fischer, former director of the Institute of Polynesian Languages and Literatures in Auckland and author of *Island at the End of the World*. Over the years, scholars have tried to decipher the script, but their attempts have been hampered by a lack of data. Only twenty-six *rongorongo* tablets have survived to the present day, some only have a few lines of script, and the originals are all overseas; the Museo Rapa Nui only has replicas. The British Museum has three tablets, none of which is currently on display.

Pakarati emphasised the importance of including Rapanui people in attempts to decipher *rongorongo* but was not confident that the script will ever be fully understood. 'It is a source of great admiration and awe towards our ancestors,' he told me. 'But on the other hand, [it is] as much a mystery as for the rest of the world.'

* * *

English pirate Edward Davis, captain of the *Bachelor's Delight*, may have been the first European to spot Rapa Nui in 1687. An account by one of his crewmen referred to a 'small flat island' in this patch of the Pacific. But the first confirmed European contact came thirty-five years later in an incident that gave rise to the name Isla Pascua, or Easter Island. After visiting the Juan Fernández Islands—an archipelago more than 400 miles off the coast of Chile where Scottish sailor Alexander Selkirk was marooned for over four years, a castaway story that inspired the Daniel Defoe novel *Robinson Crusoe*—Dutch navigator Jacob Roggeveen spotted Rapa Nui on Easter Sunday, 1722. Despite only spending a day on the island, he and his crew killed twelve Rapanui.

It was half a century before the next European visitors. In 1770, a Spanish expedition led by Felipe González de Ahedo 'claimed' the island for the Spanish crown, a process that apparently involved asking Rapanui chiefs to 'sign' a contract in a language they could not read and then firing a twenty-one-cannon salute. Four years later, in March 1774, James Cook arrived on the sloop *Resolution*, having spent the previous 100 days at sea on a mission that aimed to find the then undiscovered continent—at least from a European perspective—of Antarctica. Spotting several large statues from the water, he sailed around the island before anchoring off 'a small sandy beach' near the present-day location of Hanga Roa. Cook was so ill at this point that he only briefly set foot on the island. But his crew stayed longer, exchanging goods with the Rapanui—'medals and other trifles' for drinking water, chickens, bananas and sweet potatoes—and exploring the coastline. According to an account by the ship's naturalist, Johann Reinhold Forster, they quickly came across some *moai*:

> We first stood directly across the country under the high hill, till we came to the other Side of the Island [Ovahe, near Anakena], & there we found 7 stone pillars, 4 of which were still standing, & 3 were overturned ... One of the standing ones had lost its hat ... In what manner they contrived these structures in [is] incomprehensible to me, for we saw no tools with them ... The Images represent Men to their waist, the Ears are large & they are about 15 foot high & above 5 foot wide; they are ill shaped & have a large solid bonnet on their head like some of the old Egyptian divinities.

The crew also clashed with the Rapanui, firing shots at a man who ran off with a bag belonging to the ship's artist, William Hodges. As well as noting the toppled *moai*—Roggeveen's account, from fifty-two years earlier, only mentioned upright statues—the men recorded that the Rapanui appeared to be short of supplies and drinking water, which suggests there may have been unrest on the island in recent years. The caveat, of course, is that the crew's accounts were based on brief encounters with people who were likely to be extremely reluctant to show off their possessions to newcomers, given their previous experiences. They may also contain errors or embellishments: Hodges' paintings, for example, show the *moai* facing out to sea, rather than inland.

SMALL EARTHQUAKES

Nevertheless, the eighteenth century was undoubtedly a period of rupture on the island. Conflicts—probably driven by a combination of factors including European contact, power struggles, scarcity of food and other resources, and a loss of faith in the power of the *moai*—saw statue carving come to an end. Every *moai* on the island was toppled, and *ahus* were damaged or destroyed. As potent symbols of family, community, village and tribal power and authority, they made for obvious targets. (All of the statues standing today were restored to their upright position in the twentieth century.)

In response to this period of unrest, the Rapanui developed a new way to restore political and religious order on the island, the result of which was the Birdman contest.

* * *

For many in the global north and elsewhere in South America, Rapa Nui is as synonymous with ecocide as it is with megalithic statues and staggering remoteness. A notion that islanders overexploited their resources and destroyed their environment—cutting down forests, depleting the soil, wiping out seabird colonies—triggering a catastrophic population collapse, has become pervasive. This contentious theory was popularised by US author, biophysicist and geographer Jared Diamond in his 2005 book *Collapse*, the follow-up to the bestselling *Guns, Germs, and Steel*. 'The parallels between Easter Island and the whole modern world are chillingly obvious,' he wrote. '[The island's] isolation makes it the clearest example of a society that destroyed itself by overexploiting its own resources.' The schlocky 1994 Kevin Costner-produced film *Rapa-Nui* promoted similar views.

This theory has long been challenged by the Rapanui and widely contradicted by scientific research. In June 2024, a study using AI and satellite imaging to map the island's ancient 'rock gardens' found that the population 'could not have exceeded

STOLEN FRIEND

4,000' people, as compared to the 15,000-strong high-point population touted by some supporters of the ecocide theory. This was followed three months later by a DNA analysis published in *Nature* that rejected the idea the island underwent a population collapse in the 1600s prior to European contact. By contrast, reported the *Financial Times*, the 'island's population appeared instead to have increased to about 3,000 until the 1860s, when it plunged as a result of Peruvian slave raids and a severe outbreak of smallpox'. Furthermore, the study found evidence of contact between the Rapanui and Indigenous peoples on mainland South America dating back to 1250–1430 CE, predating European contact by at least three centuries.

What emerges from these pieces of research is a story of Rapanui ingenuity, innovation and adventure. Rapa Nui is tiny—just over 63 square miles—lacks rich soils and has limited fresh water. Unlike elsewhere in Polynesia, there are few accessible lagoons and reefs to aid fishing and shellfish harvesting. These shortcomings forced the islanders to be creative. In the past, I've explored the subterranean world of Ana Te Pahu, one of a series of lava tubes. These natural formations, some of which extend for miles, were used to create favourable microclimates in which to grow crops such as pineapples, taro and bananas, as well as collect rainwater.

The story of the Rapanui is also one of resilience against almost insurmountable odds—not only to reach the island in the first place but also to withstand the devastation, exploitation and disease of the mid-1800s. During this period, around 1,500 Rapanui were 'blackbirded': kidnapped in slaving raids. They were taken to Peru to toil in horrific conditions alongside other enslaved Polynesians and indentured Chinese labourers in guano mines, harvesting tonnes and tonnes of nutrient-rich seabird excrement, an immensely valuable commodity used as fertiliser in Europe and North America. The Peruvian trade was dominated by a British firm, Antony Gibbs & Sons. The Rapanui population was further devastated by epidemics of diseases such as smallpox and tuberculosis (tragically, after international pressure prompted the Peruvian government to end the use of enslaved labour on its guano islands, some of the fifteen previously enslaved Rapanui who were eventually repatriated to Rapa Nui were infected with smallpox). Meanwhile, Christian missionaries arrived to convert islanders and clamp down on their culture, lifestyle and religion, including the Birdman contest.

* * *

On my most recent visit to Rapa Nui, I stayed in a guesthouse hidden down a rambling warren of lanes on the northern edge of Hanga Roa. It was run by a talkative musician in his early twenties who told me he was working on a 'ukulele Rapanui reggae' album. Heading into the town centre, sharing the road with a group of semi-feral horses, I skirted a pretty, flower-filled cemetery and the three *moai*-topped *ahus* of Tahai, a popular spot to watch the sunset.

On the southwest coast of the island, Hanga Roa is a small, low-rise settlement. After picking up a fried tuna empanada with chilli sauce, I wandered along the waterfront, past the harbour, a small *moai*, a football pitch and a series of small beaches. Most of the businesses catered for tourists, the income from whom is vital for the local economy. Alongside plenty of hotels and guesthouses, restaurants served ceviche, sushi and locally caught spiny lobsters called *rape rape*, souvenir shops sold *moai* fridge magnets and Birdman statuettes, and posters advertised cultural shows featuring *umu*, a traditional meal in which meat, fish and vegetables are cooked in a hole filled with hot volcanic rocks.

Hanga Roa is an attractive town with a tranquil vibe, but for much of its history it resembled a ghetto. In the late 1860s, the missionaries were replaced by a series of rapacious ranchers, who forced the Rapanui off their ancestral lands and effectively ran the island as personal fiefdoms. The first was Jean-Baptiste Onésime Dutrou-Bornier, a violent and ruthless French Crimean War veteran. After marrying a Rapanui woman, he ousted missionaries, transported hundreds of Rapanui to labour on plantations in Tahiti and seized control of the island through coercion, deception and strategic alliances. Having failed to persuade the French government to declare Rapa Nui a protectorate, Dutrou-Bornier was killed by islanders in 1876.

He was replaced by Alexander Ari'ipaea Salmon, scion of the powerful British–Jewish–Tahitian dynasty, which backed Dutrou-Bornier's venture. His father, Alexander Salmon, was born into a wealthy family in London and travelled via California to Tahiti, where he married into the Tahitian royal family. Herman Melville memorably described him in his novel *Omoo: A Narrative of Adventures in the South Seas* as an adventurer who 'rose late, dressed theatrically in calico and trinkets, assumed a dictatorial tone in conversation, and was evidently on excellent terms with himself'.

In 1888, Chile annexed Rapa Nui, nudged along by British diplomats, who were keen to prevent France from claiming the island. After purchasing Salmon's holdings, the government attempted to settle a few Chilean families on Rapa Nui. When that plan failed, it changed tack and leased the island to a Chilean businessman, Enrique Merlet. He swiftly instructed his foreman, Alberto Sánchez Manterola, to build a 'magnificent' 10-foot stone wall. Manterola then ordered a group of fifty Rapanui, wrote anthropologist Pablo Seward in his paper 'Between "Easter Island" and "Rapa Nui"', 'to build such an enclosure, "for cattle." The enclosure of 1,000 hectares, little did the Rapanui know, was in reality meant for them.'

The wall surrounded much of present-day Hanga Roa, and the Rapanui required a permit to leave; without one, they could be shot. It essentially turned the village into a 'concentration camp', added Seward.

The violence, turmoil and repression of the nineteenth century decimated Rapanui society. Political and social structures were shattered, and the population plunged by around 95 per cent. The 1877 census recorded just 111 Rapanui islanders.

* * *

For an insight into the next phase of Rapa Nui's history, I headed to the southern outskirts of Hanga Roa, along empty streets lined with eucalyptus trees and wooden bungalows with luxuriant gardens, to meet James Grant-Peterkin, the British honorary consul and one of only a handful of foreigners to speak the Rapanui language.

Grant-Peterkin originally came to Chile to teach English in the mid-1990s but found that life in Santiago did not provide the kind of 'cultural change and experience' he had hoped. So, he took advantage of a cheap flight to Rapa Nui, a place he had been fascinated with since childhood. Grant-Peterkin spent three months on the island doing an assortment of jobs—waiting tables, working in a hotel—and fell in love with the place. 'I then went to university in the UK and diverted all of my studies towards linguistics so that I could come back here and, basically, have an excuse to study the linguistics on the island—the mix between Rapanui and Spanish that they speak,' he explained:

> So I spent my year abroad here and then, on graduation, came back out again. I've been here, pretty much, ever since. It's a fascinating place to have as your home. One takes it almost for granted when you live here, but to go—I don't know—jogging past *moai* in the morning is still pretty special.

Grant-Peterkin lived on Rapa Nui for two decades until 2023, building a home, setting up a tour company and writing a book, *A*

STOLEN FRIEND

Companion to Easter Island. His role as honorary British consul involved helping British visitors—and, often, tourists of other nationalities—who found themselves in medical, legal, financial or travel difficulties. 'It doesn't happen much here, but if anyone finds themself in the island's prison, then we get involved,' he added.

As we chatted over coffee, I asked Grant-Peterkin about the British role in the twentieth-century history of Rapa Nui. In 1903, Merlet's lease was acquired by Williamson, Balfour & Co., a Scottish-founded Chile-based company with interests in nitrate and wool. It set up a concession, the bluntly titled Easter Island Exploitation Company, 'and operated the whole island as a giant sheep ranch, bringing the animals over from Chile and the manager, administrator, vets and so on from Britain,' said Grant-Peterkin. At one stage, there were some 70,000 sheep on the island. To control them, the Compañía, as it was commonly known, constructed Scottish-style stone walls across the island, using the *ahus* as building material.

The repression of the Rapanui continued throughout this period. They were denied basic rights, including Chilean citizenship, and the presence of the Chilean state—and whatever partial and haphazard protections it might have offered—was visible only in brief annual visits by the Chilean navy. For the rest of the year, the Compañía's representatives were firmly in charge. In a powerful piece for Cultural Survival, an Indigenous-led NGO, Marisol Hitorangi, spokeswoman of the Hitorangi clan, wrote that during this period her people 'were tortured'. 'They were forbidden to freely circulate, grow crops, or keep animals, and were forced to work, threatened with leprosy injection[s] if they did not follow orders,' she continued. 'In the ghetto there was no drinking water and no food, so people survived by eating rats.'

Understandably, these brutal conditions resulted in a series of uprisings. A first-hand, if not exactly impartial account of one in 1914 is provided by British archaeologist and anthropologist

Katherine Routledge, who arrived in March of that year after securing permission from Williamson, Balfour & Co. to work on the island. Over the following sixteen months, she conducted interviews with the Rapanui, recorded their oral histories and studied their culture while excavating *moai* and historic sites and taking photographs. The work made a huge contribution to the academic study of Rapa Nui.

Beyond her research, Routledge's time on the island was eventful, to say the least. Rapa Nui, she wrote in *The Mystery of Easter Island*, 'bears no resemblance to the ideal lotus-eating lands of the Pacific; rather, with its bleak grass-grown surface, its wild rocks and restless ocean, it recalls some of the Scilly Isles or the coast of Cornwall'. She, her husband and their small team initially stayed at Mataveri with Percy Edmunds, the Compañía's manager.

After a few months, Routledge—who referred to the Rapanui as 'Kanakas'—witnessed a 'curious development ... which turned the history of the next five weeks into a Gilbertian opera'. An elderly Rapanui woman named Angata arrived at Edmunds' house and announced that God had come to her in a dream and told her that 'the chairman of the Company, was "no more," and the island belonged to the Kanakas, who were to take the cattle and have a feast the following day'. A few hours later, Edmunds was handed a 'declaration of war', which described the company's control over the island as a 'big robbery'. The Rapanui raised a flag to mark the new 'republic', a red, white and blue tricolour, and seized sheep and cattle, some of which were roasted for wedding feasts.

After dissuading the well-armed but heavily outnumbered Edmunds from attempting to put down the uprising by force, Routledge suggested mediation, safe in the knowledge that a Chilean naval ship, the *Baquedano*, was currently heading to the island for a routine visit. Initial negotiations, led by her husband, failed, so Routledge arranged a meeting with the 'prophetess' herself. A 'frail old woman with grey hair and expressive eyes', Angata was friendly but refused pleas to end the sheep raids and stop the seizing of company possessions. 'Food comes from God,' she said, 'I wish for no money.'

The situation built to a crisis point until the arrival of the *Baquedano*, whose crew subdued the uprising and detained some of the instigators. After forcing the Rapanui to return some of the sheepskins and other items they had seized, 'three of the four ringleaders were set at liberty, and no corporate punishment was inflicted'. Angata died six months later, but the uprising she sparked secured incremental improvements for the Rapanui, who continued to fight for their rights, sometimes by force. Shortly after leaving the island, Routledge wrote that she heard that 'a white [employee] of the Company has been murdered ... and thrown into the sea'.

In 1914, Rapa Nui was also the unexpected site of geopolitical conflict. On 12 October, after the revolt had died out, a German naval fleet commanded by Admiral Maximilian von Spee arrived on the island. Routledge's party did not know that the First World War had recently broken out, and von Spee kept the news to himself. He had earmarked the island as a covert rendezvous for his East Asia Squadron. Initially, relations were cordial. Routledge's party sought the assistance of a German doctor and handed over mail to send home to the UK (almost all of the letters ultimately reached their recipients). The naval officers in turn purchased meat from Edmunds and photographed Routledge's excavations. They 'were courteous and always saluted when we met,' she noted.

But the bonhomie soon came to an end. A crew member let slip to a German tobacco planter who had arrived on the *Baquedano* that war had broken out. The squadron had stayed longer than the twenty-four hours permitted in a neutral port, prompting Routledge to write a letter in protest, which she signed 'under the grandiloquent title of "Acting Head of the British Scientific Expedition"'. As well as erecting a signal point, von Spee deposited the crews of a captured French coal barque and a British sailing ship on the island. Yet, somewhat mysteriously, the Chilean representative on Rapa Nui—the schoolmaster—managed to persuade him to depart.

Leaving behind a dysentery epidemic that killed at least eight Rapanui—though Routledge believed the disease could have been introduced by the *Baquedano*—von Spee sailed to the Chilean mainland. On 1 November, his squadron sank two Royal Navy ships near the city of Concepción, killing more than 1,600 sailors. The Battle of Coronel was the Royal Navy's first defeat in more than a century and rocked British confidence in its sea power. But the battle was avenged five weeks later, when von Spee's squadron was destroyed off the Falklands. The Royal Navy sunk four of his ships, killing more than 1,800 sailors, including von Spee and two of his sons. Nevertheless, the admiral was commended for his bravery in Germany, and a pair of warships were named after him, including the *Admiral Graf Spee*, which was scuttled off the coast of Montevideo in 1939 following the first naval conflict of the Second World War, the Battle of the River Plate.

* * *

During the global economic chaos of the 1930s, the Chilean government briefly considered selling Rapa Nui, with Britain, the United States, Germany and Japan all mooted as potential buyers. Ultimately, Williamson, Balfour & Co.'s lease was extended instead, but the island's wool industry was declining, a trend exacerbated by the Second World War. Meanwhile, the Rapanui remained in appalling conditions. Many preferred to take their chances in a small boat on the perilous Pacific rather than stay on the island. Others took action to demand their rights, including in a major strike in 1928 in which Rapanui police officers joined forces with Compañía workers. According to a report by the Chilean government's representative on the island at the time, Carlos Recabarren, they called for improvements to their daily wages and food rations and a share in the company's profits.

This was not the only attempt by the Rapanui to shake off the intense oppression they faced. As Pakarati and Miguel Fuentes noted in their paper 'Towards a Characterization of Colonial Power on Rapa Nui (1917–1936)', Indigenous resistance, including 'various acts of disobedience, theft, insubordinations, and strikes ... [represented] a true and constant challenge to the actions of colonial powers on the island, represented by State institutions and the Company'.

In 1953, Williamson, Balfour & Co.'s reign over the island came to an end, with Chile's navy taking control, prohibiting the Rapanui language in the process. But a strong civil rights movement was growing on the island and within the Rapanui diaspora, alongside increasing international awareness of the plight of the islanders. In 1965, the Rapanui elected their own mayor—albeit with limited powers—and the following year finally won full Chilean citizenship and the right to vote in national elections.

* * *

Outsiders regularly portray Rapa Nui and its people as a kind of museum exhibit, frozen in time, enigmas waiting to be unravelled. It is a lazy prejudice. Over recent decades, Rapanui calls for greater self-governance, land rights and cultural preservation, alongside improved infrastructure, healthcare and education provision have intensified. Protesters have occupied various buildings and sites that are now in the hands of private companies; some demonstrations have been met with violence from the police and security forces. The Rapanui have also made submissions to the Inter-American Commission on Human Rights, denouncing human rights violations since Chile's annexation of the island in 1888 and seeking recognition of land rights.

There have been some partial and uneven successes, including securing greater local control over the national park, which was initially created in 1935 and covers most of the island, and the surrounding marine reserve, which is one of the largest in the world, spanning an area larger than France and containing 142 endemic species.

Alongside the ongoing struggle for economic, political and cultural rights, tourism poses another challenge. It started to develop at scale during the 1960s and is now central to the island's economy, with around 100,000 people visiting annually during the 2010s. Tourists are a vital source of revenue but a major burden on the island's creaking infrastructure and fragile ecosystems. As I saw at Orongo, the climate emergency, rising sea levels, coastal erosion and wildfires pose further threats to islanders and *moai* alike.

More than a century on, the impact of Williamson, Balfour & Co. and its predecessor ranchers can still be felt today. Alongside extensive damage to historic sites, the tens of thousands of sheep that were grazed on the island have left a lasting impact on the local environment. Beyond a handful of Rapanui families with British surnames—the legacy of relationships between Compañía staff and local women—the 'only physical remnants of that time are a few rotting outhouses that were used on the sheep farms,' explained Grant-Peterkin.

The British presence on the island also lives on in the Rapanui language, he added. During the Williamson, Balfour & Co. era, islanders came up with names for items they had not previously encountered. As all Rapanui words end in a vowel, hammer became 'hamara', blanket 'prankete', onion 'oniana', beer 'pia' and book 'puka'. Other words were more problematic. On hearing English phrases such as 'open the door', Grant-Peterkin continued:

STOLEN FRIEND

The Rapanui must have realised that they didn't have a word to convey this type of physical entrance into a house, since it had never existed in their ancient culture. 'Door' is a tricky word to convert into something Polynesian-sounding, and it may well be that they didn't fully understand the mechanics of the phrase. So what word did they agree on for 'door'? You guessed it: 'opani'.

* * *

Back in London, I visited the British Museum to see Hoa Hakananai'a, who now resides in the 'Living and Dying' gallery alongside a granite statue of the Egyptian deity Amun, a Buddhist conch-shell trumpet and a painting by artists from the Aboriginal community of Tjuntjuntjara. The story of his abduction is told on the body of a tattooed man. In the mid-1880s, Swedish ethnographer Knut Hjalmar Stolpe arrived in Tahiti, where he met a heavily inked Rapanui dock worker in Papeete. The man, whom Stolpe called Tepano, was covered with striking imagery, apparently self-applied. Describing him as a 'living chronicle of Easter Island', the ethnographer was particularly taken by the tattoo on his right forearm, which depicted an incident that had taken place around fifteen years earlier, and asked about its significance:

> Tepano gave the surprising answer, that it represents the dragging down of one of the large stone statues of Easter Island to the beach. The ten people, pulling on the rope, are 'English sailors', the large man with the staff is the 'First Officer', the other one the 'Second Officer'. The small figure, which is standing on the lying statue, is a dancing tribal chief.

The tattooed man's identity remains unclear: Tepano was a name commonly given to Rapanui men who had converted to Catholicism; it is the Polynesian version of Stephen. In their book *The Iconic Tattooed Man of Easter Island*, Adrienne L. Kaeppler and Jo Anne Van Tilburg argued that he is probably Vaka Ariki, whose name loosely translates as 'Canoe Chief'. A member of a high-ranking family who may even have risen to Tangata Manu, he later converted to Christianity, laboured on plantations and ultimately ended up in Tahiti. 'The tattoo he incised on his right forearm, depicting the removal of Hoa Hakananai'a from Orongo, reveals a man of spontaneous passion and, perhaps, substantial anger,' wrote Kaeppler and Van Tilburg.

The removal took place in November 1868. Commodore Richard Powell, captain of HMS *Topaze*, was keen to bring one of Rapa Nui's famous statues back to Britain. After taking their first *moai*, Moai Hava, from Mataveri, they set off for Orongo, where they dismantled a ceremonial house and transported the 4-tonne Hoa Hakananai'a down the slope of the volcano to the shore on a sled before transferring him to their ship. The *Topaze* returned to the UK the following year, and Hoa Hakananai'a was given as a gift to Queen Victoria, who subsequently passed it on to the British Museum. At present, he is on permanent display at the museum. The smaller, less finely worked Moai Hava, who was given directly to the museum by the admiralty, has been lent to institutions around the UK but is not currently on permanent display.

They are not alone. There are *moai* in museums in France, the United States, New Zealand, Belgium and mainland Chile, while around 900 remain on Rapa Nui. But Hoa Hakananai'a is particularly significant. Created around 1000–1200 CE, he is one of only a handful of *moai* sculpted from basalt—most are made from softer, more porous lapilli tuff—while his unique petroglyphs, which were added later, provide an insight into the Tangata Manu religion.

In recent years, there have been growing calls for the return of the *moai*—and other items of Rapanui heritage, such as *rongorongo* tablets—by both islanders and the Chilean government. As Anakena Manutomatoma, who serves on Rapa Nui's development commission, told the BBC, the repatriation of Hoa Hakananai'a was 'an absolute priority' for the islanders: 'The British taking the *moai* from our island is like me going into your house and taking your grandfather to display in my living room.'

A delegation from the island visited the British Museum in 2018, and a reciprocal trip was carried out the following year. Rapanui sculptor Benedicto Tuki has even offered to make the British Museum an exact replica in return. A bland, but carefully worded statement on the British Museum's website 'recognises the significance' of the *moai* to the Rapanui people and 'acknowledges the impact of their removal'. But as with many items, from the Parthenon Sculptures to the Benin Bronzes, the institution—still reeling from humiliating revelations in 2023 of the theft of some 2,000 items from its collection—does not plan to return them to their homeland. This inaction prompted a grassroots Chilean campaign to bombard the museum's social media accounts in early 2024 with the message 'return the *moai*', forcing the institution to switch off the comment function on some of its posts. The Chilean president, Gabriel Boric, echoed the sentiments of the campaign in an interview with journalists in January 2024: 'The English should give us back the *moai*.'

* * *

After safely storing Hoa Hakananai'a on board, HMS *Topaze* sailed to the UK via the Chilean port of Valparaíso, whose fortunes were soaring in the late nineteenth century as a result of its prime location on the Pacific coast and a multinational population with a strong British core.

8

JEWEL OF THE PACIFIC
VALPARAÍSO

A tall, narrow structure with tight staircases, porthole-style windows and colourful and clashing décor, La Sebastiana sits high on Cerro Florida, one of a chain of hills forming an amphitheatre around the port of Valparaíso. The house is a treasure trove of eclectic, surreal and sometimes unsettling knick-knacks: an embalmed scarlet ibis dangling from the ceiling, a wooden horse from a Parisian carousel, a hollow ceramic cow once used to serve rum punch, a music box that has fallen silent. There are crinkled maps of Chile, Patagonia and South America, multi-shaded drinking glasses, a bronze door knocker shaped like a human hand and a maritime-themed study featuring a desk stained with green ink.

Named after the Spaniard who built it, La Sebastiana is the former home of Nobel Prize-winning poet Pablo Neruda, who called it his 'house in the sky'. Seeking a peaceful spot away from the capital, Santiago, to think and write, Neruda had the property redesigned in his own eccentric image before moving into it in 1961. The panoramic views of a city he lovingly described as a 'heap, a bunch of crazy houses' and compared to a 'wounded whale' were a major draw. From the tower at the top of the building, Neruda gazed down on hills covered with brightly painted houses tumbling towards a skinny ribbon of land densely populated by municipal buildings, banks, shops and warehouses, which gave way in turn to a waterfront dominated by a busy port into which a procession of merchant and naval ships sailed to and fro.

The poet liked to encourage guests to look across to the rooftop terrace of a particular house where he claimed a woman would often sunbathe naked. Despite providing them with a telescope and a steady supply of his signature Champagne-and-cognac cocktails, no one else ever saw her.

By the time Neruda arrived, Valparaíso—known locally as Valpo—was long past its heyday, a city of crumbling buildings, falling trade and increasing poverty. The poet was also in physical decline. A strong supporter of the democratically elected socialist government of Salvador Allende, for whom he served as ambassador to France, he died in suspicious circumstances on 23 September 1973, shortly after the right-wing military coup of General Augusto Pinochet. Fifty years on, the cause of his death remains the subject of rumour and conjecture, amid persistent allegations that he was murdered by the dictatorship.

Looted after the coup, La Sebastiana was painstakingly restored in the 1990s after the return of democracy and turned into a museum, as were Neruda's other homes in Santiago and, along the coast, in Isla Negra. It offers a glimpse into the poet's magpie-like interests and turbulent (and troubling) personal life. Amid the horde of exotic and idiosyncratic possessions gathered by Neruda during his travels, it is easy to miss a rather stiff portrait of a Scottish naval officer and politician, Thomas Cochrane, 10th Earl of Dundonald. The subject of the painting is now little known in the UK but was once central to British connections with both South America's struggle for freedom and the port of

JEWEL OF THE PACIFIC

Valparaíso, for a time one of the most important trading hubs in the Americas, nicknamed the 'Jewel of the Pacific'.

* * *

Jet-lagged after a long flight from Heathrow, I dozed for most of the 80-mile bus ride from Santiago to Valparaíso, waking fitfully amid the vineyards of the Casablanca Valley and then again as we passed a series of ominous roadside billboards. They were completely black except for a pointed question: 'You are happy?' After skirting the upmarket seaside resort of Viña del Mar, known for its leafy streets, casino and annual music festival, I got off at Valparaíso's bus station. Outside the terminal, street vendors did a brisk trade in deep-fried empanadas, kebabs cooked on mini barbecues and knock-off sports gear in the shadow of Chile's National Congress, an oversized and unheralded monolith built during the Pinochet dictatorship.

Although Valparaíso's famous forty-five hills rose in the background, the first-time visitor could be forgiven for thinking that the city's architectural reputation and UNESCO World Heritage Site status were a little undeserved. With the Pacific hidden behind dusty blocks to my right and grey clouds massed overhead, I walked into the centre along scruffy, fume-choked streets stalked by guilty-looking dogs and harassed shoppers. The roads heaved with traffic and, unexpectedly, a man leading a mule laden with sacks of vegetables.

But, gradually, remnants of the city's illustrious past emerged from the gloom. A huge Greco-Roman-style library, a gracefully aging cinema. Farther on, in the centre of a strip of palm-lined parkland running down the centre of busy Avenida Brasil, stood the Arco Británico. Vaguely resembling a miniature Marble Arch, it was surrounded by a small garden, the flower beds planted with white roses, the benches spattered with bird droppings and melted ice cream. The monument was donated by the local British community—or 'colony' as its members styled themselves—in 1910 to mark the centenary of Chilean independence. A lion that would have looked more at home in Trafalgar Square reclined on the top of the arch, the sides of which featured the busts of four men whose names are unfamiliar in Britain (and Ireland) today but resonate throughout Chilean history: Bernardo O'Higgins, Roberto Simpson, Jorge O'Brien and Thomas Cochrane.

A short walk away, beyond a taxi stand, a father teaching his young daughter to roller skate, a pair of weed-smoking teenagers and a white marquee with a banner proclaiming 'Real Miracles', was another monument to Cochrane. A statue stood above the prow of a ship, surrounded by a half-filled pond, gazing inland. Panels on the side described some of the key naval victories of a man who—along with O'Higgins, Simpson, O'Brien and many other British and Irish soldiers and sailors—played a vital role in South America's wars of independence.

* * *

The defeat of Napoleon at Waterloo in 1815 left Britain awash with unemployed soldiers—as many as half a million, according to some estimates. Thousands of them decided to fight for the aspirant nations in Spanish-controlled South America. Many were simply mercenaries; others sought adventure or a sense of purpose; and some regarded themselves as freedom fighters.

In 1817, a representative of 'El Libertador' Simón Bolívar visited London on a recruitment drive. Over the following two years, more than 6,000 men sailed from Britain to fight in South America, alongside significant supplies of arms and other equipment. 'These men formed the nucleus of the British Legion and were regarded by Bolívar as vital reinforcements, while the rifles, artillery and other military equipment, provided on credit by British merchants, were no less urgent,' wrote historian John Lynch in an essay for *History Today*.

JEWEL OF THE PACIFIC

Officially, Britain was neutral during the wars of independence but nevertheless sought to prevent other European nations from militarily aiding Spain. The government was also quick to recognise the independence of the new nations, though this was far from a benign gesture: it 'came at the cost of commercial treaties being imposed by Britain on these new countries,' noted William Edmundson in *A History of the British Presence in Chile*. The point was underscored by an 1824 letter from the British foreign secretary, George Canning, in which he stated: 'Spanish America is free and if we do not mismanage our affairs ... she is English.'

A Chilean perspective on this story is provided by the Museo Marítimo Nacional, which is housed in an old naval college on top of Cerro Artillería just north of the city centre. Naval cadets in smart uniforms and primary school pupils in red-and-black tracksuits gathered for photos in the closely cropped grounds, which were studded with cannons and offered views, through the mist, across horseshoe-shaped Valparaíso Bay. Towers of shipping containers, evoking a giant game of Tetris, rose in the port alongside looming blue cranes. Offshore, a trio of warships formed a cordon, as if protecting the city from attack.

Unsurprisingly, given its military focus, the museum struck a bombastic, nationalistic tone. The interior courtyard was filled with torpedoes, cannons, anchors, flags and plaques. Inside, the first room was dedicated to O'Higgins, the Chilean-born son of Irish and Basque parents. His father, Ambrosio, was born in Sligo before emigrating to South America, where he rose through the ranks of the Spanish imperial establishment and was ultimately appointed captain general of Chile and then viceroy of Peru. As a young man, Bernardo O'Higgins studied in London—a commemorative bust can be found in the London borough of Richmond—before rising to command Chilean military forces against the Spanish Empire. He subsequently became the country's first head of state—or 'supreme director'—in 1817 and is considered one of the continent's great 'liberators' alongside Bolívar and José de San Martín. 'In contrast with his father's anglophobia,' wrote Eric Richards in *Britannia's Children*, 'O'Higgins wanted "to make Chile the England of South America", and he advocated English and Irish immigration as the best guarantee of progressive political institutions in South America.'

O'Higgins championed the adoption of a British-style constitutional system but was ousted in 1823, partly because of criticism of a controversial £1 million loan he secured from the British government that came—predictably enough—with decidedly unfavourable repayment terms. He set sail from Valparaíso on a British ship, spending the rest of his days in exile in Peru. Despite the sour departure, his name adorns streets, squares, monuments and national parks across Chile, from Puerto Williams in the south to the city of Arica in the north.

Alongside a collection of medals, swords, portraits, prints and statues, the museum immortalised O'Higgins in stained glass, as if he were a saint. Cochrane, his friend and fellow national hero, was similarly deified. The room dedicated to him showcased his uniforms, telescopes, fishing rods, pistols and handkerchiefs, as well as models of his ships, paintings of him and his homes and letters he wrote to O'Higgins, encased in plastic and hanging from a rail. I sat on a bench made from a mock crate of 'British East India Fine Tea' and read about his life.

Prior to his arrival in Chile, Cochrane had had a storied and controversial career. The Lanarkshire man joined the Royal Navy as a midshipman and quickly rose up the ranks. Commanding the sloop *Speedy*, he captured more than fifty vessels in the Mediterranean during the Napoleonic Wars, making tens of thousands of pounds for himself in prize money. In one famous incident, he led a daring 'fireship' attack—a manoeuvre in which a vessel is set alight and/or filled with combustibles and rammed into the enemy—against a French squadron. These successes prompted Napoleon to dub him the 'Sea Wolf', while his escapades would go on to inspire the character Captain Jack Aubrey, hero of Patrick O'Brien novel *Master and Commander* and portrayed in the 2003 film adaptation of the book by Russell Crowe.

Cochrane also became an MP but was expelled from parliament in 1814 after being convicted of stock exchange fraud, despite protesting his innocence. The judgment ended his career in the Royal Navy, which had already been curtailed after he attempted to have a superior officer court-martialled. These episodes prompted him to seek his fortunes elsewhere, and Cochrane accepted an invitation to found Chile's first navy and command it against Spanish forces. The nascent Chilean fleet was modelled on the Royal Navy and heavily staffed with British officers and sailors. Cochrane led it with customary aplomb, playing a crucial role in securing the freedom of both Chile and Peru, notably during the vital battle for the heavily fortified city of Valdivia in February 1820—a victory, the display boards noted, that effectively 'ended the last vestiges of Spanish power in mainland Chile and opened up the way for Chilean and Peruvian independence'.

In the Peruvian port of Callao, he later captured the Spanish flagship *Esmeralda*. (A clash with the *Esmeralda* two year earlier had cost O'Brien, another former Royal Navy officer who valiantly served in the Chilean fleet as captain of the *Lautaro*, his life. Simpson, the fourth figure on the Arco Británico, served alongside Cochrane and O'Brien and eventually rose to the rank of rear admiral of the Chilean navy.) 'Lord of the Sea, we call you, singing, to battle. Spanish chains deny us the seas,' wrote Neruda in his poetry collection *Lord Cochrane de Chile*. Like O'Higgins, he is commemorated with statues, street names and even a town in Chile. As well as the room dedicated to him at the Museo Marítimo Nacional, Valparaíso's oldest surviving house—built in 1843—now hosts the Museo Lord Cochrane, though its scant exhibits are limited to cannons, a commemorative brass plaque and a replica of Cochrane's gravestone.

Also like O'Higgins, Cochrane ultimately left the Chilean navy under a cloud, after falling out with his superiors. He went on to lead the navies of Brazil and Greece, as the countries sought to throw off the shackles of Portuguese and Ottoman rule, respectively, before returning to Britain, where he was reinstated into the Royal Navy. He died in 1860 and was buried in Westminster Abbey. In *The Autobiography of a Seaman*, published shortly before his death, he wrote with pride and palpable anger about his 'chequered' career:

> In one respect I will boldly assert that this narrative of my life is worthy of example. It will show the young officer that, in spite of obstacles, warm attachment and untiring devotion to my noble profession enabled me to render some services to my country upon which I may be allowed to reflect with satisfaction, even though this be accompanied with bitter reflection as to what the all-powerful enmity of my political opponents cruelly deprived me of further opportunity to accomplish.

* * *

Cochrane was not the first British maritime link with Valparaíso. Francis Drake raided the port in 1578 and captured the Spanish ship *Los Reyes*. According to local legend, he seized more loot than his vessels could carry and was forced to stash some of it in a near-inaccessible sea cave. The pirate was such a fearsome presence along the Pacific coast of the Americas that long after his death Chilean and Peruvian parents would utter the ominous warning 'Here comes Drake' in a bid to quieten their misbehaving children.

Almost two and a half centuries on, there was an unexpected skirmish between British and US forces in Valparaíso's harbour in 1814. During this period, the US was harrying Britain's profitable whaling fleet in the Pacific, and the Royal Navy was dispatched in response. Although Valparaíso was a neutral port, a vicious battle broke out, resulting in the capture of USS *Essex* and *Essex Junior* and scores of casualties, the vast majority on the US side.

At the time of Cochrane's departure, Valparaíso was embarking on a transformation from a quiet fishing port to a major mercantile hub. Chilean independence ended the Spanish monopoly on trade, and Britain, the dominant sea power of the era, pounced. Over the course of the nineteenth century, shipping traffic along the Pacific coast of the Americas grew substantially, aided by the California gold rush, rising demand for Chile's abundant copper and other natural resources and the growth of industries such as the wool trade. The ample commercial opportunities on offer in Valparaíso attracted a cosmopolitan mix of migrants, sailors, vagabonds and merchants from around the world, particularly Britons. They came to dominate the lucrative import/export, wholesale, financial, banking and commercial sectors, taking advantage of Britain's global dominance, the international strength of the pound and enviable lines of credit.

During the 1810s and 1820s, the number of British residents in Valparaíso grew dramatically, from two to 2,000, according to one contemporary account. A vivid portrait of the fast-developing port is provided by Cochrane's friend Maria Graham, née Dundas, a Cockermouth-born travel writer, editor, artist, botanist, translator and historian whose life story rivals that of the Sea Wolf when it comes to adventure. After spells in India and Italy, she travelled to Chile with her husband, naval officer Thomas Graham, the captain of HMS *Doris*, whose voyage was intended to preserve 'amicable relations with the government of Chile' for the 'protection of the subjects of his Britannic Majesty who are engaged in lawful commerce'. But when he died en route, succumbing to a fever off Cape Horn in 1822, Graham made the bold decision—for the era at least—to stay in Valparaíso rather than return home.

Her book *Journal of a Residence in Chile* is a valuable counterpoint to the preponderance of male accounts of the time. It provided a first-hand description of the powerful November 1822 Valparaíso earthquake, describing the impact on the surrounding landscape, notably how it lifted the beach several feet above the sea. The influenced geologist Charles Lyell's seminal *Principles of Geology*, which was published in 1830, and was later supported by Darwin in *The Voyage of the Beagle*. Graham also offered a window into British perceptions of the relationship with Chile in the early nineteenth century. In her view, Chile's independence was down, almost entirely, to O'Higgins' education in England and the daring efforts of Cochrane, with whom she became friends in Valparaíso.

Graham's book gives a sense of Valparaíso's strong British character in the 1820s: 'English tailors, shoemakers, saddlers, and inn-keepers, hang out their signs in every street; and the preponderance of the English language over every other spoken in the chief streets, would make one fancy Valparaiso a coast town in Britain.' Not that Graham was entirely impressed by her fellow countrymen and women. There was, she wrote,

> a sad proportion in the English society here of trash. However, as vulgarity, ignorance, and coarseness, often disguise kindness of heart, and as I have experienced the latter from all, it scarcely becomes me to complain of the roughness of the coat of the pineapple while enjoying the flavour of the fruit.

After a year in Valparaíso, Graham departed in January 1823, sailing with Cochrane to Brazil, where she became governess to Princess Donna Maria, later Queen of Portugal. Over the following decades, Anglo-Chilean trade continued to grow and with it the British commercial presence in Valparaíso. Firms such as Williamson, Balfour & Co., Duncan Fox and Antony Gibbs & Sons became mainstays of the local economy, and

British and Anglo-Chilean shops, factories, warehouses and wholesalers proliferated.

The expanding British community also put down roots. As the century wore on, they built homes on the hills overlooking the downtown area, initially Cerro Alegre and then neighbouring Cerro Concepción. Alongside their business ventures, they founded churches, masonic lodges, benevolent societies, social clubs, schools, a hospital, music and theatre groups and a company of the volunteer fire service, which still has the Union flag on its uniform today.

Sport was another focus. The British community set up football, rowing and tennis clubs and staged regular horseracing events. Cricket was played in the port as early as 1818, when a match took place between 'the officers of the *Andromache* and those of H.M.S. *Blossom* [which] led to the establishment of a club, the members of which met twice a week, and dined under canvas,' according to General William 'Guillermo' Miller, a Kent-born soldier who fought against the Spanish in José de San Martín's Army of the Andes, helped to capture Valdivia alongside Cochrane and later became 'grand marshal' of Peru.

Chile's oldest sports club, the Valparaíso Cricket Club, was founded in 1860, and the country's first international match, against Argentina, took place in 1893; it took the visitors three and a half days to reach Santiago, a journey that involved crossing the Andes by mule. The Valparaíso region later produced an England cricketer. All-rounder Freddie Brown, who was born to English parents in Lima, Peru, started his playing career along the coast at St Peter's School in Viña del Mar. He went on to play test cricket for England from 1931 to 1953, captaining the 1950–51 team on a tour of Australia.

* * *

From the Museo Marítimo Nacional, I followed a street named after Cochrane through the Barrio Puerto. The port district was grimy and rundown. Waiters drummed up trade outside cheap seafood restaurants, and a fishmonger in a blood-spattered apron and orange trousers deftly filleted fish, flicking the scales on to the pavement to be fought over by tough tabby cats. Patrons ducked in and out of dive bars. There were plenty of dilapidated buildings, some abandoned and semi-collapsed, others on the verge. Tangles of wires crisscrossed above the street; I counted twenty leading to one particular house. Walls were covered with graffiti, murals and frayed posters advertising the forthcoming derby between local footballing rivals Santiago Wanderers and Everton. Small groups idled on the cobbles, passing around spirit bottles and joints.

Dominated by the naval HQ, a blue-grey wedding cake of a building, Plaza Sotomayor marked the transition zone into the financial district. Trolleybuses rattled in the distance, and the streets were lined with conservative, imposing architecture. Many were relics of a time when British interests dominated the banking sector. Opposite the stately Turri clocktower, a 1920s Elizabeth Tower lookalike at the tip of the wafer-thin Edificio Edwards, named after a wealthy family with British origins and extensive financial and media interests, stood the former Banco de Londres. Now a branch of Santander, the elegant interior was filled with bronze- and marble-work imported from the UK, as well as a memorial to employees who fought in the First World War. British residents and Anglo-Chileans played a key role in the development of the city's banking sector: they helped to found and run the Bank of Valparaíso and by the early 1860s owned around a third of its capital. Transactions in the city were often carried out in sterling; indeed, an 1895 law declared that the currency was legal tender throughout Chile.

As well as Calle Prat, the city's equivalent of Wall Street, some of Valparaíso's most atmospheric bars and restaurants are also found in the area. El Cinzano livens up in the evenings when aging crooners take to the stage, while J. Cruz Malbrán—a museum as much as a restaurant, cluttered with kitsch trinkets—is the birthplace of the *chorrillana*, a life-shortening pile of steak strips, onions, eggs and French fries. I resisted and headed instead to Bar Inglés, which dates back to the early 1900s and has opened, shut and been revamped on various occasions in recent years. When I visited in 2017, it had just been saved from closure, something that would have been a 'catastrophe for the city, an irreparable loss', according to a letter from a city resident to *El Mercurio de Valparaíso*.

Tucked away behind a somewhat forbidding exterior, the latest refurbishment had retained a pub-like feel, with a long bar and floors, walls and tables of dark wood. The décor was a window into Chilean perceptions of modern-day Britain—a museum piece, in short. There were pictures of the royal family—Princess Diana featured prominently—the Beatles, the Rolling Stones, David Bowie, Freddie Mercury, Roger Moore and a young, partially dressed Helen Mirren draped in a Union flag. The most recent images were of Amy Winehouse and Daniel Craig. There were images of bowler hats on the beer mats and red telephone boxes on the toilet doors. Alongside black-and-white photos of Valparaíso in the early twentieth century and the badges and flags of various local nautical organisations, glass frames enclosed yellowed receipts from British companies that were once mainstays of the local economy: La Casa Inglesa; H. McManus; Williamson, Balfour & Co.; Edmundson & Co.

As 'We've Only Just Begun' by the Carpenters started up in the background, I ordered a beer from a bartender in a white waistcoat and black tie and scanned the tables hoping for the larger-than-life characters who pop up with suspicious regularity in travel books. But there were only a pair of elderly gents tucking into *milanesas* and a mother and son, the latter sipping a Coke and playing Roblox on his phone.

Bar Inglés has two entrances at either end of the building. 'So that when someone's wife came to look for them, they could slip out of the other door,' said Iain Hardy, with a smile, when I met him at his office a five-minute walk away from the bar. Britain's honorary consul in Valparaíso, Hardy's great-grandfather moved over from Scotland in 1876 and found a job with the Pacific Steam Navigation Company. After a couple of years, he set up a custom brokerage outfit, and it became a family business. 'Anybody who wants to import or export in Chile has to go through a broker, and my father and grandfather were brokers before me, so we've got quite a lot of history. Customs brokerage is still a big business in Valparaíso today.'

Hardy's great-grandfather saved up for seven years before he could afford to bring his fiancée over from Scotland, along with both of their mothers:

> He'd already built a house here, and they had six sons, one of whom was my grandfather. All the young were sent back to be educated in Scotland [in the early days]. But my parents decided to educate my generation in South America, which I think is quite right. After three generations, you're part of the land.

Hardy estimated that there were around 400 British citizens living in and around Valparaíso, while the local Anglo-Chilean community was three to four times bigger. Showing me round the office, whose walls were covered with black-and-white photos of his relatives, Valparaíso in the early twentieth century and firms such as Duncan Fox and Williamson, Balfour & Co., he told me there were still British schools, societies and churches in Valparaíso, Viña del Mar, Santiago and beyond, as well as events such as the annual Caledonian Ball: 'It's still well attended, but not that many kilts.'

The honorary consul—who attended a British school in Buenos Aires, where 'all our lessons were in English, and rugby was very much the main sport'—said Argentina's connections with Britain were quite different from Chile's. 'The British influence there was probably a lot stronger, but the long-term connections, I would say, are much stronger here.' As I left, he added: 'In Chile, we—I have to say "we" not "they"—like to think of ourselves as the British of South America.'

* * *

The Barrio Puerto is encircled by undulating hills that are connected to the downtown by a set of wheezing *ascensores*. These funicular lifts were installed in the late nineteenth and early twentieth centuries to ease the aching limbs of *porteños*—a name residents of Valparaíso share with their counterparts in Buenos Aires and other ports in South America—as they travelled between the relatively small business and commercial district and their homes in the *cerros* above.

At their height, there were thirty-one *ascensores*, but only sixteen still run today, and invariably at least one or two are out of operation at any given moment. They feel refreshingly unmodernised, climbing the steep slopes with a chorus of creeks, groans, judders and jolts. I took the appropriately named Reina Victoria funicular up to Cerro Alegre, the 'Happy Hill' upon which the British community first settled. Named after the recently departed Queen Victoria, it opened in 1903 and ascends a 52-degree slope, a short but atmospheric journey from the cafés and bars of Plaza Aníbal Pinto. The upper station leads on to a pedestrian strip much-frequented by tourists, with walls covered with murals and houses painted in varying shades of blue, purple, yellow, mint green, pale pink and orange.

The echoes of Valparaíso's former prosperity, and its British connections, are particularly loud on Alegre and Concepción, where streets and businesses carry names such as Atkinson, Brighton, Templeman and Leighton. Alongside counterparts

SMALL EARTHQUAKES

from Germany, France, Italy, Switzerland and beyond, British merchants lived in houses that harked back to the old country: sash windows, neatly tended gardens, clothes from Liberty, toys from Hamleys. Crucially, they gazed across to the port and the Pacific beyond, through which a steady stream of ships, many of them British, sailed in and out.

In 1858, an Anglican cathedral, St Paul's, was built in a Neo-Gothic style and later equipped with what was reputedly the finest organ in South America. It has conservative cream walls and a dull green corrugated-iron roof, amid the turquoise, purples, pinks, blues and yellows of the surrounding houses. A Presbyterian church was built in the lower town, and a 'dissidents' cemetery constructed on Cerro Panteón, beside the main cemetery, which had been reserved for Catholics.

A steep walk up from the downtown, the Cementerio de Disidentes was patrolled by the caretaker's two elderly Alsatians, who kept watch over the weathered tombstones, chipped mausoleums and occasionally headless cherubs. As in its counterpart in Punta Arenas, the names on the graves reflected Valparaíso's multicultural heritage, demonstrating how immigrants had woven themselves into the fabric of the city: Roberto Sherrington; James, Herbert, Santiago, Josefina, Rosa and Louis Bennett; Carvallo-Miller; Roberto, Jaime and Jean Clark de Shand; Alfredo R. Christie; Carlos Fernando Middleton Soffia.

Valparaíso's diverse population gave the city a vibrant atmosphere at the turn of the twentieth century. Looking back on this era in her 1957 book *Child in Chile*, former British resident Bea Howe wrote:

> The place was full of young men of all nationalities, all working hard, all playing hard, and all determined to make their fortunes in this smiling land of great opportunities. Many 'younger sons' belonging to English families with old historic names had come out to Chile and were still coming, attaching them to English business

firms ... There were German barons too by the score, and Italian counts, some genuine, others not.

* * *

The good times for Valparaíso—and its British community—came to an abrupt end in the early twentieth century. The first hammer blow was an 8.2-magnitude earthquake that struck the city on the evening of 16 August 1906, killing more than 3,000 people, injuring many more and razing countless buildings to the ground. Howe, who was living nearby at the time, wrote that the fires sparked by the quake were so strong the sky burned red:

> Whole streets lay in ruins and where houses had not been struck down by the earthquake they had been gutted by the fierce fires that had raged all through the night. A thick brown pall of smoke and dust covered the whole of the stricken town while the air smelt of the dead. Wholesale looting took place ... and robbery of the dead. Even the old were not spared ... Martial law was declared and every bandido or robber caught red-handed was shot and his body strung up on a wooden cross at a street corner to serve as a public warning to others.

Eight years later, Valparaíso was hit by another near-fatal blow. On 15 August 1914, shortly after the outbreak of the First World War, the first ship travelled through the newly opened Panama Canal, rerouting international shipping traffic and deflating, at a stroke, Valparaíso's once buoyant economy. Previously, vessels that wanted to travel between the Atlantic and the Pacific were forced to go round Cape Horn or journey through the Strait of Magellan, calling at Valparaíso en route. Now they had a handy shortcut through the isthmus of Central America. Over the following decades, the erstwhile 'Jewel of the Pacific' steadily lost its sheen. The Great Depression and the Second World War also took heavy tolls on the city, and local businesses increasingly shifted to nearby Santiago.

SMALL EARTHQUAKES

The Anglo-Chilean community declined alongside Valparaíso. Before the start of the First World War and the opening of the Panama Canal, British banks held around 25 per cent of deposits in Chile, and the UK provided a third of the country's imports. But the British presence and influence in Chile as a whole fell significantly, the victim of its waning power on the international stage, particularly over the global financial system, and the break-up of the empire, alongside the rising dominance of the United States and its companies in Latin America. In 1875, there were some 1,785 British citizens in Valparaíso; by the early 1950s, the number had plunged to 419.

For much of the century, Valparaíso's economy remained in the doldrums, and crime and poverty rates were high. Yet the decline helped to preserve the city's glorious architecture, and cheap rents attracted writers, musicians, artists and dreamers—including Neruda—who gave the place a distinctly alternative, leftfield culture. Today, this 'heap' is one of the most interesting—and idiosyncratic—cities in South America. In recent decades, many of the *cerros* have undergone a rapid gentrification, despite several devastating wildfires, notably in 2014 and 2024, disasters that claimed over 150 lives and destroyed thousands of homes. Attracted by the bohemian vibe, sweeping views and formerly cheap rents and house prices, Chilean and foreign buyers snapped up properties, many of which were swiftly repurposed to cater for rising numbers of tourists. Inevitably, this pushed up house prices and rents while easing out local residents and eroding both the sense of community and the arty atmosphere for which the city was famous.

Nowhere is the process more evident than on Alegre and Concepción, centrepieces of the city's 'historic quarter', which was named a UNESCO World Heritage Site in 2003. These residential areas are warrens of precipitous cobbled streets, narrow alleyways and crumbling townhouses. Many of the latter have

JEWEL OF THE PACIFIC

been restored, renovated and transformed into hotels and guesthouses, cafés, restaurants, ice cream parlours and bars, art galleries and souvenir shops. A melody of languages drifts along the streets, and there is just enough urban decay to provide an edge, though even that is disappearing.

There are flourishing creative, cultural and culinary scenes, such as the former prison, which has been turned into a cultural centre. Valparaíso is also renowned for its street art, murals and graffiti, which cover walls, underpasses, flyovers, public transport and sometimes entire buildings. The tradition emerged in the years of the Pinochet dictatorship as a form of non-violent—and safely anonymous—protest and resistance. Some pieces are playful, others overtly political, referencing the recent mass demonstrations and heated referendum over a new constitution.

As a prominent piece of graffiti, pointedly written in English, made clear: 'Tourism it's worse than Trump. No gentrification.'

* * *

On my last evening in Valparaíso, I met up with one of the city's British residents. A former guidebook writer, Janak Jani had lived in Valpo for years, running a guesthouse, but was now preparing to leave. On a balmy evening in the garden of a Cerro Alegre bar, we chatted about travel, gentrification and Anglo-Chilean history over expertly mixed pisco sours. The British legacy in and around Valparaíso, he explained, was not limited to architecture such as the Arco Británico, the former Banco de Londres, the townhouses on Alegre and Concepción and St Paul's Cathedral.

> In Viña del Mar there are still churches where mass is said in English. You have fourth- and fifth-generation descendants who have never been to the UK but still think of themselves as British. Lots of British things have left a mark on the culture, even though Chileans now don't know where they came from.

A classic example is that Chileans typically have four meals a day: breakfast, lunch, dinner and *la once*, literally 'the eleven'. Also known simply as *onces*, the custom was inspired by the tradition of elevenses brought over by the British community in places like Valparaíso. Eaten in the late afternoon, it generally features some combination of sandwiches—or bread, butter, cheese and jam— and cakes, pastries, tarts and doughy croissants known as *medialunas*. 'Chilean maids would serve it in British homes, and then, I believe, go home later in the day and imitate it with their family,' said Jani. '*Onces* is now also code for having a drink— "eleven", representing the eleven letters in the spirit *aguardiente*. Lots of words have made it into Chilean Spanish, too. Like "gasfiter", for plumber, even though there's a word for plumber in Spanish. Horse races are often called "derbies".'

On the walk back to my hotel, I passed the former home of British painter and teacher Thomas Somerscales, a whitewashed building with blue trim, tiled terraces and statuesque palm trees that now served as a boutique hotel. Somerscales arrived in Valparaíso with the Royal Navy in 1864 and was left to convalesce in the city having caught malaria earlier in the voyage in Panama. The Yorkshireman ended up spending three decades in Valparaíso, teaching at a local British school while forging a successful career as an artist.

Somerscales initially focused on landscapes and seascapes, particularly in and around his adopted city. But it was his depictions of Chile's naval victories that really earned him a place in the country's artistic pantheon. His change of focus was prompted by the War of the Pacific, which broke out in 1879 over a swathe of the Atacama Desert, one of the most extreme environments on earth. The conflict centred on the nitrate industry, which was vital to the Valparaíso economy and dominated by British tycoons, whose outsized influence can still be felt today.

9

GHOST TOWNS

ATACAMA

Yellow tsunami 'hazard zone' signs, planted like sunflowers on street corners, marked our drive out of Iquique and up the 2,600-foot *cordillera* that backdrops the city. White-tipped waves raced across the Pacific, and Cerro Dragón, the world's largest urban sand dune, loomed in the distance, rearing menacingly over the *barrios* below. A pair of paragliders drifted across the pale blue, cloudless sky. Part of this highway collapsed during an 8.2-magnitude earthquake in 2014, said my guide Jaime. The quake triggered a 6.5-foot-high tsunami that pummelled Iquique, claiming the lives of six people and destroying or damaging hundreds of buildings, including a women's prison, whose inmates took the opportunity to break out.

Leaving the city behind, we drove inland. The morning mist gradually evaporated, the temperature ramped up and the Atacama Desert stretched into the distance. Arid, barren, inhospitable. Half an hour into the journey, the car was enveloped in a billowing dust cloud that obscured the sky and reduced visibility to a few feet. Slowing to a crawl, Jaime explained it was the

SMALL EARTHQUAKES

result of tank exercises at a nearby army range. Eventually, the dust cleared, and the ochre landscape returned into view; it looked as if the region had been drenched in powdered cumin.

Shortly afterwards, an odd sight appeared on the horizon: a rusting skeleton of what looked like a marooned ship. As we drew closer, the surrounding structures slowly materialised. Clumps of huts and warehouses, a line of train tracks and, finally, a set of houses but not a person in sight.

* * *

The Atacama is the driest desert on earth beyond the poles. It averages less than a millimetre of rain a year; some areas have not seen a single drop in centuries. As a region, the Atacama is loosely defined: in popular usage, it refers to the northern quarter of Chile, a 600-mile plateau stretched taut like fresh bedsheets between the Pacific and the Andes, though some geographers include within it the coastal strip of southern Peru and areas of neighbouring Bolivia and Argentina.

The mountains in the east form a rain shadow over the Atacama, whose extreme aridity has produced an otherworldly landscape, a realm of blindingly white salt flats, smouldering volcanoes, undulating sand dunes, grumbling geothermic fields, gaping canyons and seemingly endless tracts of rust-coloured dust and brittle grey rock. Beyond a few coastal cities such as Iquique, a scattering of remote villages centred around oases, herds of stoic llamas and flocks of candy-pink flamingos tip-toeing through jade-green lakes, the stark region is sparsely populated by humans and animals alike. Conditions are so hostile that NASA uses the region to test out its Mars exploration vehicles.

Yet Indigenous peoples have lived in the Atacama for more than 11,000 years. The north of the region was home to the Chinchorro culture, whose members used expert mortuary practices to preserve the bodies of the dead. Hundreds of mummies dating back more than 7,000 years—predating their counterparts in Egypt by two millennia—have been discovered near the city of Arica, which lies some 200 miles north of Iquique. The Chinchorro were one of many cultures in the Atacama, and languages such as Quechua and Aymara are still widely spoken.

Over the last 200 years, the region has been an arena for conflict and geopolitical struggles, the source of immense wealth and a dumping ground for dictators, the birthplace of political movements and a place of repression, a playground for travellers and a laboratory for studying the nature of life itself. These stories are tied to a pair of natural resources found in abundance in the barren expanses. Biological life may be virtually non-existent in parts of the Atacama, yet the region has, counterintuitively, powered an agricultural revolution in the global north.

It started with seabirds. Tens of millions of cormorants, pelicans and boobies populate islands off the coast of northern Chile and southern Peru. For centuries, Indigenous peoples such as the Chincha gathered the resulting excrement, which was rich in nitrogen, phosphate and potassium thanks to the birds' nutrient-rich diet, and used it as fertiliser. The great mounds of this guano—which reached heights of 150 feet on some islands—were preserved by the hot, bone-dry climate of the Atacama.

During the fifteenth and sixteenth centuries, most of this area was part of Tawantinsuyu, the Inca Empire. Innovative agricultural practices—including the use of terraced fields to create microclimates and complex irrigation systems—allowed the Inca to overcome challenging conditions such as scant rainfall, thin soils and fluctuating temperatures and played a vital role in their imperial expansion across what is now Peru, western Bolivia, southwest Ecuador, southwest Colombia, northwest Argentina and northern Chile.

This included the use of guano, which helped to sustain the agricultural growth that provided food for more than 8 million people. The Inca administrators recognised the importance of the resource and put in place some of the first state conservation measures to protect it. As Garcilaso de la Vega, son of an Inca noblewoman and a Spanish conquistador, recorded in his book *Royal Commentaries of the Incas*, the first edition of which was published in 1609:

> Along the entire coast, from Arequipa [a city in southern Peru] to Taracapa [*sic*: Tarapacá, the region around Iquique], which is a distance of over two hundred and fifty leagues, the only fertilizer used was that of seagulls, unbelievably numerous flocks of which were to be found there. These birds, both large and small, live on islands not far from the shore, which are covered with such quantities of their droppings that they look like mountains of snow. Under Inca rule, the birds were protected by very severe laws: it was forbidden to kill a single one of them, or even to approach their islands during the laying season, under penalty of death.

Although Indigenous peoples in the Atacama continued to use guano, it was largely ignored by the Spanish, who were blinded by fever dreams of gold and silver. Yet in the mid-nineteenth century, the resource became a valuable commodity once again. At this point, the newly independent Peruvian government was in a bind. Wrestling with political and economic instability, the country was lumbered with large debts to British banks, which had financed the fight against Spanish colonial rule a few decades earlier, while its legendary mines were floundering.

Fortunately, or so it seemed, Peru was home to the greatest guano reserves on the planet, notably on the Chincha Islands off the coast of the northern Atacama. At the start of the century, the German naturalist and explorer Alexander von Humboldt brought samples of Peruvian guano back to Europe to be studied. Influential work by his similarly illustrious countryman Justus von Liebig—the pioneering chemist behind Fray

Bentos in Uruguay—later reemphasised the value of the resource as a fertiliser.

With Europe and North America grappling with depleted soils, growing populations and the momentous changes of the Industrial Revolution, guano seemed like a gift from the heavens, and a British businessman, Spanish-born William Gibbs, moved swiftly to monopolise the industry. His family company, Antony Gibbs & Sons, which had been operating in South America since the 1820s, signed deals with the Peruvian and Bolivian governments to become the sole exporter of guano in 1842. The trade made Gibbs one of the richest men in the UK, with his firm earning around £100,000 annually—roughly equivalent to £8 million today—at its height. This wealth allowed him to purchase and remodel a lavish estate—Tyntesfield, near Bristol—and inspired a popular music hall song: 'William Gibbs made his dibs, selling the turds of foreign birds.' Between 1840 and 1870, around 12 million tons of guano were exported from Peru, boosting the coffers of the Peruvian government in the process, which paid off its debts and launched an ambitious programme of public works.

But the guano trade was built on the backs of enslaved and indentured labour. People were trafficked from China in the wake of the First Opium War, as well as Rapa Nui and Polynesia, and forced to toil in horrific conditions to dig out the 'white gold' alongside Indigenous and working-class Peruvians, convicts, conscripts and army deserters. The trade had unexpected geopolitical consequences. Britain's monopoly on Peruvian guano fuelled US imperialism. The 1856 Guano Islands Act authorised US citizens to seize any unclaimed island with guano reserves. This land 'may, at the discretion of the President, be considered as appertaining to the United States,' the law asserted.

Guano also provided the impetus for major public health reforms in London. Working after dark, 'night soil' men had long emptied the thousands of cesspits in the capital, selling the contents to farmers to use as fertiliser. But the mass import of guano removed the need for 'night soil'. This combined with London's growing population, the loss of the city's remaining farmland and the popularity of the recently invented water closet, which meant sewers originally designed to carry rainwater now transported raw sewage into rivers. The result was the spread of disease, the pollution of the Thames and its tributaries and, ultimately, the Great Stink of the hot, dry summer of 1858. The stench was so bad it prompted the temporary closure of the Houses of Parliament. Belatedly spurred into action, the government commissioned Joseph Bazalgette, chief engineer of the Metropolitan Board of Works, to create a modern sewage system for London. The bulk of his network of tunnels and pumping stations is still in use today.

* * *

To appreciate the immense scale and uncanny qualities of the Atacama, you need to travel overland. My 1,200-mile journey began on an overcast day on the southern fringes of the desert in the pleasant but underwhelming city of La Serena, a seven-hour drive north of Santiago. To kill time before my bus, I took a shared taxi known as a *colectivo* to the Elqui Valley, a 'heroic slash in the mass of mountains, but so brief that it is nothing but a torrent through two green banks,' according to poet Gabriela Mistral, who was born in the region.

Known for its wine production, orchards and observatories, the Elqui Valley has long drawn hippies, dissidents, new agers and others seeking escape, enlightenment or some combination of the two. Hemmed in by mountains, we passed field upon field of grapevines, cacti-covered badlands and a reservoir upon which rode a single kiteboarder. At a bar in Vicuña, a tranquil town with a huge plaza, a museum dedicated to Mistral and a quietly prosperous air, I sipped a glass of pisco from a local distillery.

GHOST TOWNS

A clean, floral, fruity grape brandy, pisco dates from the sixteenth century, when the Spanish introduced grapes to their South American colonies, initially to produce wine for Sunday mass. To extend the life of the sweet wine—a product of the hot, dry climate—distillation was introduced and pisco created. Peru and Chile both claim it as their national spirit—the central element of a pisco sour—and both claim to have been the originators. The rivalry even led to the Chilean National Congress's decision in 1936 to change the name of an Elqui Valley town from La Unión to Pisco Elqui.

British pirates such as Francis Drake played an inadvertent role in the development of the spirit in Chile. Their attacks on coastal settlements in the sixteenth and seventeenth centuries prompted residents to move inland to safer climes such as the Elqui Valley, where they took advantage of the fertile soils and microclimates ideally suited for viticulture. This boosted pisco production, and the area is now the heart of the industry in Chile.

Memories of the pirate raids persisted in the region into the nineteenth century. When Charles Darwin visited the nearby port of Coquimbo in 1835, he met an 'old lady' who told him 'how wonderfully strange it was that she should have lived to dine in the same room with an Englishman; for she remembered as a girl, that twice, at the mere cry of "Los Ingleses", every soul, carrying what valuables they could, had taken to the mountains'. Meanwhile, Bartholomew Sharp, a British pirate who ransacked Coquimbo, lives on in a Chilean saying to describe the arrival of an unwelcome guest: 'Charqui has arrived in Coquimbo', with *charqui*—which derives from the Quechua word for dried meat ('ch'arki') and later evolved into the English word 'jerky'—a corruption of Sharp.

The next morning, I travelled 280 miles north to the city of Copiapó, entering the Atacama proper. At the bus station, the newsagent stocked copies of *The Lord of the Rings* and a biography of Leon Trotsky, while a nearby supermarket sold a selection of Waitrose-branded 'English quality' goods: peanut butter, chocolate biscuits, mayonnaise, instant decaf coffee. An electronic display at the front of the bus provided the driver's name and how long they had been driving on this particular shift. Before departure, a woman walked down the aisle of the bus selling roasted corn wrapped in paper, while a passenger hummed his way through a series of Jackson 5 numbers.

Beyond La Serena's drab suburbs, punctuated with palm trees with chubby pineapple-like trunks and pieces of graffiti ('End the genocide against the Mapuche'; 'Quality education now'), we drove through scrubland and rocky, hilly terrain, with the platinum waters of the Pacific to our west. There was extensive road-building work underway. Bulldozers, steamrollers and diggers lined the highway, alongside impromptu settlements to house the workers and migrants heading south to Santiago.

We passed through Vallenar, a town founded by Bernardo O'Higgins' father, Ambrosio, and originally named San Ambrosio de Ballenary, after the latter's birthplace in Sligo. From this point, the heat rose and the desert grew starker as we neared Copiapó, an inland city founded to exploit silver, gold and copper reserves in land originally occupied by the Diaguita people. By the time we arrived in the early afternoon, the sun was searing and would remain so for the rest of my time in the Atacama.

Laid out in South America's familiar grid system, Copiapó is a difficult place to love, with a spray of ugly modern towers, the result of the grubby, short-lived wealth brought by mining. The city briefly hit the international headlines in 2010 when thirty-three men working in a mine to the north were trapped 2,300 feet underground by a cave-in for sixty-nine days before being rescued.

Copiapó allowed me to break my journey north and make a detour to Caldera, a small coastal city surrounded by semi-desert.

GHOST TOWNS

There I swapped my bland, chain hotel in Copiapó for a guesthouse with a samurai sword and a plastic eagle in the reception, pebble-dashed interior walls that grazed your skin at the slightest brush and a room with children's bedspreads and no external windows. A wistful, down-at-heel place, Caldera was once a busy port, shipping silver, copper, cobalt, manganese and coal around the world. It was home to the country's first railway line, which was built by a US businessman and ran to Copiapó, and attracted a stream of British officials, merchants, miners and sailors; an Irish visitor in 1889 counted nine British or Anglo-Chilean insurance companies alone.

Copper and grapes still pass through the port, but Caldera's heyday had clearly long gone. Remnants of its former glory were limited to a church with a Gothic spire built by British carpenters, a few grand but decaying nineteenth-century buildings and the old railway station, now a museum and cultural centre. The beach looked appealing from a distance, but up close the water was covered by an oily sheen. Near the fishing jetty, four odorous sea lions poked their heads above the water, open mouths raised to the sky, waiting in vain for the circling seagulls to drop their catch. Despite being the start of the summer season, there was only a handful of Chilean tourists, who were eating crab gratin and paella in a seafood restaurant on the waterfront; most headed a few miles up the coast to the more glamorous and expensive beach resort of Bahía Inglesa. Centred on a picturesque stretch of powdery sand lapped by iridescent waters, 'English Bay' took its name from seventeenth-century British pirate Edward Davis (who may have been the first European to spot Rapa Nui in 1687).

Wandering out of Caldera, along streets named Edwards, Picton and Lenox, I reached the sun-bleached Cementerio Laico de Caldera, the first secular cemetery in Chile, opened in 1876. The attendant came over to chat, explaining that people from across Europe, China, Japan and the Middle East were buried here, but the English, Welsh, Scottish and Irish were the second highest demographic, after Chileans. Pointing out the graves of engineers, sailors, millwrights and nurses from Cornwall, Caernarfon, Kent and Ayrshire, he said that foreign workers during the nineteenth-century boom years were called 'vampires' as they only came out to work at night when it was cooler.

* * *

Amid widespread unhappiness at the British stranglehold over the guano industry, the Peruvian government ended the export monopoly of Antony Gibbs & Sons in 1861. But the company quickly found an opportunity to exploit another unheralded Atacama resource. The desert was home to the world's largest reserves of sodium nitrate, also known as Chilean saltpetre, a powerful fertiliser also used in the manufacture of explosives.

Indigenous peoples in the Atacama had carried out small-scale nitrate mining for centuries, including under the Inca. But it was only in the second half of the nineteenth century, thanks to advances in the refining and extraction processes, increasing demand for fertilisers in Europe and North America and the waning of the guano age, that global attention turned to the region's abundant reserves. The first major *oficinas salitreras*—self-contained mining and refining settlements, the largest of which resembled small cities—opened in the late 1860s and were soon connected by a railway network.

When Antony Gibbs & Sons moved into the industry, the map of western South America looked very different from today, with the Atacama proper then divided between Chile, Peru and Bolivia. The nitrate fields belonged to the Bolivian province of Antofagasta and, to the north, the Peruvian province of Tarapacá, which included the city of Iquique and also held significant guano reserves. Although Chile had few nitrate reserves of its own, Chilean businesses and workers were commonplace in the neighbouring regions.

But national frontiers in this part of the world had long been contested. In the late nineteenth century, Chile, Peru and Bolivia had oligarchic governments, were heavily in debt—generally to British banks—and had entrenched rivalries. In 1879, war broke out. The initial trigger was the Bolivian government's decision to increase taxes on a powerful Anglo-Chilean company operating in the region, the Antofagasta Nitrate and Railway Company, whose key shareholders included Antony Gibbs & Sons and Agustín Edwards Ossandon, scion of a wealthy Chilean family with British roots. This went against an agreement Bolivia had previously signed with Chile, and, urged on by the firm's stakeholders, the Chilean government seized the port of Antofagasta the following year. In response, Bolivia and Peru—which had a joint defence pact—declared war on Chile.

The resulting conflict, the War of the Pacific, lasted five years, claimed thousands of lives and had ramifications for all three countries that are still felt today. Chile emerged victorious, claiming the nitrate regions of Antofagasta and Tarapacá, and even, for a time, occupying the Peruvian capital, Lima. The war dramatically expanded its territory and made nitrate the centrepiece of the national economy for the next four decades. By contrast, Bolivia was left landlocked. In some respects, the country has never recovered from the defeat: the lost coastline—which was rich in metals such as copper as well as nitrate—has become a phantom limb and a source of enduring anger. Bolivia has taken its case to the International Court of Justice and every 23 March marks what it regards as a historic injustice with the Day of the Sea commemorations.

Peru's territorial losses were also significant, if not quite as debilitating. They were compounded by the 1865–79 Chincha Islands War, in which Spain temporarily seized the guano-rich archipelago, prior to the start of the War of the Pacific. Shorn of its nitrate reserves, with the guano age shuddering to a halt as a result of over-exploited reserves, and back in debt to British banks, Peru fell into civil war.

* * *

The real winners of the War of the Pacific were British robber-baron firms such as Antony Gibbs & Sons, which dominated the nitrate industry for the next forty years. According to James G. Blaine, US secretary of state between 1876 and 1881: 'It is a perfect mistake to speak of [the War of the Pacific] as a Chilean war on Peru. It is an English war on Peru, with Chile as the instrument.' As William Edmundson noted in *A History of the British Presence in Chile*, the British share of total nitrate output rose from around 13 per cent before the war to 60 per cent in the immediate aftermath.

No one benefitted more than John Thomas North, the 'Nitrate King'. The son of coal merchant, he was born in Leeds in 1842 and apprenticed as a teenager to millwrights and engineers before finding work with Fowler's Locomotive and Steam Plough Works. The job took him to Peru, where he made his fortune, with business interests ranging from coalfields to railways. Commonly suspected of helping to instigate the War of the Pacific, North took advantage of inside information and contacts—notably Robert Harvey, the Peruvian government's nitrate 'inspector general'—and bought up Peruvian nitrate concessions at bargain prices during the conflict. The tycoon almost certainly knew the Chilean government intended to honour these concessions after the end of hostilities—not least because British banks and bondholders, as Edmundson stated, 'threatened Chile's credit in Europe if their claims were not met'.

Through his Liverpool Nitrate Company Ltd—which had Harvey as a director—North became the major force in the

Atacama. Following the end of the war, he and his counterparts ramped up production, creating a highly industrialised landscape—known as the nitrate *pampa*—with railway links to ports in one of the harshest terrains on earth. This set off a stock market boom in London and helped turn the Atacama into something resembling a state within a state.

The backbreaking, labour-intensive work to exploit the unrefined saltpetre, known as *caliche*, was carried out by tens of thousands of working-class and Indigenous people from southern Chile, Peru, Bolivia and Argentina. The managers, engineers, chemists and senior staff were generally foreign, predominantly British. From the 1870s, they oversaw a decades-long nitrate boom. At the height of the industry, British firms owned around a third of the 118 *oficinas salitreras*.

* * *

An eight-hour bus journey took me to Antofagasta, where the British history became even more apparent. On the edge of the coastal city, tucked between a five-star hotel, a trio of charmless apartment blocks and a school playground, stood what looked like the ruins of an ancient citadel. Brick terraces rose up a slope, supported by sturdy walls, battlements and a tower with narrow windows that resembled the arrowslits used by archers in medieval castles. With tall, desolate hills behind and the Pacific in front, the structure felt impregnable.

The Ruinas de Huanchaca were actually the remains of a foundry built in the 1890s to process silver from the Pulacayo mine in southwestern Bolivia, to which it was linked. Owned by the British-backed Huanchaca Mining Company of Bolivia, it was briefly the most modern foundry in South America, but plummeting silver prices, a flooded mine and technological advances led to its closure in 1902. Later ravaged by a fire, which provided the misleading aged sheen, the ruins now served as a stage for everything from car shows to ballet performances. The onsite museum housed a prototype Mars rover tested in the Atacama and fossilised teeth the size of a human hand from a 100-tonne prehistoric shark.

At the turn of the twentieth century, the British were among the biggest foreign communities in Antofagasta. They left behind a replica of London's Elizabeth Tower in the central Plaza Colón, a gift to mark the centenary of Chilean independence. Scanning the menu of a nearby restaurant, I noticed that a rare steak was described as 'Inglesa'.

Initially following the route of the Antofagasta (Chili) and Bolivia Railway, I headed northeast into the interior, catching a bus to San Pedro de Atacama, northern Chile's tourist hub. The scenery grew more dramatic as we ascended to an 8,000-foot plateau, climbing hills and cutting through mountains, the terrain shifting from chalky red to caramel brown and burnt orange. Although located in an oasis, San Pedro de Atacama provided little respite from the blistering temperatures. A monitor at the town's museum warned of 'extreme heat' and advised visitors to spend no more than fifteen minutes in the sun. It was the first time in a week I'd encountered foreign tourists en masse. San Pedro de Atacama's popularity comes from the surrounding area, which is home to some of the most mesmerising landscapes in South America: gleaming salt flats, high-altitude geyser fields, wind-sculpted sand dunes and lagoons dotted with flamingos.

The region is also a hub for astronomy and astro-tourism, the lack of light pollution and 300-odd cloud-free days a year resulting in a series of observatories. South of Antofagasta, the European Southern Observatory is currently building the Extremely Large Telescope (ELT), whose 128-foot main mirror will form the 'world's biggest eye in the sky'. Drawing comparisons with the scientific breakthroughs of Galileo Galilei four centuries ago, its developers hope the ELT 'will track down Earth-like planets around other stars, and could become the first telescope to find evidence of life outside of our Solar System. It will also probe the furthest reaches of the cosmos, revealing the properties of the very earliest galaxies and the nature of the dark Universe.'

Such revelations remained out of reach for me in San Pedro de Atacama. But as the dark sky flickered with stars, planets, constellations, nebulas, clusters and other celestial bodies, the cosmos felt both impossibly large and incredibly close.

* * *

Heading northeast from San Pedro de Atacama, the bus cut through the so-called 'Valley of Death'. The only signs of humanity were the road ahead, the odd abandoned tyre and several shrines—some with shaded seating areas and Chilean flags, one ostentatiously augmented with a car mounted on a platform. After a change of buses in Calama, a six-hour journey took me from the salmon-pink desert to a greyer, rockier zone. Just north of the city, we skirted Chuquicamata, one of the world's deepest open-pit mines. This multi-billion-dollar concern and other mines in the Atacama have made Chile the world's biggest producer of copper, responsible for a quarter of global output.

Zigzagging along a mountain road, we passed a much smaller mine with a handwritten 'for sale' sign outside and María Elena, the last nitrate plant still operating in the Atacama, its layout designed to resemble the Union flag. The only major settlement on the route was the coastal city of Tocopilla, trapped between the sea and steely mountains. A centre for copper-processing and deep-sea fishing, it was a jumble of mismatched houses with ill-fitting doors and barred windows, held together by rust and peeling plaster. A few residents had attempted to brighten things up, painting their homes yellow or blue, but they were the exception. The port was run down, and several buildings lacked roofs. A lame dog slumped outside a strip club named 'The Gentleman of the Night', and everything was caked in dust. As we left the city, the highway lined with rubble, a slab of rock carried the message: 'A city blessed by Jesus.'

The landscape shifted to tumbling sand dunes as we approached Iquique, a bigger, smarter and more prosperous city backed by red-smudged hills. Modern high-rises encircled the centre, whose architecture looked like a seaside take on the historic San Telmo neighbourhood of Buenos Aires, with wooden boardwalks, palm trees and a mix of restored and attractively peeling Victorian and Georgian-style mansions, the former homes of nitrate managers and engineers, weatherboarded and painted in ice-cream shades. There was a faded old theatre and restaurants and bars spilling out on to the street. Children splashed in the fountains of Plaza Prat, in the centre of which stood another British-style clocktower. Streets were named Thompson and Wilson.

On a berth near the busy port, the scent of fishmeal in the air, was a replica of the *Esmeralda*. Named after the Spanish flagship captured by Cochrane off the coast of Peru during the war of independence, the original was built in Kent and initially captained by a British-born Chilean naval officer, Roberto Simpson, who is commemorated alongside Cochrane on the Arco Británico in Valparaíso. It later took part in a battle off Iquique that has assumed almost mythical status in Chile.

I had a lunch of ceviche at El Wagon, a seafood restaurant decked out with vintage paraphernalia: gas lamps, shovels, old bottles, Pernod posters and pin-up photos. English-language posters carried slogans such as 'Chilean nitrate of soda is the best natural nitrogenous fertiliser for tobacco', 'Crops thrive on Chilean nitrate. The natural fertiliser. Containing vital elements' and 'By using Chilean nitrate of soda bring prosperity into view.'

* * *

In 1889, William Howard Russell, an acclaimed Irish reporter for the *Times*, was preparing for a holiday in Egypt with his wife when he had a chance meeting with the Nitrate King at a party in London. Having risen from 'mechanic to millionaire', acquiring the honorific title 'colonel' from the Tower Hamlets regiment of volunteer engineers along the way, North invited Russell over to the Atacama to report on the transformation of 'wastes without a sign of life or vegetation ... into a centre of commercial enterprise ... animated industry and prosperous life'. A stalwart foreign correspondent who had covered the Crimean War and the Indian Rebellion of 1857, Russell swiftly decided that Egypt could wait. He and his wife subsequently sailed to Chile with North and his entourage.

In the resulting book, *A Visit to Chile and the Nitrate Fields of Tarapacá, etc.*, published in 1890, Russell provided a glimpse into North's wealth, power and monopolistic business practices, though the man himself always remains just out of focus. After docking in Valparaíso, the reporter sat in on a meeting between North and the Chilean president, José Manuel Balmaceda, in neighbouring Viña del Mar. Championing a policy of 'Chile for the Chileans', Balmaceda had ambitions of nationalising the nitrate industry and the infrastructure on which it depended. North, naturally, was keen to head off any curtailment of his activities. According to Russell, the meeting was amicable, with North presenting the president with a gift: the capstan of the wrecked *Esmeralda* mounted as a shield.

Nevertheless, Balmaceda later cancelled North's nitrate railway concession, amid a constitutional crisis. As Edmundson noted in *A History of the British Presence in Chile*, the British government intervened diplomatically on North's behalf, to the disappointment of his business rival William Gibbs, who protested that 'North's company monopoly was actually detrimental to British capital invested in the region.' A civil war broke out in Chile in 1891, with Balmaceda accusing North and his British counterparts of funding the unrest. The president was overthrown and subsequently committed suicide. John Gordon Kennedy, Britain's minister resident and consul-general to Chile, later refused to deny a *Times* report that 'British and Chilean business interests had instigated the rebellion' against Balmaceda.

In his epic collection *Canto General*, Neruda wrote about North, the 'powerful gringo', and his dealings with Balmaceda:

> The smooth sterling pounds
> weave like golden spiders
> an English cloth, legitimate,
> for my people, a suit tailored
> with blood, gunpowder and misery.

After meeting Balmaceda, Russell and North sailed north to Iquique, the second most important port in Chile after Valparaíso thanks to the nitrate industry, where they were warmly welcomed by the large British 'colony'. The Nitrate King's monopolistic influence quickly became apparent. Alongside a chain of highly profitable *oficinas salitreras* and the railway network upon which the nitrate was transported to port, North supplied drinking water to parched Iquique via a trio of specially designed 800–900-tonne ships. He also had a bank and was involved in a 'flourishing company' to supply gas to the city's residents.

Russell and North were hosted and wined and dined in style by the British residents, who had grown rich on the back of the nitrates boom, lived in stucco-covered mansions painted cream, blue or orange, and frequented the local racecourse, cricket ground and theatre. 'With money in your purse there is very little you can desire which you cannot buy in Iquique,' wrote Russell. A few days after their arrival, an 'enthusiastic gentleman' even approached North seeking finance for a 'revolution' in Peru.

Yet Russell was also struck by the city's precariousness:

> Day after day the wonder of this artificial existence was at work under our eyes, but it was only on reflection that its strangeness

struck you, and that you were led in a vague way to think what would happen if water and food failed, if the condensers and steamers ceased to work ... and if the provision stores gave out.

After a leisurely stay, Russell and North boarded a private train at the Nitrate Station, a 'little Crewe full of life and energy', filled with British train drivers, engineers and clerks, 'piles of jute-bags' from Dundee, fuel from Cardiff, 'machinery from Leeds and Glasgow'. It transported them up to the nitrate *pampa*, the 'sandy, salty, waterless waste' littered with *oficinas*, silver mines and trenches left over from the War of the Pacific.

They stopped at the Ramirez *oficina*, the largest nitrate producer in Chile at the time. Owned by North's Liverpool Nitrate Company, it produced around 14,000 tonnes of nitrate a month. Russell's account provides an insight into the stark differences in status and lifestyles of the predominantly British administrators, managers and senior staff and their Chilean, Peruvian, Bolivian and Argentine workers. The former rushed to show their loyalty to North, 'firing off squibs and crackers, cheering and waving flags'. They could enjoy plush hotels, restaurants and bars such as the one at the Pozo Almonte *oficina*, 3,371 feet above sea level, which offered foie gras, Périgord truffles and bottles of Château Lafite. 'I dare no more than hint at the orgies here, of which drunkenness is the most innocent incident.' At the Primitiva *oficina*, meanwhile, the house of British chemical engineer James Thomas Humberstone was set around a Spanish-style patio, styled like an Indian bungalow, kitted out with imported furnishings and staffed with men in white linen uniforms armed with broadswords.

By contrast, the workers subsisted in 'squalid-looking settlements' and shantytowns that lacked sanitation and were surrounded by an industrial landscape of boilers, chimneys, tanks, vats, crushers, corrugated-iron workshops and offices, mounds of waste materials, railway lines and mules pulling carts, hissing steam and noxious smoke clouding the air. They worked shifts lasting twelve hours or more at high altitude in the torrid heat, overseen by private police forces and paid in '*fichas*'. These tokens could only be used in the company's own shops, which sold food, drink and supplies at inflated prices. The practice continued even after it was made illegal by the Chilean government in 1924.

Dissent was met with repression that sometimes escalated into massacres. In 1907, for example, day labourers went on strike demanding a pay rise and improved living and working conditions. Thousands of nitrate workers and their families marched to Iquique as the strike spread across northern Chile, prompting President Pedro Montt to declare a state of emergency. Six workers were killed by the army at the Buenaventura *oficina*. Their funerals took place the following day, and around 15,000 miners and their families gathered at the Santa María school in Iquique, where they were attacked by the army. Soldiers stormed the building, firing indiscriminately, and killed an estimated 2,000 to 3,600 men, women and children, before tipping their bodies into mass graves.

The event became a seminal moment for trade unionists and leftists in Chile, memorialised in folk band Quilapayún's 1970 *Santa María de Iquique* album and echoing out during the rise and overthrow of Allende's democratically elected socialist government.

* * *

When you reach the summit, the only way is down. The First World War was a high water mark for the British and Anglo-Chilean nitrate firms as demand soared from Allied ammunition factories. At this point, the Atacama was one of the most valuable places on earth, and nitrate accounted for as much as 80 per cent of Chile's exports. But while the war prompted a short-term profit surge, it also triggered the collapse of the

GHOST TOWNS

industry. Germany's nitrate supplies were cut-off by a British-led blockade during the conflict, which forced the country to seek out alternatives. Chemists Fritz Haber and Carl Bosch subsequently developed an industrial process that combined nitrogen in the air with hydrogen to produce ammonia, launching the era of artificial fertilisers.

After the war, this method proved to be a cheaper and quicker way to supply farmers and arms manufacturers in Europe and beyond than the nitrate refineries of the Atacama. Haber and Bosch both won the Nobel Prize, while British investment in Chilean nitrate slowly fizzled out during the 1920s. With the world gripped by the Great Depression, the industry as a whole soon followed suit. The *oficinas salitreras* were shut down, dismantled and stripped for parts, leaving behind islands of empty buildings, broken machinery and precipitous slag heaps.

These ghost towns are now time capsules, my guide Jaime explained, as we pulled into Santa Laura, 30 miles east of Iquique. Stepping out of the air-conditioned vehicle, the intense heat felt like a physical force. My feet kicked up clumps of crumbly white *caliche* as the desert winds whistled past, covering us in a sheen of dust and grime. Founded in 1872, Santa Laura was once staffed by a workforce of 870, but Jaime and I had the eerie site all to ourselves. The *oficina* and its neighbour, Humberstone, are the best-preserved nitrate towns, having escaped the fate of their counterparts by chance. 'After Santa Laura [and Humberstone] were abandoned, they were occupied by homeless people in the 1960s,' said Jaime:

> There was rubbish everywhere, graffiti, the bodies of dead dogs. Santa Laura and Humberstone were then bought by a businessman who planned to sell off the remains for scrap. But he went bankrupt first, which actually protected it. They were taken over by a non-profit organisation, cleaned up and made UNESCO World Heritage Sites in 2005.

SMALL EARTHQUAKES

Santa Laura is now an adventure park for industrial archaeology enthusiasts, a treasure trove of Victorian-era technology that includes a factory with metal-cutting machines, coolers and compressors; a power station with a gas engine made in Halifax and steel beams from Lanarkshire; furnaces and water pumps; a 'sheep dip' to clean the hoofs of the plant's hardworking mules; and the remains of a railway station, steam engine and train carriages. Preserved in the dry desert air, the machinery looked as if it could be cranked back into operation with little trouble.

The 'marooned ship' I'd spotted from the road proved to be a leaching plant, its smokestack doubling up as a mast. Pierced by bullet holes, presumably from a spot of target practice, the rusted corrugated-iron walls creaked and groaned in the wind. As I watched, an errant board flew off the roof. There was still a distinct smell of iodine—a by-product of the nitrate-refining process—giving the sense that it was a kind of steampunk hospital.

As we explored the site, I asked Jaime about the War of the Pacific. 'Many English people fought with us in the war—they helped to sink the Peruvian ship that came to rescue their city,' he said, adjusting the ear flaps of his cap. But, he continued, the conflict was really about Britain. 'The Bolivians, Chileans and Peruvians just provided the soldiers.' Over the years, I've spent a lot of time in Bolivia, and feelings still run high—to put it mildly—over the loss of the mineral-rich coastline in conflict. Jaime wasn't impressed:

> Bolivia—blah, blah, blah—they signed the agreement after they lost the war. Then they went to The Hague to try and get access to the sea, and they didn't like what was decided, and so they went back again. A few years ago a US diplomat came over and said we should give Bolivia back some of its land. We said, when you give Texas back to Mexico, we'll give the land back to Bolivia.

* * *

GHOST TOWNS

Beyond the scarred landscape and redrawn borders, the nitrate industry left an enduring legacy in Chile. The protests, strikes and uprisings of its workers—including the creation of a short-lived 'anarchist republic' at the nitrate town of La Coruña, which came to a bloody end at the hands of the army—helped to lay the foundations for the country's trade union movement and left-wing political parties. But the response of successive governments to calls for social justice and progressive reforms—particularly the use of the military to crack down on dissent—also created a template. As historian Michael Monteón argued in *Chile in the Nitrate Era*, the 'nitrate era is, therefore, the precursor of the modern Chilean state and contemporary forms of repression'.

The Atacama remained a lawless zone for much of the twentieth century. Previously, Chilean parents had evoked the spectre of British pirates to scare their children into behaving. After the collapse of the nitrate industry, the isolated port of Pisagua took their place. Far-right governments, presidents and dictators turned the former boomtown into a concentration camp. Gay men were sent here in the late 1920s by the Carlos Ibáñez del Campo dictatorship, followed by interned citizens of Axis nations when Chile entered the Second World War on the side of the Allies. In the late 1940s, overseen by a young Augusto Pinochet, then an army captain, Pisagua was used to detain around 500 socialists, communists and anarchists.

After rising to power in a military coup in 1973, Pinochet used the town as a concentration camp for some 800 political dissidents, who faced horrific conditions, torture—reportedly at the hands of a notorious Nazi fugitive, Walther Rauff—and often summary execution. A mass grave containing twenty bodies was discovered here in 1990. Other nitrate towns were also used as detention and torture camps under Pinochet, including Chacabuco, which had been named a heritage site by Allende. Under Pinochet, Chacabuco was used to detain 2,000 political prisoners at a time—including children—surrounded by electric fences and enduring horrific treatment. Elsewhere in the nitrate *pampa*, the armed forces used the abandoned towns and towering slag heaps for target practice and military drills.

Pinochet himself had close ties to Britain. As files declassified in 2020 revealed, the Foreign Office's secretive Information Research Department (IRD) sought to protect what it considered to be 'British interests' in Chile during the 1960s and '70s. After failing to prevent the election of Allende—over fears he would 'be manoeuvred by the communists, either willingly or otherwise, and that the end-product might well be a Government on the Cuban pattern'—it conducted a propaganda campaign to damage and discredit his presidency while legitimising and boosting his opponents.

The IRD's actions were part of a widespread British programme of covert activity in South America during the Cold War that aimed to disrupt trade unions and left-wing parties, shape media coverage and distribute propaganda, as well as influence elections and prop up right-wing dictators. This included teaching members of Brazil's 1964–85 military dictatorship the 'English System' of interrogation. During twenty hours of testimony to Brazil's Truth Commission in 2014, one of the regime's most notorious torturers, Colonel Paulo Malhães, explained that he was taught 'interrogation techniques that didn't leave physical marks' in Britain, the BBC reported. Britain, he told prosecutor Nadine Borges, was 'the best place to learn' psychological torture. (Shortly after testifying, Malhães was killed during a burglary at his home.)

In 1973, the Conservative government of Edward Heath welcomed the Pinochet coup, with Foreign Secretary Alec Douglas-Home writing: 'For British interests ... there is no doubt that Chile under the junta is a better prospect than Allende's chaotic road to socialism, our investments should do better, our loans may be successfully rescheduled, and export credits later resumed.' Pinochet became a close ally of Margaret Thatcher, allowing a British surveillance team to use a Chilean military base in Punta Arenas to monitor Argentine air force operations during the Falklands War while also supplying crucial intelligence reports. Under his catastrophic rule, Chile was also a testing ground for the debilitating free market, untrammelled deregulation and swingeing privatisation policies to which Thatcher also subscribed.

Despite government opposition, around 2,500 Chileans fleeing persecution came to the UK as refugees. They were supported by a powerful solidarity movement led by British left-wing politicians, academics, activists and trade unionists. In East Kilbride, for example, workers at the town's Rolls-Royce plant took a stand and refused to repair the engines of Chilean Hawker Hunters—which had been used to bomb Allende's presidential palace in Santiago during the coup—essentially grounding Pinochet's air force. 'Dictatorship was a red flag to a bull with me. It still is,' said engineer Bob Fulton, who participated in the solidarity action, in the 2018 documentary *Nae Pasaran*.

In 1998, eight years after the end of his dictatorship, Pinochet was arrested in London for crimes against humanity on the basis of an international warrant issued by Spanish judge Baltasar Garzón. He was supported by Thatcher, who claimed Britain owed the dictator a debt of gratitude for his help during the Falklands War. Despite the British courts dismissing Pinochet's claim for immunity, Home Secretary Jack Straw controversially allowed him to return home due to ill health—after 503 days under house arrest—in the face of fierce domestic and international opposition.

* * *

We drove on to Humberstone, which was larger and more extensively restored than Santa Laura. Originally known as La Palma, the town was founded in 1872 by a nitrate firm set up by James Thomas Humberstone, an entrepreneur and chemical engineer from Dover, who pioneered the innovative 'Shanks system', which had a major impact on the industry. One of the biggest *oficinas salitreras*, La Palma passed through several foreign owners before being taken over by the Chilean government, which renamed it Humberstone in 1932. At its height, the town had a population of some 3,500. 'Though it had the capacity for twice that number. The industry was collapsing in the 1930s and the government just wanted to give people jobs,' said Jaime.

Much of the surviving architecture dates from the 1920s and '30s, with a strong Art Deco style. As a result, Humberstone has the vague feel of west coast Americana. Much more so than Santa Laura, it resembled a small but complete city, with tidy rows of prefabricated houses; the size and amenities of each one outlining the rank of the occupant. Some have been turned into mini museums. One of the most evocative was filled with letters that shed light on day-to-day life in the *oficina*: one revealed a 'strike' by housewives who refused to cook for their husbands until they received better quality charcoal for the ovens; another complained about the cost of building a new tennis court.

As well as the homes, there was a host of other buildings, including a hospital, radio station and shops, as well as a main square and market area. The hotel had a restaurant, bar and billiard room; there was a separate entrance at the back for workers, who were forbidden from using the front door, a reminder of the strict hierarchy in place during the tail-end of the nitrate era, even after marginal improvements to employment conditions. There was also a large swimming pool with a diving board, a school with graffiti-covered desks and a clocktower stuck permanently at 4 o'clock. My favourite building was a glorious theatre-cum-cinema, which once screened musical performances and Mexican films. Now hushed, it was supposedly haunted.

GHOST TOWNS

The restoration work was ongoing when I visited, but it already felt as if it had gone too far. The haunting, abandoned character of Santa Laura had been replaced by an ersatz, film set vibe on Humberstone. But when I wandered to the edge of town, beyond the factories, warehouses and a solitary train engine, the desolation returned. The scorching, shadeless desert stretched into the distance, a reminder that despite the ambitions of the nitrate barons, the Atacama remained untamed.

EPILOGUE

OPEN VEINS

It's hard to feel farther away from the Atacama than on a cold, damp mid-winter morning in southeast London. From Falconwood Station, I crossed an overpass and followed a residential road past a cemetery and a string of mock-Tudor homes, one of which had a spindly monkey-puzzle tree (*Araucaria araucana*), an evergreen hailing from southern Chile and Argentina, in the front garden.

As the wind rose and rain began to fall, I reached Avery Hill Park, a sweep of green with a playground, café, basketball court and football and cricket pitches. There was a handful of dog-walkers and a few parents with pushchairs. Parakeet screeches intermingled with the roar of a tree surgeon's chainsaw. The only anomaly was a huge Victorian hothouse at the northern edge of the park, which lies in the borough of Greenwich. Topped with a statue of Mercury—the Roman god of merchants and travellers, as well as tricksters and thieves—the domed conservatory was showing its age. The glass was clouded, fingers of moss clasped the red-brick walls, and the tropical room was temporarily closed.

Inside, a gardener coiled up a hosepipe while listening to Classic FM, the broadcast interrupted by a weather forecast warning of impending gales and potential flooding. The centrepiece of the main room, the temperate house, was an impressive Canary Island date palm whose fronds brushed the ceiling. Cacti, succulents, pines, rubber plants and agaves from countries such as Chile, Bolivia and Peru, as well as Japan, Mexico, Australia and South Africa, filled the surrounding beds. I was visiting at the wrong time of year, the gardener explained, advising me to return in the spring when the bird of paradise plant's brilliant orange and neon-blue flowers emerge and the water lilies begin to bloom.

The adjoining room had a pond with cream-and-grey koi carp and a marble statue of a sea nymph reclining nude on a snub-nosed fish. At the side, propped up behind a bench, was a cardboard cut-out of a portly man, extravagantly bewhiskered and equipped with a plumed hat, red ceremonial jacket and sword: the Nitrate King.

* * *

During the reign of Queen Elizabeth I, the Avery Hill site was owned by the mistress of the royal laundry. Two centuries later, it came into the possession of a wealthy Scottish sugar refiner. John Thomas North bought the estate in 1888 and spent £200,000 of his nitrate fortune on expanding and improving the mansion and its grounds. This included constructing an elaborate 'winter garden'—inspired by the Crystal Palace, which hosted the 1851 Great Exhibition—and filling it with exotic specimens from across the globe so that his family had somewhere pleasant to relax during 'inclement weather'.

His efforts were not to everyone's taste, with a waspish *New York Times* journalist writing:

> Avery Hill is glaringly new. There are 600 acres, 30 of which are covered by the swelling house, conservatories, stables, and kennels. The floor of the palace is tesselated in colored marble. There is a hall of statues, another of pictures, another of Mexican onyx columns.

EPILOGUE

> The dining room is ornamented with sporting trophies, the bedrooms are luxurious, the bath Turkish, the light electric. There are prizewinners in the stables ... [and] Russian hounds which were a present from the Grand Duke Alexis.

North—who alongside his South American empire invested heavily in a rubber company in King Leopold II of Belgium's Congo Free State colony, whose resources were plundered through 'genocidal exploitation', to quote Anti-Slavery International—didn't have much time to enjoy Avery Hill. After losing a parliamentary election as a Conservative candidate, he died suddenly in his City of London office on 5 May 1896. It was likely the result of heart problems, though a *New York Times* obituary noted that he was 'seized with illness after eating oysters and died within half an hour'.

North's family eventually sold Avery Hill for a mere £40,000 to a prominent psychiatrist, but the estate remained unoccupied until 1902, when it was purchased by London County Council and turned into a public park. The Turkish bath was destroyed during the Blitz, but the mansion survived, was later used as a teacher training college and is now part of a University of Greenwich campus. At the time of writing, there are controversial plans to turn the building into a boys' school.

The winter garden has survived too, just. Grade II-listed, the structure is the second biggest glasshouse in the UK after its counterpart at Kew Gardens, but it is in desperate need of restoration and sits on Historic England's 'Heritage at Risk' register.

* * *

There are ghosts from Britain's lost history in Argentina, Chile and Uruguay scattered across South London. With a morning to spare, you could visit the *James Caird*, the lifeboat that carried Shackleton to safety on South Georgia, in Dulwich College, paintings of whaling ships and guano vessels in the National

SMALL EARTHQUAKES

Maritime Museum in Greenwich, and Hither Green's Manor House Library, formerly owned by the Baring banking family, whose fortunes were once intertwined with Buenos Aires. Farther afield, Hoa Hakananai'a remains—for now, at least—in the British Museum, silent and inscrutable, while Valparaíso-based painter Thomas Somerscales' depictions of Chilean naval battles are part of the Tate's collection. A statue of José de San Martín stands alongside fellow *libertador* Simón Bolívar in the leafy surrounds of Belgrave Square, while Thomas Cochrane, their contemporary in Chile, is interred in Westminster Abbey. To the north, in Walthamstow, is St Mary's, the church school attended by Yokcushlu, Orundellico and El'leparu after the trio were kidnapped from their home in Tierra del Fuego.

Beyond the capital, Kirkstall Abbey, a ruined Cistercian monastery donated to the city of Leeds by North, is open to the public, as is Tyntesfield, guano tycoon William Gibbs' lavish Victorian Neo-Gothic pile near Bristol. The latter is now owned by the National Trust, which, to its credit, has run a 'William Gibbs: Saint or Sinner?' tour, exploring the dubious origins of Gibbs' wealth. If you need sustenance at any point, Fray Bentos products can still be found in most supermarkets.

Moreover, Britain's shared history with Argentina, Chile, Uruguay and the rest of the continent in general continues to develop. South Americans have lived in the UK since the eighteenth century, and they are now part of one of the fastest-growing communities in the country. Studies suggest there are 250,000 people with Latin American heritage in the UK, including 145,000 in London; the true figures are almost certainly higher. Latin Americans 'remain one of the most invisible' groups in the UK, according to Cathy McIlwaine, a professor at King's College London who has carried out extensive research on the subject, not least because of a lack of adequate, up-to-date data.

EPILOGUE

But their profile is rising due to the work of organisations such as the Coalition of Latin Americans in the UK and Let's Talk Latinx, which set up the #StandUptoInvisibility campaign, events such as the Festival of Latin American Women in the Arts (aka FLAWA) and websites like LatinoLife. Colombian-born, London-based artist Oscar Murillo was a joint winner of the Turner Prize in 2019. British-Brazilian author Yara Rodrigues Fowler was named on Granta's Best of Young British Novelists list in 2023. South and Central American cafés and restaurants in Elephant and Castle, the Old Kent Road, Tottenham and beyond serve up empanadas, *cazuelas*, ceviche and steaks. Argentine and Uruguayan footballers—including Liverpool's World Cup-winning midfielder Alexis Mac Allister, whose family has Irish and Scottish roots—star in the Premier League.

And while the nitrate, guano, whaling and sheep-ranching booms have long passed, another natural resource in northern Chile, northwest Argentina and southwest Bolivia is now attracting fevered international attention. The giant, high-altitude salt flats of the 'Lithium Triangle' are home to an estimated 75 per cent of the ultra-light metal that powers the digital age, a vital component for the rechargeable batteries in our phones, laptops and electric cars. A 'white gold' rush is underway, evoking hopes, fears and echoes from the past.

'History never really says goodbye,' the late Uruguayan writer Eduardo Hughes Galeano told an interviewer in 2013. 'History says, see you later.'

LIST OF ILLUSTRATIONS

1. The Palace of Running Waters, Buenos Aires.
2. The Torre Monumental (aka the Torre de los Ingleses), Buenos Aires.
3. Street art in the Ciudad Vieja, Montevideo.
4. The electricity switchboard of the former meatpacking plant at Fray Bentos.
5. The caves that sheltered the first Welsh settlers in Patagonia, Puerto Madryn.
6. Ty Nain, a Welsh Patagonian tearoom in Gaiman.
7. The prow of the *Yelcho* and a statue of Captain Luis Pardo—who rescued Ernest Shackleton's stranded crew—on the waterfront in Punta Arenas.
8. Parque Nacional Torres del Paine, Patagonia.
9. King penguins on a beach in South Georgia.
10. The rusting whaling station at Grytviken, South Georgia.
11. A view of the Beagle Channel from Isla Navarino, Tierra del Fuego.
12. Estancia Harberton, the oldest ranch in Tierra del Fuego.
13. The view from the ruins of Orongo to the islets of Motu Nui and Motu Iti, Rapa Nui.
14. The *moai* of Tahai, Rapa Nui.
15. Colourful houses in the port-city of Valparaíso.

LIST OF ILLUSTRATIONS

16. The crumbling nitrate town of Santa Laura in the Atacama.
17. Humberstone, the best-preserved nitrate town in the Atacama.
18. Nitrate King John Thomas North's glasshouse in Avery Hill Park, London.

All photos © Shafik Meghji.

SELECT BIBLIOGRAPHY

Preface: 'Not Many Dead'

Cockburn, Claud, *In Time of Trouble: An Autobiography*, London: R. Hart-Davies, 1956.

Graham-Yooll, Andrew, 'A Little History of the Buenos Aires Herald: Pâté, Brandy and Bomb Threats', *Buenos Aires Times*, 03/08/19.

Thomson, Hugh, 'Andrew Graham-Yooll Obituary', *The Guardian*, 18/07/19.

1. Forgotten Colony: Buenos Aires

'5 de julio: La Defensa de Buenos Aires', Ministerio de Defensa, https://www.argentina.gob.ar/noticias/5-de-julio-la-defensa-de-buenos-aires

'150th Anniversary of Welsh Voyage to Patagonia', ITV News, 30/05/15.

'Argentina Profile: Timeline', BBC News, 05/11/19, https://www.bbc.co.uk/news/world-latin-america-18712378

An Authentic Narrative of the Proceedings of the Expedition under the Command of Brigadier-Gen. Craufurd, until Its Arrival at Monte Video; With an Account of the Operations against Buenos Aires under the Command of Lieut.-Gen. Whitelocke, London: n.p., 1808.

Baldock, Hannah, 'The "Other" Harrods Shows Argentina is in Recovery', *The Independent*, 14/06/03.

Baring Archive, 'A Brief History of Barings', https://baringarchive.org.uk/history/a-brief-history-of-barings/

Bayarri, Gabriel, 'Uki Goñi: Racism Persists in Argentina; Interview with

SELECT BIBLIOGRAPHY

the Author Highlights Concerns about the Rise of the Right', Latin America Bureau, 17/08/23.

Blanchard, Peter, 'An Institution Defended: Slavery and the English Invasions of Buenos Aires in 1806–1807', *Slavery & Abolition: A Journal of Slave and Post-Slave Studies* 35, no. 2 (2014): 253–72.

Borges, Jorge Luis, 'Autobiographical Notes', *New Yorker*, 11/09/70.

'Buenos Aires: Thousands Protest against Education Cuts', BBC News, 24/04/24, https://www.bbc.co.uk/news/world-latin-america-68886411

Caddick-Adams, Peter, 'Britain's "Forgotten" Invasion of Argentina', BBC News, 10/08/06, http://news.bbc.co.uk/1/hi/magazine/4779479.stm

Centenera, Mar, 'Argentina Gripped by One of the Largest Protests in 20 Years: "Public education is an inalienable right"', *El País*, 24/04/24.

Dema, Verónica, 'Descubrí el exclusivo barrio inglés escondido en Caballito', *La Nacion*, 01/11/13.

Droller, Federico, Martín Fiszbein and Santiago Pérez, 'The Age of Mass Migration in Argentina: Social Mobility, Effects on Growth, and Selection Patterns', National Bureau of Economic Research, 02/08/22, https://www.nber.org/papers/w31448

'Ellis Island', The Statue of Liberty–Ellis Island Foundation, https://www.statueofliberty.org

Estrada, Ezequiel Martínez, *X-Ray of the Pampa*, Austin: University of Texas Press, 1971.

Farrell, Joe, 'An Adventurer Worth Remembering', Historic Environment Scotland, 17/01/18, https://blog.historicenvironment.scot/2018/01/adventurer-worth-remembering/

Fay, Stephen, *The Collapse of Barings*, New York: W.W. Norton, 1997.

Ferns, H.S., 'The Baring Crisis Revisited', *Journal of Latin American Studies* 24, no. 2 (May 1992): 241–73.

——— *Britain and Argentina in the Nineteenth Century*, Oxford: Clarendon Press, 1960.

Friends of Manor House Gardens, 'About the Gardens', www.friendsofmanorhousegardens.com

Ghosh, Palash, 'Blackout: How Argentina "Eliminated" Africans from Its History and Conscience', International Business Times, 06/04/13.

Goñi, Uki, 'The Hidden History of Black Argentina', *New York Review of Books*, 08/02/21.

SELECT BIBLIOGRAPHY

—— 'Legendary Buenos Aires Cafe to Make Way for Nike Shop', *The Guardian*, 21/08/11.

Graham-Yooll, Andrew, *The Forgotten Colony: A History of the English Speaking People in Argentina*, Buenos Aires: LOLA, 1999.

'La historia de Frank Brown: El payaso angloargentino dueño de uno de los circos más espectaculares de América', *La Nacion*, 06/05/17.

'Inmigracion 1857–1920', Dirección Nacional de Migraciones, https://www.migraciones.gov.ar/pdf/museo/inmigracion1857-1920.pdf

'IOM Migration Profile for Argentina Reveals a Country in Search of New Horizons', IOM, 10/08/09.

Jauncey, James, *Don Roberto: The Adventure of Being Cunninghame Graham*, n.p.: Scotland Street Press, 2023.

Jemio, Diego, 'Cecilia Grierson: A Scottish Descendant Who Was a Pioneer in Argentina', *The National*, 14/12/08.

Kaplan, Paul D., 'What Prior Market Crashes Taught Us in 2020', *Morningstar*, 23/07/20.

King, John, 'Civilisation and Barbarism: The Impact of Europe on Argentina', *History Today*, 08/08/84.

Lopez, Jonathan, 'Argentina's Inflation up to 288% in March, but Central Bank Cuts Rates on "Pronounced Slowdown"', Independent Commodity Intelligence Service, 12/04/24.

López, Mario Justo, Jorge E. Waddell and Juan Pablo Martínez, *A History of the Railways in Argentina: Railway Policies between 1857 and 2015*, trans. Paddy Farrell, Carapachay: Lenguaje Claro Editora, 2023.

'The Making of a President: Javier Milei's Life before Politics', *Buenos Aires Times*, 21/11/23.

Martínez, Tomás Eloy, *Santa Evita*, New York: Doubleday, 1997.

McGill, Sean, 'The Edinburgh Teacher Who Introduced Football to Argentina in the 1800s', Edinburgh Live, 19/12/22.

Meter, Alejandro, 'Argentina in the Era of Mass Immigration', Oxford Bibliographies, *Latin American Studies*, June 2014.

'Milei Says He'll Privatize Argentina's Train Service if Elected President', *Buenos Aires Herald*, 18/10/23.

Mitten, Andy, 'Meet David Olaoye, the First English Professional to Play in Argentina', ESPN, 06/12/17, https://www.espn.co.uk/football/story/_/id/37487751/david-olaoye-english-professional-play-argentina

SELECT BIBLIOGRAPHY

Morrone, Beatriz, *Cecilia Grierson: Soy una obrera del pensamiento*, n.p.: UNLP, 2018.

Muro, Valentín, 'Meet the Argentine Songwriter Who Defied Dictatorship with Children's Songs', Culture Trip, 04/03/20.

Novillo-Corvalán, Patricia, 'Juan Filloy's Caterva and the Geopolitics of the Joycean Novel in Argentina', *Textual Practice* 36, no. 2 (2022).

Petroni, Agostino, 'Chimichurri: The Argentinian Sauce Eaten as a Ritual', BBC Travel, 01/06/21, https://www.bbc.co.uk/travel/article/20210531-chimichurri-the-argentinian-sauce-eaten-as-a-ritual

Platt, D.C.M., 'Foreign Finance in Argentina for the First Half-Century of Independence', *Journal of Latin American Studies* 15, no. 1 (1983): 23–47.

Rock, David, *The British in Argentina: Commerce, Settlers & Power 1800–2000*, Basingstoke: Palgrave Macmillan, 2019.

Shaxson, Nicholas, *Treasure Islands: Tax Havens and the Men who Stole the World*, London: Vintage, 2012.

The South American Handbook 1924 (Replica Edition), n.p.: Footprint, 2014.

'The South Sea Company and the Slave Trade', Curiosity Collections, Harvard Library, https://curiosity.lib.harvard.edu/south-sea-bubble/feature/the-south-sea-company-and-the-slave-trade

'St John the Baptist Anglican Cathedral', Cathedral Anglicana, www.catedralanglicana.org.ar

Stones, H.R., *British Railways in Argentina 1860–1948*, Bromley: P.E. Waters, 1993.

'Stories of Homecoming: We're on the March with Argentina's Scots', *The Scotsman*, 14/12/08.

Weightman, Brian, 'A Tainted Inheritance', Glasgow Life, 14/06/23.

'What Was the South Sea Bubble?', Royal Museums Greenwich, https://www.rmg.co.uk/stories/topics/south-sea-bubble#:~:text=The%20South%20Sea%20Bubble%20was,in%20Central%20and%20Southern%20America

Wilson, Jonathan, *Angels with Dirty Faces: The Footballing History of Argentina*, London: Orion, 2016.

'Women and Independence in Latin America: An Exploration of Women's Involvement in the Latin American Wars of Independence', University of Nottingham, https://www.nottingham.ac.uk/GenderLatam/?lang=en&linkID=110

2. Everything but the Moo: Uruguay

Barnett, Tracy L., 'Moira Millán: "A telluric movement is awakening the women of the earth"', Esperanza Project, 03/12/21.

Brummer, Alex and Stuart Millar, 'Heirs and Disgraces', *The Guardian*, 11/08/99.

Campomar, Andreas, *¡Golazo! A History of Latin American Football*, n.p.: Riverrun, 2015.

Cannon, Geoffrey, 'Latin Titan. Eduardo Galeano', ResearchGate, May 2015, https://www.researchgate.net/publication/326763647_Latin_titan_Eduardo_Galeano

Cansler, Clay, 'Where's the Beef?', *Distillations Magazine*, 14/12/13, https://www.sciencehistory.org/stories/magazine/wheres-the-beef/

Clubbe, Dan, 'The "Other" Liverpool FC: They Won the League in 2020 but Play in Blue!', This Is Anfield, 27/03/22, https://www.thisisanfield.com/2022/03/meet-the-other-liverpool-fc-who-play-in-blue/

Da Cruz, Martin, *From Beauty to Duty: A Footballing History of Uruguay 1878–1917*, Brighton: Pitch Publishing, 2022.

'Edmund Vestey', *The Herald*, 13/12/07.

Galeano, Eduardo, *Open Veins of Latin America: Five Centuries of the Pillage of a Continent*, London: Serpent's Tail, 2009.

Goedecke, Catharina, 'Justus von Liebig: Great Teacher and Pioneer in Organic Chemistry and Agrochemistry', Chemistry Views, 01/05/23, https://www.chemistryviews.org/justus-von-liebig-great-teacher-and-pioneer-in-organic-chemistry-and-agrochemistry/

Graham-Yooll, Andrew, *Uruguay: A Travel and Literary Companion*, Buenos Aires: LOLA, 2008.

Harford, Tim, 'How Formula Milk Shaped the Modern Workplace', BBC News, 24/07/17, https://www.bbc.co.uk/news/business-40281403#:-:text=The%20appeal%20of%20formula%20quickly,now%20shapes%20the%20modern%20workplace

Hayward, Tim, 'A Unified Theory of Corned Beef', *Financial Times*, 18/04/20.

SELECT BIBLIOGRAPHY

'História del Pueblo', Villa General Belgrano: El Destino Que Queremos, https://villageneralbelgrano.gob.ar/historia-del-pueblo/

Hudson, W.H., *The Purple Land, Being One Richard Lamb's Adventures in the Banda Oriental, in South America, as Told by Himself*, Berkeley: Creative Arts Book Company, 1979.

'Interview: Cold War Steve', Thames & Hudson, 09/05/19, https://thamesandhudson.com/news/interview-cold-war-steves-festival-of-brexit/

Kirkbride, Phil, 'Everton Announce New Deal that Includes Talent Identification and Pre-season Opportunities', *Liverpool Echo*, 09/10/20.

Knightly, Phillip, *The Rise and Fall of the House of Vestey: The True Story of How Britain's Richest Family Beat the Taxman—And Came to Grief*, London: Warner, 1993.

Montevideo Cricket Club website, www.mvcc.com.uy

Nicholls, Andy, 'The Incredible Story of Tank "Fray Bentos" Is Being Told at the Tank Museum', *Bournemouth Echo*, 22/08/17.

'The Oldest Rugby Club in the Americas Turns 162', Americas Rugby News, 19/06/23, https://www.americasrugbynews.com/2023/07/19/the-older-rugby-club-in-the-americas-turns-162/#:~:text=The%20oldest%20rugby%20club%20in%20the%20Americas%20turns%20162%20today,first%20rugby%20club%20in%20Uruguay

Rabinowitz, Joel, 'Liverpool Win Another Major Trophy: A Small Club in Uruguay's Love Affair with the Reds', Liverpool.com, 10/09/19, https://www.liverpool.com/liverpool-fc-news/features/liverpool-football-club-montevideo-uruguay-16890801

Russell, Polly, 'The History Cook: Lemco', *Financial Times*, 31/08/12.

'Scottish Influence in Shaping Uruguayan Football', Scottish Football Museum, https://www.scottishfootballmuseum.org.uk/news/scottish-influence-in-shaping-uruguayan-football/#:~:text=Anglo%2DScot%2C%20William%20Leslie%20Poole,first%20football%20club%2C%20in%201891

Sengupta, Arunabha, 'Earlier Meetings between Uruguay and England': Cricket Country, 24/07/14, https://www.cricketcountry.com/articles/earlier-meetings-between-uruguay-and-england-150353/

Shaxson, Nicholas, *Treasure Islands: Tax Havens and the Men Who Stole the World*, London: Vintage, 2012.

SELECT BIBLIOGRAPHY

Tallentire, Mark, 'A Hundred Years on, Everton Face Everton for the First Time', *The Guardian*, 03/08/10.

'What You Need to Know about the Battle of the River Plate', Imperial War Museum, https://www.iwm.org.uk/history/what-you-need-to-know-about-the-battle-of-the-river-plate

3. Y Wladfa: Argentine Patagonia

'El 2,9% de la población en viviendas particulares se reconoció indígena o descendiente de pueblos indígenas': Censo 2022 República Argentina, https://censo.gob.ar/index.php/el-29-de-la-poblacion-en-viviendas-particulares-se-reconocio-indigena-o-descendiente-de-pueblos-indigenas/#:~:text=Este%20valor%20representó%20el%202,Negro%20(6%2C4%25)

Andrews, Evan, '10 Surprising Facts about Magellan's Circumnavigation of the Globe', History.com, 17/10/23, https://www.history.com/news/10-surprising-facts-about-magellans-circumnavigation-of-the-globe

'The Blue Books of 1847', National Library of Wales, https://www.library.wales/discover-learn/digital-exhibitions/printed-material/the-blue-books-of-1847

'Brazil's Welsh Colony Items Online at People's Collection Wales', BBC News, 14/10/15, https://www.bbc.co.uk/news/uk-wales-mid-wales-34526778

Brooks, Walter Ariel, 'The Welsh Language in Patagonia: A Brief History', *Voices Magazine*, 25/10/18.

Davies, Lewis, R. Berwyn Jones et al. 'A Collection of Letters Sent by Some of the Founders of the Welsh Settlement, 1865–6', trans. Emlyn Jones and Sioned Jones, People's Collection Wales, January 2025, https://www.peoplescollection.wales/items/13491#?xywh=-205%2C-56%2C1164%2C1111

Davies, Steph, *Hiraeth: Stories from Welsh Patagonia*, n.p.: Parthian Books, 2015.

Devine, Darren, 'How the Penguin and Dylan Enriched Our Use of English', Wales Online, 01/12/10, https://www.walesonline.co.uk/news/wales-news/how-penguin-dylan-enriched-use-1877886

Drake, Francis, *The World Encompassed by Sir Francis Drake*, London: Nicholas Bourne, 1628.

SELECT BIBLIOGRAPHY

Durrell, Gerald, *The Whispering Land*, New York: Viking Press, 1962.

Dyson, Steph, 'Where Is Patagonia? Everything You Need to Know about Chilean and Argentine Patagonia', Worldly Adventurer, 06/10/23, https://worldlyadventurer.com/where-is-patagonia/

Edmundson, William, *A History of the British Presence in Chile: From Bloody Mary to Charles Darwin and the Decline of British Influence*, Basingstoke: Palgrave Macmillan, 2009.

Falkner, Thomas, *A Description of Patagonia and the Adjoining Parts of South America*, London: C. Pugh, 1774.

Gobat, Michel, 'The Invention of Latin America: A Transnational History of Anti-imperialism, Democracy, and Race', *American Historical Review* 118, no. 5 (December 2013): 1345–75.

Gómez, Leila, 'Moira Millán on Land Struggle and Terricidio', *ASAP Review*, 25/09/23.

Hopcian, Emily, 'Here's Why Patagonia Is a Climber's Paradise', *National Geographic*, 08/03/18, https://www.nationalgeographic.com/adventure/article/patagonia-chile-argentina-climbers-paradise

Jasper, Heather, 'An Unexpected Destination Inspired a Beloved Children's Book', Fodors.com, 25/09/23, https://www.fodors.com/world/south-america/argentina/experiences/news/argentina-inspired-antoine-de-saint-exuperys-classic-book-the-little-prince

Johnson, Ian, 'We Shouldn't Romanticise the Actions of the Welsh Who Colonised Patagonia', *Nation Cymru*, 19/11/20, https://nation.cymru/opinion/we-shouldnt-romanticise-the-actions-of-the-welsh-who-colonised-patagonia/

Langman, Jimmy, 'A New Magazine for Patagonia', *Patagon Journal*, 12/10/09, https://www.patagonjournal.com/index.php?option=com_content&view=article&id=415%3Aa-new-magazine-for-patagonia&catid=60%3Aeditor&Itemid=264&lang=en

Larson, Carolyne R. (ed.), *The Conquest of the Desert: Argentina's Indigenous Peoples and the Battle for History*, Albuquerque: University of New Mexico Press, 2020.

Lublin, Geraldine, *Memoir and Identity in Welsh Patagonia: Voices from a Settler Community in Argentina*, Cardiff: University of Wales Press, 2024.

SELECT BIBLIOGRAPHY

—— 'Welsh Key Words: Gwladfa', *Planet*, https://www.planetmagazine.org.uk/planet-online/240/Geraldine-Lublin

'Manuscripts Relating to Patagonia', National Library of Wales, https://www.library.wales/discover-learn/digital-exhibitions/manuscripts/modern-period/manuscripts-relating-to-patagonia#:-:text=Patagonia%20manuscripts%20by%20theme&text=The%20Library's%20collection%20of%20material,council%2C%20church%20and%20business%20records

Matthews, Abraham, *Hanes y Wladfa Gymreig yn Patagonia*, Aberdare: Mills & Evans, 1894.

Moss, Chris, *Patagonia: A Cultural History*, Oxford: Oxford University Press, 2008.

'Patagonia 150 Years on: A "little Wales beyond Wales"', BBC News, 30/05/15, https://www.bbc.co.uk/news/uk-wales-32919137#:-:text=They%20had%20little%20idea%20of,Mimosa%2C%20would%20be%20arduous%20enough

Pigafetta, Antonio, *The First Voyage around the World 1519–1522: An Account of Magellan's Expedition*, Toronto: University of Toronto Press, 2007.

'Pueblos originarios de Chile: Tehuleche', Museo Chileno de Arte Precolombino, https://precolombino.cl/wp/culturas-americanas/pueblos-originarios-de-chile/tehuelche/

'Report on the Welsh Language Project, Patagonia 2020', British Council, https://wales.britishcouncil.org/sites/default/files/welsh_language_project_report_2020-21.pdf

Rhys, William Casnodyn, *A Welsh Song in Patagonia: Memories of the Welsh Colonization*, n.p.: Lulu, 2005.

Serafini, Paula, 'Moira Millán: Urgent Situation of Indigenous People in Patagonia', Latin America Bureau, 16/04/24, https://lab.org.uk/moira-millan-urgent-situation-of-indigenous-people-in-patagonia/

Simon, Matt, 'Fantastically Wrong: Magellan's Strange Encounter with the 10-Foot Giants of Patagonia', *Wired*, 17/09/14.

Taylor, Lucy, 'Global Perspectives on Welsh Patagonia: The Complexities of Being Both Colonizer and Colonized', *Journal of Global History* 13, no. 3 (2018): 446–68.

SELECT BIBLIOGRAPHY

'The Treachery of the Blue Books', Open University, https://www.open.edu/openlearn/history-the-arts/methodism-wales-17301850/content-section-8

'Voting Paper for an Election Held in the Welsh Settlement in Patagonia, 1876', People's Collection Wales, https://www.peoplescollection.wales/items/8224#?xywh=-9%2C-1%2C855%2C598

'Voyage', Project Hiraeth, www.project-hiraeth.com

Williams, Glyn, 'Welsh Settlers and Native Americans in Patagonia', *Journal of Latin American Studies* 11, no. 1 (1979): 41–66.

4. The Golden Fleece: Chilean Patagonia

'1878 Revolt in a Chilian Penal Settlement', Patagonia Bookshelf, https://patlibros.org/clip/txt/CL033.htm

Aagesan, D., 'Crisis and Conservation at the End of the World: Sheep Ranching in Argentine Patagonia', *Environmental Conservation* 27, no. 2 (2000): 208–15.

Bayer, Osvaldo, *Rebellion in Patagonia*, trans. Paul Sharkey and Joshua Neuhouser, Oakland: AK Press, 2016.

'The British Club, Punta Arenas (1899–1981)', Patagonia Bookshelf, https://patbrit.org/eng/clubs/paclub.htm

'Circuito Antártico de Punta Arenas y El Estrecho de Magallenes', Instituto Antártico Chileno, https://www.inach.cl/wp-content/uploads/2013/04/guia-circuito.pdf

Claro, Hernan, 'Cementerio de Punta Arenas, uno de los más bellos de Chile', Chile.Travel, 06/10/24, https://www.chile.travel/blog/cementerio-municipal-de-punta-arenas-uno-de-los-mas-bellos-de-chile/

Darwin, Charles, *Voyage of the Beagle*, London: Penguin, 1989.

Dixie, Lady Florence, *Across Patagonia*, London: Richard Bentley and Son, 1880.

Edmundson, William, *A History of the British Presence in Chile: From Bloody Mary to Charles Darwin and the Decline of British Influence*, Basingstoke: Palgrave Macmillan, 2009.

Harambour-Ross, Alberto, 'Sheep Sovereignties: The Colonization of the Falkland Islands/Malvinas, Patagonia, and Tierra del Fuego, 1830s–1910s', ResearchGate, September 2016, https://www.researchgate.net/publica-

SELECT BIBLIOGRAPHY

tion/330346742_Sheep_Sovereignties_The_Colonization_of_the_Falkland_IslandsMalvinas_Patagonia_and_Tierra_del_Fuego_1830s-1910s

Keller, Tait, 'The Ecological Edges of Belligerency: Toward a Global Environmental History of the First World War', *Annales: Histoire, sciences sociales* 71, no. 1 (2016): 61–78.

'Lady Florence Dixie (1855–1905)', Humanist Heritage, https://heritage.humanists.uk/lady-florence-dixie/#:~:text=She%20was%20a%20supporter%20of,on%20her%20criticisms%20of%20religion

'Mártires Obreros', Consejos de Monumentales Nacionales de Chile, https://www.monumentos.gob.cl/monumentos/monumentos-publicos/martires-obreros

Mistral, Gabriela, *Desolación*, n.p.: Tor, 1945.

Moss, Chris, *Patagonia: A Cultural History*, Oxford: Oxford University Press, 2008.

'Museum and Private Collection Puerto Bories', The Singular, www.thesingular.com

'Mutiny in Punta Arenas, November 1877', The British Presence in Southern Patagonia, https://patbrit.org/eng/events/pamutiny.htm

'Our History', The Singular, www.thesingular.com

'Patagonian Rebellion Collection', University of Massachusetts Libraries, http://findingaids.library.umass.edu/ead/mums353

'Pueblos originarios de Chile: Tehuelche', Museo de Arte Precolombino, https://precolombino.cl/wp/culturas-americanas/pueblos-originarios-de-chile/tehuelche/

The South American Handbook 1924 (Replica Edition), n.p.: Footprint, 2014.

5. *'Two Bald Men Fighting Over a Comb': Falkland Islands and South Georgia*

Amos, Jonathan, 'South Georgia: Bird Flu Infects Penguins at Famous Wildlife Haven', BBC News, 11/03/24, https://www.bbc.co.uk/news/science-environment-68538190

'Blue Whales Return to South Georgia after Near Extinction', British Antarctic Survey, 19/11/20, https://www.bas.ac.uk/media-post/blue-whales-return-to-south-georgia-after-near-extinction/

SELECT BIBLIOGRAPHY

Bower, Kenneth, 'Resurrection Island', *National Geographic*, December 2009.

Briggs, Johnny, 'Whaling and Seal Hunting Defined South Georgia—but then Crashed', Pew Charitable Trusts, 13/07/17, https://www.pewtrusts.org/en/research-and-analysis/articles/2017/07/13/whaling-and-seal-hunting-defined-south-georgia-but-then-crashed

Brown, Colin and Kim Sengupta, 'Sinking the Belgrano: The Pinochet Connection', *The Independent*, 03/04/12.

Calderan, Susannah V. et al., 'South Georgia Blue Whales Five Decades after the End of Whaling', *Endangered Species Research* 43 (2020): 359–73.

Campbell, Gordon, 'Antonio de la Roche and the Discovery of South Georgia', *Polar Record* 59 (2023): e20.

'Clayton, Samuel Wittewrong', Dictionary of Falklands Biography, https://www.falklandsbiographies.org/biographies/clayton_samuel

Coulthard, Seb, 'Ernest Shackleton: Death or Glory', Ends of the Earth, http://www.ends-of-earth.com/history/death-or-glory/

Darwin, Charles, *Voyage of the Beagle*, London: Penguin, 1989.

'Discovery of the Falkland Islands', Historic Dockyard Museum, https://falklands-museum.com/early-history#:~:text=Discovery%20of%20the%20Falkland%20Islands&text=However%2C%20research%20has%20unearthed%20forgotten,took%20place%20around%201518%2D19

Foley, Tim, *Crean: The Extraordinary Life of an Irish Hero*, Newbridge, Co. Kildare: Merrion Press, 2023.

Giordano, Elena, 'Argentina's Eyes Light Up over Falklands as Britain Gives Away One Overseas Territory', Politico, 04/10/24, https://www.politico.eu/article/argentina-britain-falklands-uk-overseas-territory-chagos-islands/

Hamley, Kit M. et al., 'Evidence of Prehistoric Human Activity in the Falkland Islands', *Science Advances* 7, no. 44 (October 2021).

Holmes, Vera Brown, 'Anglo-Spanish Relations in America in the Closing Years of the Colonial Era (1763–1774)', PhD diss., Bryn Mawr College, 1923.

'Jorge Luis Borges: "Traveling not only in space, but in time"', UPI,

SELECT BIBLIOGRAPHY

14/10/84, https://www.upi.com/Archives/1984/10/14/Jorge-Luis-Borges-Traveling-not-only-in-space-but-in-time/9670466574400/#:-:text=It%20was%20a%20sensation%20of,whenever%20Borges%20speaks%20or%20writes

'Largest Whale', Guinness World Records, https://guinnessworldrecords.com/world-records/69467-largest-whale

Leake, Jonathan, 'Falklands Risks Diplomatic Row with Britain over Plans to Drill Huge Oil Field', *The Telegraph*, 28/09/24.

Nicholson, Adam, 'South Georgia: The Lost Whaling Station at the End of the World', BBC News, 09/06/14, https://www.bbc.co.uk/news/magazine-27734930

'Population Status', International Whaling Commission, https://iwc.int/about-whales/population-status

Sandison, Jon, 'Shetlanders' Role in Shackleton's Funeral', Shetland.org, 18/04/22, https://www.shetland.org/blog/shetlanders-shackletons-funeral

Smith, Lewis, 'The Antarctic Island That's Richer in Biodiversity than the Galapagos', *The Independent*, 27/05/10.

'South Georgia Declared Rodent-Free', South Georgia Heritage Trust, https://sght.org/news/south-georgia-declared-rodent-free/

Stratton, Mark, 'South Georgia: Back from the Brink?', ExplorEarth, 12/12/24, https://explorearth.com/original-stories/story/south-georgia-back-from-the-brink/

'What Is the British Military Presence on the Falkland Islands?', *The National*, 14/06/22.

6. End of the World: Tierra del Fuego

Bridges, Lucas, *Uttermost Part of the Earth: A History of Tierra del Fuego and the Fuegians*, New York: Overlook Press, 2007.

'Colecciones Digitales', Museo Territorial Yagan Usi, https://www.museoyaganusi.gob.cl/colecciones

'Cristina Calderón Was the Only Full-Blooded Member of Her People', *The Economist*, 05/03/22.

Darwin, Charles, *The Descent of Man and Selection in Relation to Sex*, London: John Murray, 1871.

SELECT BIBLIOGRAPHY

——— *Voyage of the Beagle*, London: Penguin, 1989.

Drake, Francis, *The World Encompassed by Sir Francis Drake*, London: Nicholas Bourne, 1628.

FitzRoy, Robert, Philip Parker King and Charles Darwin, *Narrative of the Surveying Voyages of His Majesty's Ships Adventure and Beagle, between the Years 1826 and 1836*, London: Henry Colburn, 1838.

Freeman, Kelsey, 'Supporting Indigenous Self-determination through Collective Memory', Knight-Hennessy Scholars Stanford University, 23/07/24, https://knight-hennessy.stanford.edu/news/supporting-indigenous-self-determination-through-collective-memory

Gilliland, Haley Cohen, 'Argentina Brought Beavers to Tierra del Fuego: It Was Not a Good Idea', *National Geographic*, 25/06/19.

Gusinde, Martín, *The Lost Tribes of Tierra del Fuego: Selk'nam, Yamana, Kawésqar*, London: Thames & Hudson, 2015.

Hazlewood, Nick, *Savage: The Life and Times of Jemmy Button*, London: Sceptre, 2000.

'The History of Tierra del Fuego', Estancia Harberton, www.estanciaharberton.com

Isabella, Jude, 'The Rise of the Yaghan, Indigenous People of Tierra del Fuego Once Declared "Extinct"', Atlas Obscura, 21/02/23, https://www.atlasobscura.com/articles/yaghan-indigenous-tierra-del-fuego

Marsh, John W. and W.H. Stirling, *The Story of Commander Allen Gardiner, R.N., with Sketches of Missionary Work in South America*, London: James Nisbet, 1883.

Mason, Peter and Christian Báez Allende, 'In Heavy Chains like Bengal Tigers: Native Peoples of Tierra del Fuego on Show in London in 1889', Academia.edu, 2005, https://www.academia.edu/43161147/In_heavy_chains_like_Bengal_tigers_Native_peoples_of_Tierra_del_Fuego_on_show_in_London_in_1889

Molina, Federico Rivas, 'Cristina Calderón, Last Speaker of Yaghan Language, Dies in Chile at 93', *El País*, 18/02/22.

'Palabras de nuestro equipo', Hach Saye, www.hachsaye.com

Pennock, Caroline Dodds, *On Savage Shores: How Indigenous Americans Discovered Europe*, London: Weidenfeld & Nicolson, 2023.

Pimenta, Marcio, Nina Radovic Fanta and Caio Barretto Briso, '"We are alive and we are here": Chile's Lost Tribe Celebrates Long-Awaited Recognition', *The Guardian*, 03/10/23.

Seguel, Alfredo, 'The Selknam Are Still Alive', trans. Robert Lae Wild, *Patagon Journal*, 02/07/20, https://www.patagonjournal.com/index.php?option=com_content&view=article&id=4278:el-pueblo-selkanam-sigue-vivo&catid=197:cultura&Itemid=340&lang=en

Snow, William Parker, *A Two Years' Cruise off Tierra del Fuego, the Falkland Islands, Patagonia and in the River Plate*, London: Longman, 1857.

Wilbert, Johannes (ed.), *Folk Literature of the Selknam Indians: Martin Gusinde's Collection of Selknam Narratives*, UCLA Latin American Studies Series, Berkeley: University of California Press, 1975.

Zárraga, Cristina, *Cristina Calderón: Memories of My Yagan Grandmother*, n.p.: Oliver Vogel Ediciones, 2017.

7. Stolen Friend: Rapa Nui

Bartlett, John, '"Stolen friend": Rapa Nui Seek Return of Moai Statue', BBC News, 18/11/18, https://www.bbc.co.uk/news/world-latin-america-46222276

Davis, Dylan S., Robert J. Dinapoli, Gina Pakarati, Terry L. Hunt and Carl P. Lipo, 'Island-Wide Characterization of Agricultural Production Challenges the Demographic Collapse Hypothesis for Rapa Nui (Easter Island)', *Science Advances* 10, no. 25 (June 2024).

Delsing, Riet, 'Issues of Land and Sovereignty: The Uneasy Relationship between Chile and Rapa Nui', in Florencia E. Mallon (ed.), *Decolonizing Native Histories*, Durham, NC: Duke University Press, 2012.

Diamond, Jared, *Guns, Germs, and Steel: A Short History of Everybody for the Last 13,000 Years*, London: Vintage, 1998.

Edmundson, William, *A History of the British Presence in Chile: From Bloody Mary to Charles Darwin and the Decline of British Influence*, Basingstoke: Palgrave Macmillan, 2009.

Grant-Peterkin, James, *A Companion to Easter Island*, n.p.: Chilena del Libro, 2023.

Guy, Jack, 'Activists Bombard British Museum's Social Media with Calls for Return of Easter Island Statue', CNN, 19/02/24, https://www.cnn.

com/2024/02/19/style/british-museum-easter-island-statue-scli-intl-gbr/index.html

Hitorangi, Marisol, 'Fighting for Survival on Easter Island', Cultural Survival, 19/08/13, https://www.culturalsurvival.org/news/fighting-survival-easter-island

'January–March 1774', Captain Cook Society, https://www.captaincooksociety.com/cooks-voyages/second-pacific-voyage/january-march-1774

Jarman, Cat, 'What Happened to the People of Rapa Nui?', History Extra, 29/03/22, https://www.historyextra.com/period/medieval/rapa-nui-people-what-happened/

Kaeppler, Adrienne L. and Jo Anne Van Tilburg, *The Iconic Tattooed Man of Easter Island*, Rapa Nui: Floating World Editions, 2019.

Larsson, Naomi, 'The Struggle for Freedom on Rapa Nui', Toward Freedom, 07/10/20, https://towardfreedom.org/story/the-struggle-for-freedom-on-rapa-nui/

Long, Gideon, 'WW1 Coronel: An Unlikely Naval Battle Remembered', BBC News, 01/11/14, https://www.bbc.co.uk/news/world-latin-america-29857302

Marley, Jack Elliot, 'Easter Island Votes for World's Newest Marine Reserve', Mongabay, 27/02/18, https://news.mongabay.com/2018/02/easter-island-votes-for-worlds-newest-marine-reserve/

Melville, Herman, *Omoo: A Narrative of Adventures in the South Seas*, London: Penguin Classics, 2007.

'Moai', British Museum, https://www.britishmuseum.org/about-us/british-museum-story/contested-objects-collection/moai

Moreno-Mayar, J. Víctor et al., 'Ancient Rapanui Genomes Reveal Resilience and Pre-European Contact with the Americas', *Nature* 633 (2024): 389–97.

Pakarati, Cristián Moreno and Miguel Fuentes, 'Towards a Characterization of Colonial Power on Rapa Nui', *Rapa Nui Journal* 27, no. 1 (2013).

Peel, Michael, '"Ecocide" Did Not Kill Remote Pacific Islanders, DNA Analysis Finds', *Financial Times*, 11/09/24.

Rauen, Alexia, 'Limiting Migration to Rapa Nui', Council on Hemispheric Affairs, 23/05/17, https://coha.org/limiting-migration-to-rapa-nui/

'Rongorongo', British Museum, https://www.britishmuseum.org/collection/object/E_Oc1981-Q-1642

SELECT BIBLIOGRAPHY

Scoresby Routledge, Katherine, *The Mystery of Easter Island*, London: Hazell, Watson and Viney, 1920.

Seward, Pablo Howard, 'Between "Easter Island" and "Rapa Nui": The Making and the Unmaking of an Uncanny Lifeworld', *Berkeley Undergraduate Journal* 27, no. 2 (2014).

8. Jewel of the Pacific: Valparaíso

'The British and Chile's Opening to the World by David Woods', Anglo-Chilean Society, https://www.anglochileansociety.org/single-post/the-british-and-chile-s-opening-to-the-world-by-david-woods

Burrows, Isabelle, 'Narratives of Empire: Cultural Colonialism in Maria Graham's "Journal of a Residence in Chile during the Year 1822"', Women's Print History Project, 13/08/21, https://womensprinthistory-project.com/blog/post/83

Canales, Katy, 'Maria Graham: Trailblazer and Peepshow Maker', V&A, 18/01/17, https://www.vam.ac.uk/blog/museum-of-childhood/maria-graham-trailblazer-and-peepshow-maker?srsltid=AfmBOooNYxk2Giz713ieOpSMFblIwdDdX0-C8XvnA-H43j4fh8fLpJxX

Cochrane, Thomas, *The Autobiography of a Seaman*, London: Richard Bentley, 1861.

Edmundson, William, *A History of the British Presence in Chile: From Bloody Mary to Charles Darwin and the Decline of British Influence*, Basingstoke: Palgrave Macmillan, 2009.

Edwards, Nick, Anna Kaminski, Shafik Meghji and Sorrel Moseley-Williams, *The Rough Guide to Chile & Easter Island*, London: Rough Guides, 2018.

Graham, Maria, *Journal of a Residence in Chile, during the Year 1822*, London: Longman, Hurst, Rees, Orme, Brown and Green, 1824.

Haigh, Samuel, *Sketches of Buenos Ayres and Chile*, London: James Carpenter and Son, 1829.

Howe, Bea, *Child in Chile*, London: Andre Deutsch, 1957.

Latrille, Jorge, 'Mitos porteños: El tesoro de Sir Francis Drake', Orgullo Porteño, 08/02/18, https://orgulloporteno.cl/2018/02/mitos-portenos-el-tesoro-de-sir-francis-drake/

Long, Gideon, 'Pablo Neruda: Chilean Poet's Death Still Shrouded in

SELECT BIBLIOGRAPHY

Mystery', BBC News, 24/09/23, https://www.bbc.co.uk/news/world-latin-america-66853120

Long, Jerome, 'Simon Bolivar's Secret Weapon in South America: British Veterans', Historynet.com, 24/05/22, https://www.historynet.com/simon-bolivars-british-soldiers/

Lynch, John, 'Simon Bolivar and the Spanish Revolutions', *History Today*, 07/07/83.

MacDougall, Philip, 'The Valparaiso Incident Reassessed', *Naval History* 21, no. 2 (April 2007).

MacSwan, Angus, 'Seeking the Real "Master and Commander" in Chile', Reuters, 24/10/07, https://www.reuters.com/article/world/seeking-the-real-master-and-commander-in-chile-idUSN15368592/

Miller, John, *Memoirs of General Miller: In the Service of the Republic of Peru, Volume 1*, London: Longman, Hurst, Rees, Orme, Brown and Green, 1829.

Prain, Michelle (ed.), *Legado Británico en Valparaíso/British Legacy in Valparaiso*, Viña del Mar: Universidad Andrés Bello, Instituto Chileno Británico, RiL Editores and British Council, 2010.

Richards, Eric, *Britannia's Children: Emigration from England, Scotland, Wales and Ireland since 1600*, London: Hambledon and London, 2004.

Seminara, Dave, 'Chile through Pablo Neruda's Eyes', BBC, 28/10/14, https://www.bbc.co.uk/travel/article/20141020-chile-through-pablo-nerudas-eyes

'Thomas Cochrane', Royal Museums Greenwich, https://www.rmg.co.uk/stories/topics/thomas-cochrane

9. Ghost Towns: Atacama

'110 Years Ago: Massacre at Santa Maria School in Chile: Commemorate 21 December 1907', Socialist Party, https://www.socialistparty.org.uk/articles/26626/13-12-2017/110-years-ago-massacre-at-santa-maria-school-in-chile-commemorate-21-december-1907/

Bartlett, John, 'In Chile a Language on the Verge of Extinction, Stirs into Life', NPR, 14/10/24, https://www.npr.org/2024/10/14/nx-s1-5148780/chile-lost-language-atacama-desert#:-:text=In%20Chile%20a%20language%20once,stirs%20back%20into%20life%20%3A%20

SELECT BIBLIOGRAPHY

NPR&text=Hourly%20News-,In%20Chile%20a%20language%20once%20declared%20extinct%2C%20stirs%20back%20into,it%20to%20a%20new%20generation

Brown, Colin and Kim Sengupta, 'Sinking the Belgrano: The Pinochet Connection', *The Independent*, 03/04/12.

Buchanan, Emily, 'How the UK Taught Brazil's Dictators Interrogation Techniques', BBC News, 30/05/14, https://www.bbc.co.uk/news/magazine-27625540

'Cementerio Laico de Caldera', Consejo de Monumentales Nacionales de Chile, https://www.monumentos.gob.cl/monumentos/monumentos-historicos/cementerio-laico-caldera

Chambers, Jane, 'Living with the World's Oldest Mummies', BBC News, 25/10/21, https://www.bbc.co.uk/news/world-latin-america-58639748

Corera, Gordon, 'Latin America Politics: UK's 1960s Covert Activity Revealed', BBC News, 11/12/20, https://www.bbc.co.uk/news/world-latin-america-55230503

Darwin, Charles, *Voyage of the Beagle*, London: Penguin, 1989.

De la Vega, Garcilaso, *Royal Commentaries of the Incas*, ed. Alain Gheerbrant, New York: Avon Books, 1961.

'Death of Col J.T. North', *New York Times*, 06/05/1896.

'El día que saquearon y quemaron La Serena: La historia de los piratas en la zona', *El Día*, 09/03/22.

Diaz-Cerda, Veronica, 'General Pinochet Arrest: 20 Years On, Here's How It Changed Global Justice', The Conversation, 15/10/18, https://theconversation.com/general-pinochet-arrest-20-years-on-heres-how-it-changed-global-justice-104806

Edmundson, William, *A History of the British Presence in Chile: From Bloody Mary to Charles Darwin and the Decline of British Influence*, Basingstoke: Palgrave Macmillan, 2009.

Gambone, Larry, *The Libertarian Movement in Chile: Mutualism and Anarcho-syndicalism from 1840 to the Present*, Montreal: Red Lion Press, 1996.

'The Great Peruvian Guano Bonanza: Rise, Fall, and Legacy', Council on Hemispheric Affairs, 13/07/11, https://coha.org/the-great-peruvian-guano-bonanza-rise-fall-and-legacy/

SELECT BIBLIOGRAPHY

Halliday, Stephen, 'Sir Joseph Bazalgette (1819–1891) and the Cleansing of the Victorian Metropolis', Gresham College, 09/10/19, https://www.gresham.ac.uk/watch-now/bazalgette

'In a Nutshell', European Southern Observatory, www.elt.eso.org

Johanson, Mark, *Mars on Earth: Wanderings in the World's Driest Desert*, n.p.: Rocky Mountain Books, 2024.

Long, Gideon, 'Humberstone: A Chilean Ghost Town's English Past', BBC News, 08/02/15, https://www.bbc.co.uk/news/world-latin-america-31090757

Mayo, John, 'A "Company" War? The Antofagasta Nitrate Company and the Outbreak of the War of the Pacific', *Boletín de Estudios Latinoamericanos y del Caribe* 28 (June 1980): 3–11.

McEvoy, Kevin John, 'Before the Rubble: Britain's Secret Propaganda Offensive in Chile (1960–1973)', *Contemporary British History* 35, no. 4 (2021): 597–619.

Monteón, Michael, *Chile in the Nitrate Era: The Evolution of Economic Development, 1880–1950*, Madison, WI: University of Wisconsin Press, 1982.

Neruda, Pablo, *Canto General*, trans. Jack Schmitt, Berkeley: University of California Press, 2000.

O'Brien, Thomas F., 'The Antofagasta Company: A Case Study of Peripheral Capitalism', *Hispanic American Historical Review* 60, no. 1 (1980): 1–31.

O'Sullivan, John, 'Chile's Valuable Role in the Falklands War', *National Review*, 03/04/12.

Russell, William Howard, *A Visit to Chile and the Nitrate Fields of Tarapacá, etc.*, London: J.S. Virtue & Co., 1890.

'The Scots Who Stopped Air Strikes by a Violent Chilean Dictator', BBC Scotland, 20/02/19, https://www.bbc.co.uk/programmes/articles/50CTJnPn0RC2tXg18zfcXxy/the-scots-who-stopped-air-strikes-by-a-violent-chilean-dictator

Trickett, John, 'UK–Chile Relations and 50th Anniversary of Coup in Chile', Hansard, 14/09/23, https://hansard.parliament.uk/commons/2023-09-14/debates/EAB3D0BF-B258-41D2-AA3D-D21B3642EF9F/UK-ChileRelationsAnd50ThAnniversaryOfCoupInChile

SELECT BIBLIOGRAPHY

'Tyntesfield', National Trust, https://www.nationaltrust.org.uk/visit/bath-bristol/tyntesfield

Vergara, Eva, 'Child Victims Are the Forgotten Voices of Chile during the Pinochet Dictatorship from 1973 to 1990', Associated Press, 08/09/23, https://apnews.com/article/chile-pinochet-dictatorship-child-victims-6089cc5e561bc61345b3ff32e0346eb5

Woods, Roberta, *The Chemical Conquistador: Colonel North & His Nitrate Dream House*, n.p.: n.p., 2020.

Epilogue: Open Veins

'Death of Col J.T. North', *New York Times*, 06/05/1896.

McIlwaine, Cathy, 'An Emergent Latin/x London', Latin America Bureau, 09/02/24, https://lab.org.uk/an-emergent-latin-x-london/

McQuade, Aidan, 'Roger Casement, an Anti-Slavery Rebel', Anti-Slavery International, 03/08/16, https://www.antislavery.org/latest/roger-casement-anti-slavery-rebel/

Woods, Roberta, *The Chemical Conquistador: Colonel North & His Nitrate Dream House*, n.p.: n.p., 2020.

Younge, Gary, 'Eduardo Galeano: "My great fear is that we are all suffering from amnesia"', *The Guardian*, 23/07/13.

ACKNOWLEDGEMENTS

A huge thanks to everyone at Hurst for helping to make *Small Earthquakes* a reality, in particular Michael Dwyer for his support and enthusiasm for the proposal; my brilliant editors Alice Clarke and Tim Page, proofreader Laurence Fenton and production director Daisy Leitch; the wonderful Kathleen May, Rubi Kumari, Raminta Uselytė and Jess Winstanley in the sales, marketing and publicity teams; and Dan Mogford for a killer cover design.

Many thanks to everyone in Argentina, Chile, Uruguay, the Falklands, South Georgia, the UK and beyond who spoke to me on and off the record, shared their knowledge, showed me around, gave me lifts, checked arcane facts, sourced obscure publications and indulged my incessant questions.

A particular muchas gracias must go to the following interviewees and guides: the late Andrew Graham-Yooll; John Hunter; Marcelo Huernos; Alvaro Cuenca; Diana Cerilla; Nicolás Cremella; Alejandra Barrios Harmer; Ricardo Muza; Pía Vergara; John Rees; Seb Coulthard, Marty Garwood, Annette Bombosch, Bob Gilmore, Nate Small and the rest of the crew of the *Hebridean Sky*; Phil Middleton; Finlay Raffle; Juan Balda; Abby Goodall; Maurice Van de Maele; James Grant-Peterkin; Cristián Moreno Pakarati; Steven Roger Fischer; Iain Hardy; Janak Jani; and Jaime in the Atacama.

ACKNOWLEDGEMENTS

An additional thanks to John Hunter and James for helping to check the Buenos Aires and Rapa Nui chapters, respectively; to Janak for generously sharing his extensive library of books on Valparaíso's British connections; and to Emlyn Jones for translating some of the source material for the Welsh Patagonia chapter.

Many of the research trips for *Small Earthquakes* were made possible by my editors at Rough Guides, Lonely Planet, *Wanderlust*, *National Geographic Traveller*, BBC Travel, Adventure.com and *Geographical*. A special thanks must go to Lyn Hughes, Georgia Stephens, Ellie Cobb and Meera Dattani, as well as the teams at Journey Latin America and Senderos who provided vital help with contacts and logistics. Thanks also to the Society of Authors and the Authors' Foundation, whose grant made a huge difference during the write-up process.

Above all, I want to thank my brilliant agent Tom Cull for his advice and guidance throughout the process; Jean, Nizar and Nina Meghji for their unfailing encouragement and expert proofreading skills; and Sioned Jones for her constant love and support.

INDEX

ABCC. *See* Argentine-British Community Council (ABCC)
Across Patagonia (Dixie), 107
Adelaide (Queen), 149
Admiral Graf Spee (ship), 45–6, 198
AFA. *See* Argentine Football Association (AFA)
Africans, 7–8, 12, 19, 37, 39
'Age of Mass Migration', 11, 12
Agua y Saneamientos Argentinos (AySA). *See* Buenos Ayres Water Supply & Drainage Co.
Ahu Tongariki, 186
Alberdi, Juan Bautista, 68
All Saints' Day, 99
Allende, Christian Báez, 171–2
Allende, Salvador, 206, 244, 247, 248–9
Almetta, Liliana Ester, 1
Alumni Athletic Club, 29
Amundsen, Roald, 110
Ana Te Pahu, 191
Anderson, Wes, 3
Angels with Dirty Faces (Wilson), 30
Anglo-Argentine Tramways Company, 26
Antofagasta, 234–5, 238
Antony Gibbs & Sons (firm), 192, 214–15, 229, 234–5, 236
Aranco, Nicolás, 50
Arco Británico, 207–8, 211, 223, 240
Ardito, Nélida Beatriz, 1
Argentina, 122, 215, 237, 255–6
  border dispute between Chile and, 180
  Britain influence, 15–16, 17
  British community expansion in, 12
  clash with British forces, 123–4
  fought with British in Falklands, 123–4
  launched Conquest of the Desert, 76–7, 83, 89, 166
  occupied Montevideo, 37
  War of the Triple Alliance, 4

285

INDEX

See also Buenos Aires; Patagonia; South Georgia; Ushuaia
Argentine Confederation, 120
Argentine Football Association (AFA), 29
Argentine-British Community Council (ABCC), 25, 27
Argentines, 12–13, 16, 27, 83, 123–4
Arica, 210, 227
Artuso, Felix, 127
Asia, 94
Atacama Desert, 224, 238, 244, 247, 251
    Chinchorro culture, 226–7
    guano usage, 228–9
    nitrate mining, 234, 239
Aubrey, Jack, 211
Australia, 54, 65, 68, 78, 254
Austria, 4
Autobiography of a Seaman, The (Cochrane), 212
Avenida de Julio, 6–7
Avery Hill, 254–5
avian flu, 133
Aymara (language), 227
Ayrshire, 234

Bachelor's Delight (ship), 188
Bahía Inglesa (beach resort), 233
Bahía Wulaia, 155–6, 160–2
Balmaceda, José Manuel, 241–2
Balvanera, 1, 2
Banco de Londres, 40, 216, 223

Banco del Chubut, 10
Bank of England, 5
Bank of London, 5, 47
Bank of Valparaíso, 216
Baquedano (ship), 196–8
Bar Británico, 24, 25
Bar Inglés, 217–18
Baring Brothers, 4–6
Baring Crisis (Panic), 5–6, 43
Baring, Francis, 4
Baring, Walter, 43
Barrio Inglés, 26–7
BAS. *See* British Antarctic Survey (BAS)
Battle of Coronel (1914), 198
Battle of Passchendaele (1917), 54
Battle of the River Plate (1939), 45, 46, 198
Baxters, 58
Bayer, Osvaldo, 103, 104
Bazalgette, Joseph, 230
BBC (Broadcasting company), 129, 203, 248
Beagle Channel, 141, 147, 150, 154, 155, 178
Belgium, 94, 171, 202
Belgrave Square, 18, 256
Belle Époque, 21
Ben Nevis, 125
Benin Bronzes, 203
Bentham, Jeremy, 10, 172
Bertrab Glacier, 133–4
Bible, 96, 97, 163, 166
Big Ben, 17
Birdsall, Elizabeth, 47

INDEX

Blaenau Ffestiniog, 81
Blaine, James G., 236
Blanco en blanco (film), 179
Blood Wedding (play), 14
Blue Star Line, 54
'Boat Memory', 147, 148
Boca Juniors, 2
Bolívar, Simón, 18, 208, 210, 256
Bolivia, 87, 120, 159, 234, 235, 254
Bombosch, Annette, 133
Borges, Francisco, 31
Borges, Jorge Luis, 22, 31, 81, 123
Borges, Nadine, 248
Boric, Gabriel, 203
Bosch, Carl, 245
Bouwer, Nicholas, 5
Brazil, 41, 54, 212
    conflict between Argentina, Uruguay and, 4
    Graham and Cochrane visit to, 214
    occupied Montevideo, 37–8
    Truth Commission (2014), 248
Brea, Martha María, 1
Bridges, Lucas, 153–4, 167–70, 173–4
Bridges, Thomas, 159, 161, 162, 163–7, 168
Britain, 10, 78, 123–4, 202, 255–6
    Age of Mass Migration, 12–13
    aid to Uruguay, 37–8
    Argentina's connections with, 219
    conflict with Yagán, 143
    Graham moved back to, 19–20
    influence over Argentina, 15–16
    relationship between Buenos Aires and, 7–9
    role in development of Argentine culture, 29–30
    US forces battle with, 212–13
    See also Chile; Montevideo; Royal Navy; Uruguay
British Antarctic Survey (BAS), 126–7, 132
British Association of Magallanes, 96
British Council, 79
British Empire, 66, 67
British in Argentina:, The (Rock), 15
British Library, 178
British Museum, 178, 203
    Hoa Hakananai'a, 185, 186, 201–2, 256
    rongorongo tablets, 187–8
British School of Punta Arenas, 94–7
Britons, 8, 43, 88, 123, 213
Brown, Frank, 30–1
Brown, Freddie, 215
Browning, Robert, 136
Brussels, 171
Buenos Aires Cricket Club (BACC), 47
Buenos Aires, 24, 27, 104, 171, 256
    Anglo-French blockade of, 38
    Bridges died in, 174
    British investors domination, 43

INDEX

growth of British community in, 10
Harrods branch opened in, 22
relationship between Britain and, 7–9
water supply and sanitation, 3
Buenos Ayres Water Supply & Drainage Co., 3, 4–6, 7
Burmantofts, 2
Byron, John, 116

Caernarfon, 234
Caldera, 232–4
Calderón, Cristina, 177–8
Calderón, Lidia González, 178
Caleta Eugenia, 181
Camilenna, 162–3
Campomar, Andreas, 49, 51
Canada, 67, 78
Cannes Film Festival (2023), 179
Canning, George, 209
Canto General (Neruda), 242
Cape Desolation, 145
Cape Horn, 126, 140, 143, 150, 221
Cardiganshire, 65
Carmarthenshire, 65
Carmen de Patagones, 75
Casa Rosada, 2, 9, 25
Casablanca Valley, 207
Casnodyn Rhys, William, 70, 77
Cavendish, Thomas, 86, 115
Celman, Miguel Juárez, 5, 6
Central America, 31, 221
Central Uruguay Railway Company, 43

Centro Cultural Kirchner, 9–10
Cerro Bandera, 139, 179
Cerro Dragón, 225
Cerro Guido Conservation Foundation, 108
Cerro La Campana, 90
Cerro Sombrero, 150
Céspedes, Martina, 8
Chacabuco, 247–8
Chacarita, 28
Charles (King), 55
Charles V (Roman emperor), 141
Chartism, 65
Chatwin, Bruce, 79, 105, 109–10
Child in Chile (Howe), 220–1
Chile in the Nitrate Era (Monteón), 247
Chile, 76, 78, 103, 168, 216
  annexed Rapa Nui, 193, 200
  border dispute between Argentina and, 180–1
  Britain's shared history with, 255–6
  British presence and influence in, 222
  civil war (1891), 241–2
  Cochrane arrival in, 210–11
  colonisation of western Patagonia, 87, 106
  Darwin arrival in, 90
  entry in World War II, 247
  puma hunting banned in, 108
  support to Selk'nam people, 179
  War of the Pacific, 235
  See also Patagonia

INDEX

Chilean congress, 179, 207, 231
Chilean saltpetre, 234
Chileans, 68, 88, 178, 224, 234, 249
China, 54, 229, 234
Chincha (community), 227
Chincha Islands War (1865–79), 235–6
Chincha Islands, 228
Chinchorro culture, 226–7
cholera, 2, 159
Christian Salvesen, 129
Christie, John, 47
Chubut River, 70, 78, 81
Chubut, 68, 77, 78–80, 83, 107
Chuquicamata (copper mine), 239
Ciudad Vieja, 38–41
Coalition of Latin Americans, 257
Cochrane, Thomas, 206–7, 208, 210–11, 212, 256
Cold War, 248
Colegio Británico, 14
Collapse (Diamond), 190
Collapse of Barings, The (Fay), 5
Colonia del Sacramento, 37
Companion to Easter Island, A (Grant-Peterkin), 194–5
Concepción, 198, 219, 222, 223
Conquest of the Desert: Argentina's Indigenous Peoples and the Battle for History, The (Larson), 76
Cook, Frederick A., 168
Cook, James, 126, 143, 147, 188–9
Copiapó, 231–3
Córdoba, 17, 46

Cornwall, 234
Corporación Selk'nam, 178–9
Coulthard, Seb, 132–3, 135
COVID-19 lockdowns, 140
COVID-19 pandemic, 24, 58, 114
Cox, Robert, 22
Craig, Daniel, 217
Crean, Tom, 135
Cremella, Nicolás, 56, 58
Crimean War (1853–6), 241
Cristina Calderón: Memories of My Yagan Grandmother (Zárraga), 178
Crowe, Russell, 211
Cuenca, Álvaro, 41–4, 46–7, 51
Cueva de los Manos, 63
Cultural Survival (NGO), 195
Cunninghame Graham, Robert Bontine, 19–20, 42
Cwm Hyfryd, 78

Daily Mail (newspaper), 59
Dampier, William, 116
Darwin, Charles, 90, 120–1, 151–5, 156, 214
  views on Tierra del Fuego, 157
  visit to Coquimbo, 231
Davies, Lewis, 70
Davis, Edward, 188, 233
Davis, John, 115
de Bougainville, Louis-Antoine, 116–17
de Sobremonte, Rafael, 8
de Weerdt, Sebald, 116
Definitely Maybe (Oasis), 28

INDEX

Derby, 101
Descent of Man, and Selection in Relation to Sex, The (Darwin), 152
Desolación (Mistral), 92
Despard, George Pakenham, 159, 161
Diaguita (people), 232
Diamond, Jared, 190
Diana (Princess of Wales), 79, 82, 217
Dientes de Navarino, 140, 176
Divine Comedy (Dante), 2
Dixie, Florence, 107
Dodds Pennock, Caroline, 141–2
Don Roberto: The Adventure of Being Cunninghame Graham (Jauncey), 19
Doughty, Thomas, 64
Douglas-Home, Alec, 248–9
Drake Passage, 143, 181
Drake, Francis, 64, 84, 86, 141–3, 212, 231
Duff, James, 18
Duncan Fox, 94, 214–15, 218
Durrell, Gerald, 62
Durrell, Lawrence, 22
Dutrou-Bornier, Jean-Baptiste Onésime, 193

East Falkland, 116, 121, 124
East Kilbride, 249
Easter Island Exploitation Company, 195
Edificio Kavanagh, 2, 18
Edmunds, Percy, 196
Edmundson & Co, 217
Edmundson, William, 209, 236, 241
Edward VIII (Prince of Wales), 25–6
Egypt, 227, 241
Einstein, Albert, 14
El Anglo, 55
El Cinzano, 216–17
El País (newspaper), 177
El Pedral, 84
El Pingüino (newspaper), 109–10
El'leparu, 147, 148–9, 151, 152–3, 155–6, 165
Elephant Island, 134–5, 136
Elizabeth I (Queen), 254
Elizabeth II (Queen), 95
Elizabeth Tower, 216, 238
Ellis Island, 11, 12
Elqui Valley, 92, 230–1
ELT. *See* Extremely Large Telescope (ELT)
Endeavour (ship), 143
Ends of the Earth (website), 135
Endurance (ship), 134, 137
England, 4, 28, 66, 163–4
Epelbaum, Lila, 1
Esmeralda (ship), 211, 240, 241
Esquel, 78
Estación Constitución, 25–6
Estancia Cerro Guido, 85–6, 107–8
Estancia Harberton, 166–7
Estancia Viamonte, 172

INDEX

Europe, 4, 52–4, 77, 94, 143
  demand for fertilisers in, 234
  Fray Bentos products in, 56
  guano usage, 191, 229
  Human zoos in, 170–1
  religious persecution in, 11
  World War I impacts on, 101
European Southern Observatory, 238
Europeans, 65, 106, 115, 140–1, 145, 158
ex-*Buenos Aires Herald* (newspaper), 22
Exposition Universelle (1889), 170–1
Extremely Large Telescope (ELT), 238–9

Facebook, 98
Falkland Islands, 47, 123–4, 137, 198
  controlled and funded by UK, 122
  Darwin arrival in, 120–1
  outbreak of avian flu in, 133
  refused to ratify Paris Agreement, 125
  sheep farms, 89–90
Falklands War (1982), 18, 115, 119, 127, 181, 249
Falklands. *See* Falkland Islands
Falkner, Thomas, 64
Fay, Stephen, 5
Ferns, H.S., 5
Festival of Latin American Women in the Arts (FLAWA), 257
Financial Times (newspaper), 191
Fischer, Steven Roger, 187
FitzRoy, Robert, 144–8, 149, 151, 155–6, 178
'flensing plan', 128
Fletcher, Francis, 64
Forster, Johann Reinhold, 189
Foxley, David, 50
France, 4, 26, 38, 193, 202, 220
Fray Bentos (food brand), 56–7, 58–60, 256
Fray Bentos, 36, 53–5, 60, 100, 129
Freire, Jose, 50
Frigorífico Bories, 101–2
From Beauty to Duty: A Footballing History of Uruguay 1878–1917 (Cruz), 48
Fundación Hach Saye, 179

Gaiman, 70, 81–2
Galápagos, 157
Galeano, Eduardo Hughes, 40, 257
Galilei, Galileo, 238–9
Galtieri, Leopoldo, 123
García Lorca, Federico, 14
Gardel, Carlos, 28, 81
Gardiner, Allen, 159–60
Garwood, Marty, 118
Garzón, Baltasar, 249
Germany, 198, 220, 245
Gibbs, William, 229, 241, 256
Giebert, George Christian, 52–3

291

INDEX

Gilmore, Bob, 134
Globe Tavern, 121–2
Golazo! A History of Latin American Football (Campomar), 49
Golfo Nuevo, 62, 69, 71, 84, 115
Goñi, Uki, 12
González de Ahedo, Felipe, 188
Goodall, Abby, 175
Goose Green, 123
Graham, Maria, 213–15
Graham, Thomas, 213
Graham-Yooll, Andrew, 37, 38, 57
Grant-Peterkin, James, 194–5, 200–1
Great Depression, 25, 221, 245
Great Exhibition (1851), 254
Greece, 212
Greene, Graham, 22
Grierson, Cecilia, 30
Grove Park, 6
Grytviken, 125, 126–8, 129, 130, 136
Guano Islands Act (1856), 229
guano, 191–2, 227–30, 234, 255–6, 257
Guerra Grande ('Great War'), 38
Gusinde, Martín, 141, 170

H. McManus, 217
Haber, Fritz, 245
Halifax, 246
Hanga Roa, 183, 187, 189, 192–4
Harambour-Ross, Alberto, 89

Hardie, Keir, 20
Hardy, Iain, 218
Harmer, Alejandra Barrios, 95
Harrods, 21–2
Harvey, Robert, 236–7
Harwood, Henry, 45–6
Heath, Edward, 248–9
Hebridean Sky (ship), 115, 117–18, 125, 132–3, 134, 135
Hielo Continental Sur, 90
Historic Dockyard Museum, 122
History of the British Presence in Chile, A (Edmundson), 209, 236, 241
History of the Railways in Argentina, A (Waddell), 15
History Today (magazine), 208
Hitorangi, Marisol, 195
HMS *Achilles*, 45
HMS *Adventure*, 144
HMS *Ajax*, 45
HMS *Beagle*, 90, 144–5, 146–7, 157
    Darwin's experiences on, 151–2
    sailed to Bahía Wulaia, 155
HMS *Doterel*, 98
HMS *Exeter*, 45
HMS *Resolution*, 126, 188–9
HMS *Topaze*, 202, 203
Hodges, William, 189
Hogan, Carlos, 18
Holmes, Vera Brown, 117
Honorary Consul, The (Greene), 22
Hornopirén, 62

INDEX

Hotel de los Inmigrantes, 12, 15
Hotel José Nogueira, 93
House of Lords, 20
Howe, Bea, 220–1
Huanchaca Mining Company of Bolivia, 237–8
Hudson, W.H., 20, 42
Huernos, Marcelo, 13–14
Hughes, Hugh, 73–4
Humberstone, 245, 249–51
Humberstone, James Thomas, 243, 250
Humboldt, Alexander von, 228–9
Hunter, John, 25–9
Hurley, Frank, 134
Hurlingham Club, 27
Hurlingham, 3
Hyslop, Samuel, 106

Iceland, 131
Iconic Tattooed Man of Easter Island, The (Kaeppler and Van Tilburg), 201–2
Imperial Trans-Antarctic Expedition, 134
In Patagonia (Chatwin), 79, 105
Inca Empire, 227
India, 213
Indian Rebellion (1857), 241
Indians of Tierra del Fuego, The (Lothrop), 170
Industrial Revolution, 52, 229
Information Research Department (IRD), 248
'International Capital of the Trout', 150

International Court of Justice, 235
International Whaling Commission (IWC), 130–1
Iquique, 225, 227, 234, 239, 242–3, 244
Ireland, 20
Isla Isabel, 142
Isla Navarino, 150, 154, 163, 174, 177
Island at the End of the World (Fischer), 187
Istanbul, 176
Italy, 12, 213, 220

James Caird (boat), 135, 137, 255–6
Jani, Janak, 223–4
Japan, 131, 198, 234, 254
Jauncey, James, 19, 20
Jewett, David, 120
Johnson, Ian, 83
Johnson, S.W., 57
Jones, Lewis, 68–9, 75, 82
Jones, Michael D., 67–9, 81
Jones, R. Berwyn, 70
Jones-Parry, Love, 68–9
Journal of a Residence in Chile (Graham), 214
Journal of Latin American Studies: (Ferns), 5
Juan Fernández Islands, 188
Juan Guillermos, 87
Justo, Agustín Pedro, 20

Kaeppler, Adrienne L., 201–2

INDEX

Kawésqar (community), 106, 142–3, 145–6, 166, 174
Kennedy, John Gordon, 242
Kent, 234, 240
Keppel Island, 160, 161–3
Kevin Red, 19
Kidd, William Leslie, 102
King Haakon Bay, 135
King, Phillip Parker, 144
Kiosko Roca, 92
Kipa-Akar, 177
Kirkstall Abbey, 256
Knightley, Phillip, 55

L'Hermite, Jacques, 143
La Bombonera, 2
La Casa Inglesa, 217
La Coruña, 247
La Matanza, 3
la Roché, Antoine de, 125–6
La Sebastiana, 205–6
La Serena, 230, 232
Ladrillero, Juan, 99
Lake of Menteith, 20
Lanarkshire, 246
'Land of Fire', 141
Langsdorff, Hans, 45–6
Lasserre, Augusto, 165
Latin America, 48, 222
Latin Americans, 256–7
LatinoLife (website), 257
Leeds, 256
Leeson, Nick, 6
Lemco Dishes for All Seasons (Tuite), 53

Lennox, 180
Leopold II (King), 255
Let's Talk Latinx, 257
Lexington (warship), 120
Lichtenberger, Henry, 49
Liebig Extract of Meat Company (LEMCO), 53, 54, 60
Liebig, Justus von, 52–3, 228–9
Lima, 235
Lithuanians, 43
Little Prince and *Night Flight, The* (Saint-Exupéry), 80
Liverpool, 40, 50, 54, 69, 171
Liverpool FC, 49–50
Liverpool Nitrate Company Ltd, 236–7, 243
Llanuwchllyn, 67
Lloyd George, David, 82
Loch Ness, 154
London County Council, 6, 255
London Olympics (1908), 54
London, 53, 171, 176, 229–30, 237
  Bolívar visit to, 208
  Latin American heritage in, 256
  Pinochet arrested in, 249
Lord Northbrook pub, 6
Los colonos (film), 179
Los Reyes (ship), 212
Louis XV (King of France), 116
Lublin, Geraldine, 69, 73–4, 79
Lynch, John, 208

Mac Allister, Alexis, 257
MacLennan, Alexander, 169–70

INDEX

Macri, Mauricio, 83
Magallanes Workers' Federation, 102
Magdalena (island), 142
Magellan Times (newspaper), 96
Magellan, Ferdinand, 63–4, 92–3, 141
Magellanic penguins, 84, 174
Maître, Maurice, 170–2
Malhães, Paulo, 248
'Malvinas Argentinas', 124
Manor House Library (Hither Green), 4, 256
Manor House, 6
Manterola, Alberto Sánchez, 193
Manutomatoma, Anakena, 202–3
Mapuche, 65, 76, 83
María Elena (nitrate plant), 239
Maria, Donna (Queen), 214
Mars (planet), 226
Marta (island), 142
Mason, Peter, 171–2
Master and Commander (O'Brien), 211
Matthews, Abraham, 73
Matthews, Richard, 151, 155–6
May Revolution (1810), 9–10
McBride, John, 116
McCarthy, Timothy, 135
McClelland, Peter H., 94
McIlwaine, Cathy, 256
McNeish, Chippy, 135
Memoir and Identity in Welsh Patagonia (Lublin), 69
Mendoza, 17

Mendoza, Pedro de, 7, 24
Menéndez, José, 100, 169–70
Menéndez, Josefina, 94
Mercado del Puerto, 39–40
Merlet, Enrique, 193, 195
Mestivier, Esteban, 120
Mexico, 254
Middle East, 11, 77, 234
Middleton, Phil, 122–3, 125
Milei, Javier, 6–7, 17, 23
Mill, James, 10
Millán, Moira, 83–4
Milward, Charles Amherst, 109–10
'Miracle of the Andes', 48
Mistral, Gabriela, 92, 230
Molina, Fernanda Olivares, 179
Monari, Graciela Clarisa, 1
Mondino, Diana, 137
Monteón, Michael, 247
Montevideo Cricket Club (MVCC), 47–9, 51
Montevideo Independent (newspaper), 44
Montevideo Rowing Club, 48–9
Montevideo Waterworks Co., 40, 47
Montevideo, 37, 39, 56, 120, 198
 British community in, 42–3
 British population growth in, 48
 occupied by British forces, 8
 siege by Argentine–Uruguayan army, 38
 See also Uruguay

INDEX

Montserrat, 23
Montt, Pedro, 244
Moody, Richard Clement, 121
Morningside (firm), 5–6
Motu Nui, 184
Mount Tambora, 52
Mount Tarn, 157
Movement of Indigenous Women and Diversities for Good Living, 83
Murillo, Oscar, 257
Museo Rapa Nui, 187, 188
Museo Regional de Magallanes, 94
Muza, Ricardo, 85–6, 108
MVCC. *See* Montevideo Cricket Club (MVCC)
Mylodon, 105, 109
Mystery of Easter Island, The (Routledge), 196

Nae Pasaran (documentary), 249
Napoleon, 208
NASA, 226
National Maritime Museum (Greenwich), 255–6
Nepal, 123
Neruda, Pablo, 205–6, 211, 222, 242
New York Review of Books (magazine), 12
New York Times (newspaper), 254–5
New Yorker, The (magazine), 31

New Zealand Shipping Company, 109
New Zealand, 54, 68, 202
Newport Rising (1839), 65
Nike, 22
North America, 86, 106, 191
    demand for fertilisers in, 234
    Human zoos in, 171
    Yagán conflict with, 143
North, John Thomas, 236–7, 241–3, 254–5
Northbrook Park, 6
Norway, 131
Nostromo (Conrad), 19
Nova Cambria, 67
Nueva Helvecia, 36
Nuevo París, 49–50
"Nunca Caminarás Solo", 50

O'Brien, Jorge, 208
O'Brien, Patrick, 211
O'Higgins, Bernardo, 208, 209–10, 211, 212, 214
Okokko, 161–3
Old Christians Club (rugby team), 48
Olympic (ocean liner), 14
Omoo: A Narrative of Adventures in the South Seas (Melville), 193
On Savage Shores: How America Discovered the World (Dodds Pennock), 141–2
Open Veins of Latin America (Galeano), 41
Opium War I (1839–42), 229

INDEX

Orongo (village), 184–5, 200, 202
Orundellico, 147–8, 151, 152–4, 155–7, 160–3, 256
Ossandon, Agustín Edwards, 235
Oxford English Dictionary, 84
Oxo, 53–4

Pacific Steam Navigation Company, 218
Pakarati, Cristián Moreno, 187–8
Palace of Running Waters, 2–3, 5–6, 7, 9
Palacio Barolo, 2
Palacio Braun Menéndez, 94
Palacio de Aguas Corrientes. *See* Palace of Running Waters
Palacio José Menéndez, 93
Palermo Soho, 32
Palestine, 68
Pall Mall Gazette (newspaper), 171
Pampas, 12, 19, 33, 53, 76, 107
Panama Canal, 108, 221–2
Paraná Delta, 17
Pardo, Luis, 110–11, 136
Parque Lezama, 24
Parque Nacional Tierra del Fuego, 158
Parque Nacional Torres del Paine, 85, 105
Parthenon Sculptures, 203
Patagonia Rebelde, 103
Patagonia, 62–5, 88, 90–2, 106–7, 165
  British role in, 96–7
  Chile's colonisation of, 87, 177
  Davies impression on, 70
  growth of whaling industry, 128–9
  military campaigns against, 76–7
  sheep farms, 89
  Welsh community in, 72, 79–80, 83–4
  Welsh expansion in, 78
  workers rebellion, 102–4
Patagonians, 63, 75
'Patitos Tik Tok', 21
Pehuenche, 76
Pellegrini, Carlos, 31
Pembrokeshire, 65
Peñarol, 49
Península Valdés, 61–2, 71
Perón, Juan, 16–17, 25
Peru, 87, 120, 191–2, 211, 227, 234–5
  guano exported from, 228–9
  territorial losses, 235–6
Peru-Bolivian Confederation, 11
Phillips, Garland, 161–2
Phillips, Thomas Benbow, 67
'Phony War', 45
Picton Island, 159–60, 180
Pigafetta, Antonio, 63–4
Pinochet, Augusto, 206, 247–9
Pisagua (port), 247
Pisco Elqui, 231
Pitt Rivers Museum, 178
Planet (magazine), 73–4
Plaza Británica, 17–18

INDEX

Plaza Colón, 238
Plaza de Mayo, 9, 28
Plaza Prat, 240
Plaza San Martín, 18
Plymouth, 148–9, 151
Point Wild, 134, 135
Poland, 45
Polynesia, 185, 186, 187, 191, 229
Polynesian Triangle, 185–6
Polynesians, 191
Poole, William Leslie, 49
Poor Law (1834), 66
Pope John Paul II, 180–1
Port Egmont, 116–17
Port Famine, 86, 144, 157
porteños, 1, 5, 219
Portugal, 37
Possession Bay, 126
Powell, Richard, 202
Preston North End, 51
Primaleon (novel), 63–4
Principles of Geology (Lyell), 214
Prion Island, 132
Prosser, Natalie, 175
Prussia, 4
Puelche, 76
Puerto Bories, 100, 101–2
Puerto Madero, 13
Puerto Madryn, 71, 80, 115
Puerto Natales, 101–2, 103, 105
Puerto San Julián, 63, 64
Puerto Soledad, 116–17, 120
Puerto Toro, 181
Puerto Williams, 87, 154, 174, 176–8

Punta Arenas, 88, 103, 110, 125, 165, 249
  Harmer travelled to, 95
  multinational history, 97–8
  Shackleton travelled to, 136
Punta Carretas, 51
Punta Cuevas, 72
Punta del Este, 47
Punta Tombo, 71

Quechua (language), 33, 227, 231

Radowitzky, Simón, 173
RAF Mount Pleasant, 123
Raffle, Finlay, 127–8, 129–30
Rankülche, 76
Rano Kau, 183–4
Rano Raraku, 186–7
Rapanui (people), 188–9, 190–1, 192–4, 198–200, 203
  repression of, 195
  Routledge interviews with, 196
Rapa Nui (Easter Island), 181, 186, 188, 191, 193, 200
Rapa-Nui (film), 190
Rapanui language, 185, 194, 199, 200
Ratcliffe, Norman, 131
Rauff, Walther, 247
Rawson, Guillermo, 68
Rebecca Riots, 65
Rebellion in Patagonia (Bayer), 103
Recoleta Cemetery, 2, 97
Red Cross, 102
Rees, John, 96–7, 109

INDEX

Remembrance Day, 27
Reynard, Henry, 89, 96, 142
Rhondda, 69
Richards, Eric, 210
Río de la Plata, 7–8, 10, 33, 101
   British invasions of, 37
   enslaved Africans brought to, 12
Río Gallegos, 80, 104
Río Grande, 150–1, 172, 174
Rise and Fall of the House of Vestey:, The (Knightley), 55
Rivadavia, Bernardino, 10
River Plate Times and *Montevideo Times* (newspaper), 44
Robert II (King), 19
Roberts, David D., 81, 82
Robertson, Malcolm, 16
Robinson Crusoe (Defoe), 188
Roca, Julio Argentino, 166
Rock, David, 15, 25
Rockhopper Exploration, 125
Rodrigues Fowler, Yara, 257
Rogers, Woodes, 116
Roggeveen, Jacob, 188, 189
rongorongo tablets, 187–8, 202
Rosas, Juan Manuel de, 11
Routledge, Katherine, 196–8
Royal African Company, 8
Royal Aquarium, 171
Royal Commentaries of the Incas (De la Vega), 228
Royal Doulton, 2
Royal Navy, 8, 45–6, 87, 121, 143–4, 224
   defeat in Battle of Coronel, 198
   war with US ships, 212–13
Russell, William Howard, 240–3
Russia, 4, 11, 54, 131

Salmon, Alexander, 193
Salta, 17
San Martín, José de, 9, 18, 210, 215, 256
San Pedro de Atacama, 238–9
San Telmo, 23, 240
Santa Cruz, 103
Santa Evita (Martínez), 3
Santa Laura, 245–6, 250–1
Santa María de Iquique (album), 244
Santillán, Susana Isabel, 1
Sarmiento, Domingo Faustino, 31
Saunders Island, 116, 117
Savage: The Life and Times of Jemmy Button (Hazelwood), 148
Scandinavia, 101–2, 129, 143
Schmith, Hermann Eberhard, 105
Scotia Sea, 134
Scots, 89, 129
Scott, Robert Falcon, 54, 110
Scottish Football Museum, 49
Scottish Highlands, 119
Scottish Labour Party, 20
Scottish National Party, 20
Selk'nam (people), 140–1, 153, 166, 169, 172
   challenges faced by, 178–9
   measles epidemics, 174
Selkirk, Alexander, 188

INDEX

Seno Última Esperanza, 99–100, 103
Seward, Pablo, 193–4
Shackleton, Ernest, 54, 110–11, 134, 135, 136, 255–6
'Shanks system', 250
Sharp, Bartholomew, 231
Shaw, George Bernard, 19
Shaxson, Nicholas, 59–60
'Sheep Sovereignties', 89
Simpson, Roberto, 208, 211, 240
Snow, William Parker, 160–1
Sociedad Explotadora de Tierra del Fuego, 94, 100, 101–2, 103, 107
Somerscales, Thomas, 224, 256
Sørlle, Thoralf, 135
Soto, Antonio, 104
South Africa, 254
South American Handbook (Box), 22, 90
South American Missionary Society, 95, 159–61, 162–3, 166, 171
South Americans, 256
South Atlantic, 18, 45, 119, 123, 131, 137
South Georgia Museum, 127
South Georgia, 114–15, 131–4, 135, 137, 255–6
  first sighting of, 125–6
  seized by Argentine forces, 123–4
  whaling stations, 129–30
South Sandwich Islands, 115, 123, 131

South Sea Company, 7–8, 12
South Shetlands, 134
South Wales, 65, 66, 69
southern Brazil, 67
Southern Cross (newspaper), 31
Southern Ocean, 90, 130, 140, 150
Spain, 7, 9, 12, 37, 209, 235–6
Spanish Empire, 64, 209
St Petersburg, 185
#StandUptoInvisibility campaign, 257
Stanley Bowles, Henry, 47
Starbucks, 31
Stephenson, George, 43
Stevenson, Robert Louis, 19
Stirling, Waite, 162–4, 176
Stokes, Pringle, 144, 151
Stolpe, Knut Hjalmar, 201
Strait of Magellan, 84, 86, 88, 99, 110
  Beagle returned to, 157
  Drake impression on, 142
  FitzRoy anchored in, 145
  Panama Canal impacts on, 108
Straw, Jack, 249
Stromness Bay, 114, 135
Strong, John, 116
Sumbawa, 52
Switzerland, 220
Sydney Aquarium, 118

Tahiti, 193, 201, 202
Tarapacá, 234, 235
Tawantinsuyu. *See* Inca Empire

INDEX

Taylor, Lucy, 74, 75
Te Ara O Te Ao trail, 183–4
Te Pito O Te Henua, 185
Teatro Victoria, 44
Tehuelche, 63–5, 71, 73, 83, 106–7
   Argentina attack on, 76–7
   Welsh trading relationship with, 74, 75
Telegraph (newspaper), 125
'Templo Inglés', 40
Thames (river), 230
Thatcher, Margaret, 124, 249
Thomson, James, 144
Tierra del Fuego, 140–1, 151, 159, 165, 172, 180
   Argentine and Chilean governments aid to, 174
   Bridges aid to, 167
   Bridges visit to, 163–4
   Darwin arrival in, 152–3
   Darwin views on, 157
   European interest in, 143
   sheep farming, 169, 179
   UK's connections with, 176
Tigre, 17
Times (newspaper), 59, 88–9, 136
Titanic (ocean liner), 14
Tjuntjuntjara (community), 201
Tocopilla, 239
Torre de los Ingleses. *See* Torre Monumental
Torre Monumental, 17
Trafalgar Square (London), 20, 208

'Treachery of the Blue Books', 66, 67
Treasure Islands: Tax Havens and the Men Who Stole the World (Shaxson), 59–60
Treaty of Utrecht (1713), 7
Trelew, 70, 81
Tren de la Costa, 17
Tren de los Presos (Prisoners' Train), 173
Tren del Fin del Mundo, 173
Trevelin, 78
Trotsky, Leon, 232
Tucumán, 14
Turnpike Trusts, 65
typhoid, 2, 167

UD Engineering Co., 101
UK (United Kingdom), 54, 125, 178, 256–7
   backed by Chile, 181
   Chileans fleeing to, 249
   connections with Tierra del Fuego, 176
   Fray Bentos products, 58
   funds to Falklands, 122
   Shackleton returned to, 136
   Topaze sailed to, 202, 203
   vote right to women, 76
   World War I impacts on, 101
UNESCO, 39, 56–7
Union Cold Storage Company, 54
United States (US), 11, 67, 120, 198, 202
   battle between British forces and, 212–13

INDEX

rising dominance of, 222
westward expansion of, 12
University of Brasília study (2008), 12
Uruguay: A Travel and Literary Companion (Graham-Yooll), 37, 57
Uruguay, 39, 54, 120, 255–6
   British community in, 42–3
   British sporting links with, 47, 48, 51
   claimed independence, 37–8
   King Charles visit to, 55
   World Cup win (1930), 50
   See also Argentina
Uruguayan civil war (1839–51), 11
Ushuaia, 154, 157–8, 164, 174, 176
   Argentina expanded penal colony in, 172–3
   Argentine naval ships arrival in, 165–6
Uttermost Part of the Earth (Bridges), 169, 172

Valdivia, 211, 215
Valeria, 19
Vallenar (town), 232
Valparaíso Bay, 209
Valparaíso Cricket Club, 215
Valparaíso, 212–13, 218–19, 223, 240
   British connections with, 206–7, 214–15
   diverse population, 220–1
   Somerscales arrived in, 224

   war influence on, 221–2
Van de Maele, Maurice, 179–81
Van Tilburg, Jo Anne, 201–2
Vancouver Island, 68
Varela, Héctor B., 104
Vegan Food Awards (2019), 59
Venezuela, 54
Vergara, Pía, 108
Vernet, Luis, 120
Vestey, Edmund, 54–5, 59–60
Vestey, William, 54–5, 59–60
Victoria (Queen), 44, 46, 51, 202, 219
Victoria Cricket Club, 47
Victoria Hall, 44
Vicuña, 230
Villa Ukika, 177, 179
Vincent, John, 135
Virago (Royal Navy sloop), 88
Virgin Mary, 71
Visit to Chile and the Nitrate Fields of Tarapacá, etc., A (Russell), 241
von Spee, Maximilian, 197–8
Voyage of the Beagle, The (Darwin), 121, 151–2, 214

Waddell, Jorge, 15
Wales–Argentina Society, 79
Wall Street Crash, 25
Walsh, María Elena, 24–5
Walthamstow, 148–9, 151, 256
War of the Pacific (1879–84), 87, 224, 235–6, 243, 246
War of the Triple Alliance (1864–70), 4

INDEX

Waterloo, 208
Watson Hutton, Alexander, 29–30, 49
Watt, James, 43
'We Shall Overcome', 25
Weddell Sea, 134, 137
Welsh Language Project (1997), 79
Welsh language, 66–7, 78
West London, 101
West Point Island, 118–19
Westminster Abbey, 212, 256
Westminster Quarters (song), 17
Whispering Land, The (Durrell), 62
Whitelocke, John, 9, 37
Wilckens, Kurt Gustav, 104
Wild, Frank, 136, 137
William IV (King), 149
Williams Rebolledo, Juan, 87
Williams Wilson, John, 87, 96, 177
Williamson, Balfour & Co., 195–6, 198–9, 200, 214–15, 217, 218
Wilson, Jonathan, 30
Winehouse, Amy, 217
Winter Garden, 171
Wollaston Islands, 162
World Encompassed by Sir Francis Drake, The (Drake), 64, 142
World War I, 54, 82, 98, 122, 222
    impact on Patagonian economy, 103
    outbreak of, 101, 129, 134, 197, 221
World War II, 45, 51, 98, 122, 198

Argentine-British Squadron, 28–9
Chile entry in, 247
Worsley, Frank, 135

X-Ray of the Pampa (Estrada), 16

Y Drafod (newspaper), 82
Y Wladfa, 61–4, 65–70, 71–2, 78–81
    military campaigns against, 76–7
    reassessment of, 82–4
    Tehuelche communities role in, 73–5
Yagán (community), 142–3, 153–4, 158–60, 161, 164
    FitzRoy approached by, 147
    measles epidemics, 166, 174
    resistance to missionary settlements, 172
    support to Bridges, 167
    Yagán–English dictionary, 168, 178
yellow fever, 2
Yokcushlu, 146, 151, 152–3, 155–6, 256
    arrival in Plymouth, 148–9
    visit to Ushuaia, 165
YouTube, 27
Yrigoyen, Hipólito, 104
Yza, Ángel Ignacio, 104

Zárraga, Cristina, 178
Zimbabwe, 123
Zona Franca, 91